England's Boy King

A contemporaray sketch of Edward VI.

England's Boy King

ల⚘ర

THE DIARY OF EDWARD VI
1547–1553

EDITED BY JONATHAN NORTH

RAVENHALL BOOKS

This edition first published 2005 by Ravenhall Books,
an imprint of Linden Publishing Limited

© Ravenhall Books, 2005

All rights reserved. No part of this publication may be reproduced, stored in a retrieval system, or transmitted in any form or by any means, electrical, mechanical or otherwise without the written permission of the publisher.

British Library Cataloguing in Publication Data
Edward, VI, King of England, 1537-1553
England's boy king : the diary of Edward VI, 1547-1553
1.Edward, VI, King of England, 1537-1553 - Diaries 2.Great Britain - Kings and rulers - Diaries 3.Great Britain -History - Edward VI, 1547-1553
I.Title
942'.053'092

ISBN 190504304X

Ravenhall Books
Linden Publishing Limited
PO Box 357, Welwyn Garden City, AL6 6WJ, United Kingdom
www.ravenhallbooks.com

The diary was published in 1858 in John Nichols' *Literary Remains of King Edward the Sixth*. The text has here been thoroughly updated for a modern audience but is complete and unabridged.

Printed and bound in Great Britain
by Creative Print and Design (Wales), Ebbw Vale.

CONTENTS

Preface	7
Chronology	11
The Diary	
1547	13
1548	25
1549	29
1550	43
1551	71
1552	125
Letters written by Edward VI	181
Principal Personalities	189

PREFACE

King Edward VI's account of his own reign is an important historical source on the mid-Tudor period, a time when England was being subjected to many internal and external pressures. A sense of those pressures emerges from Edward's writings – financial problems, religious upheaval, rural unrest and continental wars – but an indication as to how Tudor government coped is also readily apparent in the narrative.

The reign was inevitably going to be difficult given the situation in Europe and the growing sense of impending crisis in England itself. Edward inherited a kingdom which had known but one authoritarian monarch for the last forty years and the boy king's accession was seen by many to be a relief from the sinister closing years of his father's reign. At the same time that seeming relaxation allowed a great deal of pent up anxiety and frustration comparatively free expression. Religious, political, clan and social faction took full advantage of the perceived shift and the result was that, in Edward's early years on the throne at least, events seem to be overshadowed by a series of plots and rebellions. Yet he and his government weathered the storm and, despite their limited means, embarked on a programme of policies which made a genuine contribution to transforming England and England's governance.

PREFACE

Edward's account, written in his own neat hand, is of all the incidents in his reign which he deemed to be memorable. He himself called it a Chronicle and he began his daily entries in it in March 1550, when he was aged 12, giving a brief summary of events up until then. He brought the diary, as Horace Walpole, David Lloyd and others termed it, to a close in November 1552, when he was only just 16 and, it seems, growing steadily weaker. By February 1553 he was seriously ill and he died in July of that year.

The diary is a genuine record as the evidence indicates that Edward did not write from dictation. He borrowed some phrases from official records and despatches but entries were created by the young monarch himself, often following his own inclinations and interests and using his own terminology. There is, for example, much on sport on tournaments, although war and fortification also capture the king's imagination. Indeed, for someone branded a pious and godly monarch, there is very little which can be called religious in this his personal narration.

Quite often Edward enters dates out of chronological sequence, seemingly adding material he thought to be of interest but which came to his notice after completing the main entry. This is especially true when describing events abroad, from where news came in slowly and in a haphazard fashion. He thus seems to have checked and corrected his work at the end of each month, a sign, perhaps, of a tidy mind. The entries are much fuller after March 1550, those for the early years being sketchy and terse and a little devoid of personal involvement. It is quite apparent that there is little emotion here. Perhaps some personal excitement creeps in every now and again but Edward is, by and large, very detached in terms of relationships. This coldness is especially evident even when mentioning close friends and relatives.

Edward's style of writing is sound and confident, his literary ability high. He makes use of the royal 'we' a great deal, or sometimes refers to himself as 'the king', but in later years the diary is much more of a first-person account.

The manuscript by King Edward filled 68 pages and it came into the possession of Sir Robert Cotton, an important collector of antiquities (Thomas Fuller calling his collection the English Vatican for manuscripts) in around 1616. The Cotton collection was acquired by the British Museum when it was founded in 1753.

Edward's diary was originally published by Bishop Burnet in his *History of the Reformation*, completed in 1719, but a more useful edition appeared in 1858 when John Nichols reproduced the work in his *Literary Remains of King Edward the Sixth*.

The version of the text we are presenting below is based on the material in that work but the language has been updated, the punctuation modernised and, in some cases, sentences restructured in order to assist the reader. Our intention has been to create an accessible text which throws much light on Edward and on his kingdom and this, necessarily, has meant that certain alterations have had to be made to Edward's original prose. We have attempted to assist the reader with footnotes and by the occasional addition of text in brackets whenever possible.

It has still not always been possible to deduce what Edward means in certain passages but this is no reflection on

PREFACE

the author of the work, merely a problem encountered by anyone attempting to read a personal document more than 400 years old. Indeed, as personal narratives go, the diary of the last of the Tudor kings is one of the best sources for the ups and downs of the mid-sixteenth century.

Jonathan North
2005

CHRONOLOGY

1537	*12 October*	Edward VI born
	15 October	Edward VI christened
	24 October	Jane Seymour dies
1540	*6 January*	Henry VIII marries Anne of Cleves
	9 July	Anne of Cleves and Henry VIII divorced
	28 July	Henry VIII marries Catherine Howard
1542	*13 February*	Catherine Howard executed
	8 December	Mary, future Queen of Scotland, born
1543	*12 July*	Catherine Parr marries Henry VIII
1546	*30 December*	Henry VIII names Edward his heir in his will
1547	*28 January*	Henry VIII dies
	20 February	Edward Tudor crowned as Edward VI at Westminster

❦ CHRONOLOGY ❧

1547	*31 March*	Henri II proclaimed King of France following the death of François I
	24 April	Charles V defeats the Protestant German princes at Muhlberg
	10 September	The English defeat the Scots at Pinkie
1549	*16 January*	Arrest of Thomas Seymour ordered
	20 March	Thomas Seymour executed
1551	*11 October*	Duke of Somerset arrested
1552	*15 January*	Treaty of Chambord, the French king allies with Protestant German princes
	22 January	Duke of Somerset executed
1553	*21 May*	Lady Jane Grey marries Guilford Dudley
	6 July	Edward VI dies
	10 July	Lady Jane Grey proclaimed queen
	20 July	Mary Tudor proclaimed queen
	8 August	King Edward buried at Westminster
	21 August	John Dudley, Duke of Northumberland, executed
	30 October	Mary Tudor crowned as Mary I

The Diary
∽ *1547* ∾

Edward, Prince of Wales.

ᘛ 1547 ᘚ

In the Year of our Lord 1537 a prince was born to King Harry the Eighth by Jane Seymour, then queen, who within a few days after the birth of her son died and was buried at Windsor Castle.[1] This child was christened by the Duke of Norfolk, the Duke of Suffolk and the Archbishop of Canterbury.[2] Afterwards he was brought up among the women until he was six years of age.[3] At his sixth year he was brought up in learning by Mr Doctor Coxe, who was later his Almoner, and John Cheke, Master of Arts; two well learned men who sought to bring him up in learning the tongues of the scriptures, philosophy and all liberal sciences. Also John Belmaine, a Frenchman, taught him the French language.[4]

---

1 Jane Seymour was the daughter of Sir John Seymour and Margaret Wentworth. Edward was born on the 12th of October 1537 at Hampton Court. Jane Seymour died twelve days later.
2 Edward does not mention the presence of his god-mother, his sister, Lady Mary, later Queen Mary I.
3 These would have included his 'Lady Maistres' (Lady Margaret Bryan), his dry-nurse (Sibil Penne, widow of Henry VIII's Barber Surgeon) and four rockers (including Jane Russell and Bridgette Forster).
4 In addition there was Sir Anthony Cooke, Roger Ascham (Edward's tutor in writing) and Philip van Wilder (his music teacher). Dr Richard Coxe was born in 1499 and had been master of Eton school. He was later Bishop of Ely. John Cheke, who was to supplement Dr Coxe, was a celebrated scholar of Greek. Belmaine was a French Protestant about whom little is known except that he received wages of £6, 12 shillings and four pence a quarter and that Edward's French lessons began on 12th of October 1546.

෴ 1547 ෴

When his tenth year was not yet ended it was appointed that he should be created Prince of Wales, Duke of Cornwall and Count Palatine of Chester. At which time, being the Year of our Lord 1547, the said king died of dropsy, as it was thought. After his death Edward, Earl of Hertford, and Sir Anthony Brown, Master of the Horse, came at once to convey the Prince to Enfield where the Earl of Hertford told him and his younger sister, Elizabeth, that their father had died.

After the death of King Henry VIII his son, Edward, Prince of Wales, was taken to Hertford by the Earl of Hertford and Sir Anthony Brown, Master of the Horse, and was afterwards taken to Enfield where he was told of the death of his father, and the same day the death of his father was announced in London where there was great lamentation and weeping. Suddenly he was proclaimed king. The next day, being the 31st of January, he was brought to the Tower of London where he stayed for three weeks.

Meanwhile the Council sat every day for the performance of the will and at length thought best that the Earl of Hertford should be made Duke of Somerset, Sir Thomas Seymour Lord Sudeley and the Earl of Essex Marquis of Northampton, and some knights should be made barons, such as Lord Sheffield, with some others.

Also they thought best to choose the Duke of Somerset to be Protector of the realm and Governor of the king's person during his minority, to which all the gentlemen and lords did agree because he was the king's uncle on his mother's side.[5] Also at this time the king was buried at

---

5 The Lord Protector, now Duke of Somerset, also assumed the titles of Lord Treasurer and Earl Marshal.

Queen Jane Seymour, portrait by Holbein.

The coronation procession of Edward VI.

Windsor with much solemnity, and the officers broke their staves, hurling them into the grave. But they were restored to them again when they came to the Tower.

Lord Lisle was made Earl of Warwick and the Lord Great Chamberlainship was given to him and Lord Sudeley was made Admiral of England. All these things were done, the king being in the Tower.

Afterwards, all things being prepared for the coronation, the king, being then but nine years old, passed through the city of London, as hitherto had been done, and came to the Palace of Westminster.[6] The next day he came into Westminster Hall and the people were asked whether they would have him as their king. They answered 'Ye, ye!' Then he was crowned King of England, France and Ireland by the Archbishop of Canterbury[7] and all the rest of the clergy and nobles, and anointed with all such ceremonies as were the custom, took his oath and gave a general pardon. And so he was brought to the Hall to dinner, Shrove Sunday, where he sat with the crown upon his head with the Archbishop of Canterbury and the Lord Protector, and all the lords sat at boards in the hall below. The Lord Marshal's deputy, for my Lord Somerset was Lord Marshal, rode about the hall to make room. Then Sir John Dymoke, champion, came in and made his challenge, and so the king drank to him and he had

---

6 This was on the afternoon of Saturday 19th February. He was accompanied by his uncle, the Lord Protector, and six knights. The procession was delayed near St Paul's so Edward could watch the performance of a Spanish tightrope-walker.

7 This was Cranmer, who gave a much shortened sermon on how the king should do his duty, especially in respect to religion.

the cup. At night the king returned to his palace at Westminster where there were jousts and barriers and afterwards order was taken for all those servants who were with his father and him as a prince and the ordinary and unordinary were appointed.

In the mean time Sir Andrew Dudley, brother to my Lord of Warwick, being in the *Pauncy* encountered the *Lion*, one of Scotland's principal ships which had hoped to take the *Pauncy* without resistance. But the *Pauncy* approached her and she opened fire, but, at length, they came very near and the *Pauncy*, shooting along all one side, burst all the deck of the *Lion* and all her tackle and at length boarded her and took her. But on the return journey she was lost at Harwich harbour by negligence, along with almost all her men.

In the month of May the French king, called Francis, died and his son, called Harry, was proclaimed as the king.[8] There also came an ambassador out of Scotland but nothing came to pass and an army was then prepared to enter in to Scotland.

Certain injunctions were sent forth which took away diverse ceremonies and a commission sent to take down images and certain homilies [sermons] were issued to be read in church.

Doctor Smith of Oxford recanted certain opinions on the mass at Paul's Cross and that Christ was not according to the order of Melchizedek.

Lord Seymour of Sudeley married the queen whose

---

8 This relates to the death of François I, France's great Renaissance monarch, and the accession of his son Henri II. François actually died at the end of March.

name was Catherine, by which marriage the Lord Protector was much offended.[9]

Great preparations were now made to go into Scotland and the Lord Protector, the Earl of Warwick, Lord Dacre, Lord Grey and Mr Brian went with a great number of nobles and gentlemen to Berwick where, on the first day after his arrival, he mustered all his company which numbered 13,000 foot soldiers and 5,000 horsemen. The next day he marched on into Scotland and so passed the Peaths. Then he burnt down two castles in Scotland and so passed straight over a bridge where 300 Scottish lighthorsemen set upon him from behind, though they were discomforted. So he went to Musselburgh where the first day after he arrived he went up the hill and saw the Scots, thinking them, as they were indeed, at least 36,000 men and my Lord of Warwick was almost taken by an ambush chasing the Earl of Huntley. But he was rescued by one Berteville[10] with 12 handgunners [hagbusiers in the text] on horseback and the ambush ran away. The 7th of September the Lord Protector thought he would get the hill, which the Scots seeing, they passed the bridge over the river of Musselburgh and

---

9 Seymour was certainly ambitious. His marriage plans were aimed at further improving his position. He had asked John Fowler to ask the king for his thoughts on his marriage. Edward had replied that Seymour should marry Anne of Cleves but then quickly changed his mind and said he should marry 'my sister, Mary, to turn her opinions.' After Catherine Parr's death, in September 1547, he then sought the hand of Edward's sister, the Lady Elizabeth. After that his fall was rapid. He was arrested in January 1549 and executed on Wednesday 20th of March on Tower hill.

10 Berteville was a French mercenary in English pay. This did not prevent him from supplying the French ambassador with information on the English army.

Thomas, Lord Seymour of Sudeley.

Queen Catherine Parr.

1547

strove for the higher ground and almost got it. But our horsemen set upon them and although they delayed them yet they were put to flight and only gathered together again by the Duke of Somerset, Lord Protector, and the Earl of Warwick and were ready to try again. The Scots, being amazed by this, fled, some to Edinburgh, some to the sea and some to Dalkeith and 10,000 of them were slain. Of the Englishmen there were 51 horsemen, which were all gentlemen, and one foot soldier lost.[11]

The prisoners taken were Lord Huntley, Chancellor of Scotland, and diverse other gentlemen and a thousand lords were slain. And Mr Brian, Sadler and Vane were made bannerets.

After this battle Broughty Craig [Bouchtekrag] was given to the Englishmen as well as Hume, Roxburgh and Aymouth which were fortified and captains were put in them and the Lord Somerset rewarded with £500 of land.

In the mean time Stephen Gardiner, Bishop of Winchester, was committed to custody for not receiving the injunctions.

A Parliament was also called whereupon all the chantries were granted to the king and an extreme law made for vagabonds and diverse other things.[12]

Also the Scots besieged Broughty Craig which was defended against them by Sir Andrew Dudley, knight, and their ordnance was taken and spoilt many times.

---

11 Edward's description of the Scottish defeat at the battle of Pinkie seems relatively accurate although English casualties were higher.

12 The acquisition of chantry lands, and their subsequent sale, would net the government more than £250,000. Nearly £50,000-worth of land was given away as gifts.

1548

Stephen Gardiner, Bishop of Winchester (1483 (?)-1555).

∽ 1548 ∾

There was a triumph in which six gentlemen challenged all comers at barriers, jousts and tournaments. And they also held a fortress with 30 men against 100 or under. This was done at Greenwich.

Sir Edward Bellingham, being sent into Ireland as deputy, replaced Sir Anthony St Leger.[13] He took O'Conor and O'More, bringing the lords that rebelled into submission. And O'Conor and O'More, leaving their lordships, had a pension of £200 apiece.

The Scots besieged the town of Haddington where the captain, Mr Wilford, sortied out against them everyday and slew many of them. The place was very weak but for the men who did very manfully. Mr Holcroft and Mr Palmer resupplied it many times, passing through the enemy. And at last the Rhinegrave[14] set upon Mr Palmer, who had nearly 1,000 men and 500 horsemen, discomforted him, taking him, Mr Bowes (Warden of the West Marches) and others, to the number of 400, prisoner and also slew a few.

Upon St Peter's day the Bishop of Winchester was committed to the Tower.

---

13 Anthony St Leger (1496-1559) had held the post since 1540.
14 The commander of some German troops sent by France to aid the Scots. Ringrave in the original.

❧ 1548 ❧

Then they [the Scots] made a great number of breaches. Then the Earl of Shrewsbury, general of the army, went with 22,000 men and burnt many towns and fortresses. The Frenchmen and Scots hearing this, raised their siege in the month of September. As they did so some came to Tiberio, who was then at Haddington, and seeing the weakness of the town, told him that all honour was due to the defenders and none to the attackers. So the siege being lifted, the Earl of Shrewsbury entered the place, resupplied it and reinforced it. After he left 2,000 armed men came at night into Haddington, taking the townsmen in their shirts, but they defended themselves with the help of the watch and, at length, with artillery firing upon them, they slew a marvellous number. They withstood many hot assaults and, at length, drove them home and kept the town safe.

A Parliament was called where a uniform order of prayer was instituted which had been made by a number of bishops and learned men gathered together at Windsor. A subsidy was granted and there was a notable disputation of the sacrament in the house of parliament.[15]

Also Lord Sudeley, Admiral of England, was condemned to death and died the March following. Sir Thomas Sharington was also condemned for making false coins, which he himself confessed. Others were also placed in the Tower.

---

15 This was the second session of the first Parliament in Edward's reign and it would sit until March 1549.

1549

Henry, Lord Grey.

1549

Home Castle was taken at night, by treason, by the Scots. Mr Wilford was badly wounded in a skirmish and taken. There was a skirmish at Broughty Craig in which Mr Luttrell, captain after Mr Dudley, burnt several villages and took Monsieur de Toge prisoner.

The Frenchmen assaulted Boulogne Berg and were manfully repulsed. They had made fagots with pitch, tar, tallow and powder to burn the ships in Boulogne harbour. But they were driven away by the Boulogners and their fagots taken.[16]

Lord Dacre was put in Mr Bowes' place as Warden of the West Marches and in Lord Grey's place, the Earl of Rutland.[17] He, after his arrival, entered Scotland and burnt many villages and took much prey.

The people began to rise in Wiltshire where Sir William Herbert did put them down, overrun and slay them. Then they rose in Sussex, Hampshire, Gloucestershire, Suffolk, Warwickshire, Essex, Hertfordshire, a piece of Leicestershire, Worcestershire and Rutlandshire, where, by honest persuasion, partly by honest men among themselves, partly by gentlemen, they were often appeased. And again because certain

---

16 Boulogne, and a few outlying villages and forts, had been in English hands since Henry VIII's last expedition to France in 1544.
17 The marches denote a border area and in this case were those parts of England bordering Scotland.

commissions were sent down to pluck down enclosures, they did not rise again.

The French king, perceiving this, caused war to be proclaimed. Hearing that our ships lay at Jersey, he sent a great number of his galleys and certain ships to surprise our ships. But they, lying at anchor, beat the French so that they had to retire with the loss of 1,000 men. At the same time the French king passed by Boulogne to Ambleteuse and took Blackness and the Almaine Camp by treason. Which done, Ambleteuse surrendered. Also, in a skirmish between 300 English foot and 700 French horsemen, six noblemen were slain. Then the French king came to Boulogne with his army and Boulogne Berg was razed. But because of the plague he was compelled to retire and Chatillon[18] was left behind as governor of the army.

Meanwhile, because there was a rumour that I was dead, I passed through London.[19]

After that they rose in Oxfordshire, Devonshire, Norfolk and Yorkshire.

Lord Grey of Wilton was sent to Oxfordshire with 1,500 horsemen and foot. His coming, with the assembling of the gentlemen of the country, did so abash the rebels that more than half of them ran away and others that tarried were slain, some taken and some hanged.[20]

The Lord Privy Seal was sent to Devonshire with his band,

---

18 Gaspard de Coligny (1517-1572).
19 This rumour sprang from Robert Allen who had predicted the king's death through astronomical calculation. He was promptly placed in the Tower 'for matters of astronomie'.
20 Grey defeated the rebels at the battle of Enslow Hill.

which being small, he remained at Hunnington whilst the rebels besieged Exeter, where there were many pretty feats of war.[21] After many skirmishes, when the gates were burnt, they in the city did continue their fire until they had made a rampart within. Also, afterwards, when they were undermined, and powder placed in the mine, those within [the city] drowned the powder and the mine in water. The Lord Privy Seal thought to go and reinforce them by a byway. The rebels cut all the trees between Exeter and Ottery St Mary. The Lord Privy Seal burnt that town and thought to return home. The rebels kept a bridge behind his back and so compelled him with his small band to attack, which he did and overcame them, killing 600 of them and returning home without any loss of men. Then Lord Grey and Spinola with their bands came to him, and afterwards Grey with 200 of Reading, and with these bands, being reinforced, he came to raise the siege of Exeter for there they had scarcity of food. As he passed from Hunnington he came to a little town which had but two roads and they had raised two bulwarks made of earth and had put 2,000 men to the defence of the same. The rest they had placed some at a bridge called Hunnington Bridge, partly along a certain hedge by a highway and the most part at the siege of Exeter. The rearward of the horsemen, of which Travers was captain, set upon one of the bulwarks, the vanguard and main body the other. Spinola's band kept them occupied at their wake. At

---

21 Here begins Edward's description of the western rising in Devon and Cornwall. This began when rebels gathered outside Bodmin on 6th of June 1549 to protest against religious reform and continued into Devon where the Lord Privy Seal, John Russell, failed to contain the rebel forces. Many rebels were angered by the introduction of the new Prayer Book.

length Travers drove them into the town[22] which the Lord Privy Seal burnt. Then they ran to a bridge nearby, from whence being driven there were about 900 of them slain in a plain. The next day another 2,000 of them were met at the entrance to a highway who first desired to talk. Meanwhile they fortified themselves but they ran away and that same night the city of Exeter was delivered from the siege.

After that they gathered at Launceston where the Lord Privy Seal and Sir William Herbert went and overthrew them, taking their chiefs and executing them. Nevertheless some sailed to Bridgewater and went about sedition but were quickly repressed. Hitherto of Devonshire.

At this time the black galley was taken.

Now to Norfolk.[23] The people suddenly gathered together on Norfolk and increased to a great number. The Lord Marquis Northampton was sent against them with the number of 1,060 horsemen. Winning the town of Norwich they kept it for one day and one night and the next day, in the morning, they departed out of the town with the loss of 100, among whom the Lord Sheffield was slain. There were taken many gentlemen and serving men to the number of 30, with which victory the rebels were very glad. But afterwards, hearing that the Earl of Warwick was coming against them, they began to gather upon a plateau upon a hill near to the town of Norwich, having the town allied to them. The Earl of Warwick came with 6,000 men and 1,500 horsemen and entered into the town

---

22 Clyst St Mary.
23 The rebellion in Norfolk began in early July and by mid-July a huge force of rebels had gathered on Mousehold Heath, outside Norwich, under the leadership of Robert Kett.

of Norwich and having won it found it so weak that he could scarcely defend it. Oftentimes the rebels came into the streets killing many of his men, and were repulsed again. Ye, and the townsmen were given to mischief themselves. So having endured their assaults three days and stopped their supplies, the rebels were constrained by lack of meat to retreat. The Earl of Warwick followed with 1,000 Germans and all his horsemen, leaving the English footmen in the town. He overcame them in plain battle, killing 2,000 of them and taking Kett, their captain, who in January following was hanged at Norwich, and his head hanged out. Kett's brother was also taken, and punished alike.

Meanwhile Chatillon attacked the pier that had been built in Boulogne harbour and, after a long bombardment of more than 20,000 shot assaulted it and was manfully repulsed.[24] Nevertheless they still continued the siege and often had skirmishes or false assaults in which they won not much. Therefore, seeing they profited little that way they planted ordnance against the mouth of the haven so that no supplies might come into it. Which our men seeing, they set upon them by night and slew many Frenchmen and dismounted many of their guns. Nevertheless the French came another time and planted their ordnance toward the sand side on the sand dunes and beat many ships at the entrance to the harbour. But yet the Englishmen sent by the king came into the harbour and refreshed the town a number of times. The Frenchmen seeing

---

24 The French had declared war in August 1549 and besieged Boulogne which had been an English possession since 1544. A peace treaty in March 1550 would end hostilities, following which Boulogne would be given up to the French.

◈ 1549 ◈

that they could not prevail that way continued their battery a little which before had fired 1,500 shots a day. But they loaded a galley with stones and gravel which they let go in the channel to sink it but it sank too near the bank and the Boulogners took it out and brought the stones to reinforce the pier.

Also at Guines there was a certain skirmish in which there was about 100 Frenchmen slain, of which some were gentlemen and noblemen.

In the meantime in England there arose great unrest, likely to increase much if it had not been foreseen. The Council, about 19 of them, were gathered in London, thinking to meet with the Lord Protector and making him amend some of his disorders. He, fearing his state, caused the secretary [Petre] in my name to be sent to the lords to know why they had gathered their powers together and that if they meant to talk to him then they should come in a peaceable manner. The next morning, being the 6th of October, and a Saturday, he commanded that the armour be brought down out of the armoury of Hampton Court, about 500 harnesses, to arm both his and my men, and for the gates of the house to be barred and for people to be raised. People came abundantly to the house. That night at 9 or 10 o'clock at night, I went to Windsor with all the people.[25] There was much watch kept every night. The lords sat in open places in London, calling for gentlemen before them, and declaring the causes of their accusations against the Lord Protector, and caused the same to be proclaimed. After which time few came to Windsor except my own men of the guard, which the lords wanted

---

25 This journey gave Edward a bad cold.

fearing the rage of the people so recently quieted. Then the Protector began to negotiate with letters, sending Sir Philip Hoby, lately come from being ambassador in Flanders, to see to his family; he brought on his return a very gentle letter to the Protector, which he delivered to him, another to me, another to my household, to declare the Protector's faults, ambition, vain glory, entering into rash wars during my youth, negligence in regard to Ambleteuse, enriching himself from my treasury, following his own opinion and doing all by his own authority, etc, etc. These letters were openly read and immediately the lords came to Windsor, took him and brought him through Holborn to the Tower.[26] Afterwards I went to Hampton Court where they appointed, by my consent, six lords of the Council to be attendant upon me, at least two, and four knights; for lords there were the Marquis of Northampton, the earls of Warwick[27] and Arundel, Lords Russell, Saint John and Wentworth; the knights being Sir Andrew Dudley, Sir Edward Rogers, Sir Thomas Darcy, Sir Thomas Wroth. Afterwards I came through London to Westminster. The Lord of Warwick was made Admiral of England. Sir Thomas Cheyney was sent to the Emperor for help which he could not obtain.[28] Mr Wotton was made

---

26 Here, on the 24th of October, the Protector confessed to a list of 29 misdemeanours.
27 John Dudley. He has been seen by many as the man who organised and instigated the arrest of Somerset.
28 Edward and his contemporaries used the word Emperor to denote the Holy Roman Emperor. Throughout Edward's reign this was Charles V. In addition to ruling the Holy Roman Empire, which consisted primarily of German and Austrian territories, Charles was King of Spain and he also governed much of Italy and the Netherlands.

Edward Seymour, Duke of Somerset.

John Dudley. Duke of Northumberland.

1549

secretary.[29] The Lord Protector lost, by his own agreement and submission, his protectorship, treasurership, marshalship, all his moveables and nearly £2,000 worth of land, by Act of Parliament.

The Earl of Arundel was committed to his house for certain crimes he was suspected of, such as plucking down bolts and locks at Westminster, giving my stuff away, etc. He was fined £12,000 to be paid £1,000 yearly, of which he was afterwards released.

PART OF THE CHRONICLE OF THE THIRD YEAR OF THE REIGN OF KING EDWARD VI

Mr Southwell was also committed to the Tower for certain seditious bills written with his hand, and was fined £500. Likewise Sir Thomas Arundel and Sir John [Arundel] were committed to the Tower for conspiracies in the western parts.[30]

Parliament devised a way to consecrate priests, bishops and deacons.

Mr Paget, surrendering his comptrollership, was made Lord Paget of Beaudesert and placed in the higher house by writ of Parliament.

Sir Anthony Wingfield, previously Vice-Chamberlain, was made comptroller. Sir Thomas Darcy was made Vice-Chamberlain.

---

29 Nicholas Wotton here replaced Sir Thomas Smith.
30 The Arundels were a rich Cornish family and they had prospered under Henry VIII. They were suspected of assisting the rebels in the western counties and were kept in prison for two more years.

I passed through London on the 15th of October. The Lord Warwick was made Lord Admiral at Hampton Court.

Guidotti had carried out a number of errands for the Constable of France to try and make peace with us and four commissioners were appointed to negotiate and they, after long debate, made a treaty as follows.

A peace concluded between England, France and Scotland by, on the English side, John, Earl of Bedford, Lord Privy Seal; Lord Paget de Beaudesert; Sir William Petre, Secretary; and Sir John Masson. On the French side: Monsieur de Rochepot; Monsieur Chatillon; Guillart de Mortier; and Bochetel de Sassy. It was made upon the condition that all titles, tributes and defences should remain; that the fault of one man, except he that goes unpunished, should not break the league; that merchant ships shall pass to and fro, that pirates and ships of war should be called back; that prisoners shall be returned by both sides; that we shall not go to war with Scotland unless a new occasion be given; that Boulogne, with the pieces of new conquest, along with two basilisks, two demi-cannon, three culverins, two demi-culverins, three sakers, 16 falcons, 94 harquebus on stands, 21 iron pieces and Lauder and Dunglass, with all their ordnance, save that which came from Haddington, shall be delivered within six months after this peace is proclaimed; and for the French to pay 200,000 ecus on Our Lady's Day in the harvest next ensuing; and that if the Scots razed Lauder, etc, we should raze Roxburgh and Eyemouth. For the performance of the peace these hostages should be delivered to Guines and Ardres:

1549

French
Marquis de Mayenne [François de Lorraine]
Monsieur [Louis] Trémoille
Monsieur d'Enghien [Jean de Bourbon]
Monsieur de [François] Montmorency
Monsieur de Hunaudaye [Jean d'Annebaut]
Vidame of Chartres [François de Vendôme]

English
My Lord of Suffolk [Henry Brandon]
My Lord of Hertford [Edward Seymour]
My Lord Talbot [George Talbot]
My Lord FitzWarren [John Bourchier]
My Lord Maltravers [Henry FitzAlan]
My Lord Strange [Henry Stanley][31]

At the delivery of the town ours should come home and at the first payment, three of theirs. And that if the Scots raze Lauder and Dunglass we must raze Eyemouth and Roxburgh and no one shall afterwards build forts there. Done with the comprehension of the Emperor.

---

31 It is interesting to note that these hostages were predominantly youths who had been Edward's schoolfellows in Latin and Greek.

1550

Nicholas Ridley.

1550

MARCH

25 March. This peace is proclaimed at Calais and Boulogne.

29 March. In London. Bonfires.

30 March. A sermon to give thanks for peace and a Te Deum sung.

31 March. My Lord Somerset was delivered of his bonds and came to court.

APRIL

2 April. The April Parliament prorogued until the second day of the term in October.

3 April. Nicholas Ridley, formerly of Rochester, was made Bishop of London and received his oath.

Thomas Thirlby, formerly of Westminster, was made Bishop of Norwich and received his oath.

4 April. The Bishop of Chichester who was before a vehement affirmer of transubstantiation, preached against it at Westminster in the preaching place.[32]

Removing to Greenwich from Westminster.[33]

---

32 This was George Day and he preached before the king on Good Friday.
33 Edward's custom was to spend the winter at either Hampton Court or Whitehall. Easter was usually spent at Greenwich and the summer at Hampton Court or Oatlands in Surrey. By autumn he was either at Hampton Court or Windsor, although he did not care much for Windsor.

ᴄᴏ 1550 ᴏᴠ

6 *April.* Our hostages passed the narrow seas between Dover and Calais.

7 *April.* Monsieur de Fernin, gentleman of the king's Privy Chamber, came from the French king through England to the Scottish queen to tell her of the peace.[34] An ambassador called Andre came from Gustavus [Vasa], the Swedish king, for a surer understanding of trade.

9 *April.* The hostages were delivered on both sides for the ratification of the league with France and Scotland, although someone said to Monsieur Rochepot, lieutenant, that Monsieur de Guise, father to the Marquis de Mayenne, was dead and therefore the delivery was put off for one day.

8 *April.* My Lord Warwick was made general Warden of the North and Mr Herbert was President of Wales. The first had 1,000 Marks of land granted to him whilst the second had 500; and Lord Warwick had 100 horseman at my[35] command.

9 *April.* Licenses were signed for the whole Council and certain members of the Privy Chamber to keep among them 2,340 retainers.

10 *April.* My Lord Somerset was taken into the Council. Guidotti, who began the peace talks, was recompensed with a knighthood, 1,000 Crowns reward, 1,000 Crowns pension, and his son with 250 Crowns pension. Certain prisoners [detained] for light matters were released. Agreed to the return of the French prisoners taken in the wars. Peter Vannes was sent as ambassador to Venice. Letters were sent to various nobles to

---

34 The Scottish queen, or dowager queen, was Mary of Guise, mother of Mary Queen of Scots.
35 Altered to 'the king's' in the text.

take a blind legate calling himself the Bishop of Armagh and coming from the Pope.[36] Commissions for the delivery of Boulogne, Lauder and Dunglass.

6 April. Three Flemish men of war tried to pass our ships without vailing bonnet which, they seeing, shot at them and drove them at length to vail bonnet and so depart.[37]

11 April. Monsieur Trémoille, Monsieur Vidame de Chartres and Monsieur Hunaudaye came to Dover, the rest remained at Calais until they had leave.

12 April. Order was taken that whosoever had benefices given to them should preach before the king in or out of Lent and that every Sunday there should be a sermon.

16 April. The three hostages previously mentioned came to London, being met at Deptford by Lord Grey of Wilton, Lord Braye and many other gentlemen, to the number of 20, and 100 serving men, and they were brought into the city and lodged there and kept in houses, every one by himself.

18 April. Mr Sidney and Mr Neville were made gentlemen of the Privy Chamber. A commission was given to Lord Cobham, Deputy of Calais; Sir William Petre, Chief Secretary; and Sir John Mason, French Secretary, to see the French king take his oath with certain instructions. Sir John Mason should be ambassador in residence.

A commission was given to Sir John Dennis and Sir William Sharington to receive the first payment and deliver the quittance.

---

36 Robert Waucop had been granted this see by the Pope but he died in Paris in 1551.
37 Vailing bonnet was removing one's hat or cap and bowing, ie paying homage to a superior.

1550

10 April. Sir John Mason was taken into the Privy Council and William Thomas[38] was made clerk of the same.

As the Emperor's ambassador desired permission by letters patent that my Lady Mary might have mass, it was denied him; and when he said we broke the league with him, by making peace with Scotland, he was answered that the French king and not I did comprehend them, except that I might not invade them without occasion.[39]

10 April. Laude being besieged by the Scots, the captain, hearing that peace had been proclaimed in England, delivered it as the peace did will him, taking guarantees that all the bargains of the peace should be kept.

18 April. Monsieur de Guise died.

20 April. Order taken for the Chamber that three of the outer Privy Chamber gentlemen should always be here, and two should lie on the pallet[40] and take the place of one of the four knights; that the esquires should be diligent in their office and five grooms should always be present, one of which was to keep watch in the bed chamber.

21 April. The Marquis de Mayenne, the Duke d'Enghien and the Constable's son arrived in Dover.

23 April. Monsieur de Trémoille and the Vidame of Chartres and Monsieur Hunaudaye came to the court and saw the Order of the Garter and the king and the knights receive communion.

---

38 Thomas became responsible for Edward's political tuition. In 1551, for example, he set the King 85 questions on political rule.

39 Here we have the first reference to Edward's difficulties with his much older sister, Mary. She, a religious conservative, had refused to have her services conform to the Prayer Book of 1549. In March she had written to the Emperor asking him if he might help her flee the country.

40 A pallet was a small camp bed.

Sir Willliam Sharington.

24 April. Certain articles touching upon a straighter friendship in trade were sent to the King of Sweden. These were first that if the King of Sweden sends bullion, he should pay no toll on our commodities. Secondly that he should bring bullion to no other prince. Thirdly, if he brought osmunds[41] and steel and copper, etc, he should have our commodities and pay customs as an Englishman. Fourthly if he brought any other he should have free intercourse, paying customs as a foreigner.

A reply was sent to the Duke of Brunswick[42] that whilst he offered the services of 10,000 men of his band the war was ended. And as for the marriage of my Lady Mary to him, there was talk of her marrying the Infante of Portugal and when this was determined he shall have an answer.

25 April. Lord Clinton, Captain of Boulogne, having sent away all his men, save 1,800, and all his ordnance, save that stipulated in the treaty, issued out of the town with his 1,800, delivering it to Monsieur Chatillon and receiving from him the six English hostages, the quittance for the delivery of the town and a safe-conduct to go to Calais. When he reached there he placed the 1,800 on the Emperor's frontiers.

27 April. The Marquis de Mayenne, Count d'Enghien and the Constable's son were received at Blackheath by my Lord of Rutland, my Lord Grey of Wilton, my Lord Braye, my Lord Lisle and many gentlemen, with all the Pensioners,[43] to the number of 100, besides a great number of serving men.

---

41 High quality iron bars.
42 This should be the Margrave of Brandenburg as it was this German prince who endeavoured to obtain Mary's hand in marriage.
43 The Pensioners were a body of mounted troops forming the king's royal guard.

It was granted that my Lord of Somerset should have all his moveable goods and leases except those that be already given.

The King of Sweden's ambassador departed home to his master.

29 April. The Count d'Enghien, brother to the Duke of Vendome, and next heir to the crown after the king's children, the Marquis de Mayenne, brother to the Scottish queen, and Monsieur Montmorency, the Constable's son, came to the court where they were received with much music at dinner.

26 April. Certain persons were taken that went about to have an insurrection in Kent upon the following May day and the priest who was the chief worker ran away into Essex, where he was laid for.

30 April. Dunglass was delivered as the treaty did require.

MAY

Joan Bocher, sometimes called Joan of Kent, was burnt for holding that Christ was not incarnate of the Virgin Mary; she had been condemned the year before but kept in the hope of conversion. On the 30th of April the Bishop of London and the Bishop of Ely were to persuade her. But she withstood them and insulted the preacher who preached at her death.[44]

The first payment was made at Calais and was received by Sir Thomas Dennis and Mr Sharington.

4 May. Lord Clinton, formerly Captain of Boulogne, came to the court where, after thanks, he was made Admiral of

---

[44] Joan Bocher, or Butcher, was an Anabaptist and had been in trouble during Henry VIII's reign for promoting Tyndale's translation of the Bible. Nicholas Ridley was Bishop of London and Thomas Goodrich was the Bishop of Ely.

1550

England following the surrender of the Earl of Warwick's patent. He was also taken in to the Privy Council and promised further reward. The captains and officers of the town were also promised rewards. Monsieur de Breze also passed through the court en route to Scotland but at Greenwich came before the king telling him that the French king would see to it that if he lacked any commodity that he had, he would give it to him as too would the Constable of France.

5 May. The Marquis de Mayenne departed for Scotland with Monsieur de Breze to comfort the queen on the death of the Duke of Guise.

The Master of Erskine and Monsieur de Morette's brother came out of Scotland for the acceptance of the peace and then afterwards had passports to go into France.

7 May. The Council drew up a book of every shire and who should be the lieutenants of them and who should remain with me, but the lieutenants were ordered to stay until Chatillon, Sassy and Bochetel had come and then they were to depart.

8 May. A proclamation was made that the soldiers should return to their homes and the Mayor of London was charged with searching through all the wards, take them and send them to their countries.

The debt of £30,000 and odd money was put over for a year and 2,500 quintals of powder were bought.

11 May. A proclamation was made that all the wool-winders should take an oath that they would make good cloth there, as the Lord Chancellor ordered them according to an Act of Parliament made by Edward III.

7 May. Lord Cobham, Secretary Petre and Sir John Mason went to the French king at Amiens and they were received by all the nobles and so brought to their lodgings, which were well dressed.

10 May. The French king took an oath for the acceptance of the treaty.

12 May. Our ambassadors departed from the French court, leaving Sir John Mason as resident ambassador.

14 May. The Duke of Somerset was taken in to the Privy Chamber as was the Lord Admiral.

15 May. It was ordered that all the lighthorsemen of Boulogne and the men-at-arms should be paid their wages and should be commanded by the Lord Marquis of Northampton, captain of the Pensioners, and all the guard of Boulogne under the Lord Admiral. And also that the chief captains should be sent with 600 of them to strengthen the frontiers of Scotland.

The comprehension of peace with Scotland was accepted so far as the league went and was sealed with the great seal of Scotland.

16 May. The Master of Erskine departed for France.

17 May. Removing to Westminster from Greenwich.

18 May. The French king came to Boulogne to visit the pieces [of artillery] lately delivered to him and to establish order in things there which, being done, he departed.

19 May. Peter Vannes went as ambassador to Venice and departed from the court with his instructions.

20 May. The Lord Cobham and Sir William Petre came home from their journey, delivering both the oath and the testimonial of the oath witnessed by many noblemen of France and also the treaty, sealed with the great seal of France. In the oath it was confessed that I was Supreme Head of the Church of England and Ireland, and also King of Ireland.

1550

23 *May*. Monsieur Chatillon and Mortier and Bochetel, accompanied by the Rhinegrave d'Andelot, the Constable's second son, and Chemault the resident ambassador, came to Durham Place[45] and on their journey they were met by Mr Treasurer and 60 gentlemen at Woolwich and they were also saluted with great peals [of bells] at Woolwich, Deptford and the Tower.

24 *May*. The ambassadors came to me, presenting the resident ambassador and also delivering letters of credence from the French king.

25 *May*. The ambassadors came to the court where they saw me take the oath for the acceptance of the treaty and afterwards they dined with me. After dinner was a pastime of 10 against 10 in the ring; on one side was the Duke of Suffolk, the Vidame of Chartres, Lord Lisle[46] and seven other gentlemen dressed in yellow. On the other side was Lord Strange, Monsieur Hunaudaye and eight others in blue.

26 *May*. The ambassadors saw the baiting of bears and bulls.

27 *May*. The ambassadors sat with me at supper after they had hunted.

28 *May*. They went to Hampton Court where they hunted and, the same night, returned to Durham Place.

25 *May*. One that thought at a marriage to assemble the people and so make an insurrection in Kent was taken by the gentlemen of the shire and afterwards punished.

29 *May*. The ambassadors had a fair supper given to them by the Duke of Somerset and afterwards went to the Thames

---

45 A large house in the Strand, originally the London residence of the bishops of Durham, then John Dudley's town house.
46 John Dudley, son of the Duke of Northumberland.

Willliam Parr, Marquis of Nothampton.

1550

and saw bears hunted in the river and also wild fire cast out of boats and many pretty conceits.

30 May. The ambassadors took their leave and the next day departed.

JUNE

3 June. The king came to Sheen where there was a marriage between Lord Lisle, the Earl of Warwick's son, and Lady Anne, daughter to the Duke of Somerset. This was done, a fair dinner was had and the dancing done when the king and the ladies went into two chambers made from boughs where first he [the king] saw six gentlemen on one side and six on another run the course of the field twice over. Their names were as follows: Lord Edward, Sir John Appleby [there then follows a space].

And afterwards came three masquers on one side and two on the other and they ran four courses each. Their names [left blank].

Last of all came the Count of Rangone with three Italians and they ran with all the gentlemen four courses and afterwards fought at tourney. And so after supper he [the king] returned to Westminster.

4 June. Sir Robert Dudley, third son of the Earl of Warwick, married Sir John Robsart's daughter after which marriage certain gentlemen tried to see who could be the first to take away a goose's head which was hanged alive on two crossed posts.[47]

---

47 Sir Robert Dudley was the fifth son of the Duke of Northumberland (the Earl of Warwick) and he married Amy Robsart. She died after falling down stairs and breaking her neck in September 1560, a time when Robert Dudley was quite possibly Elizabeth I's lover.

5 June. There was tilting and a tourney on foot with great lances as could be used on horseback.

6 June. Removing to Greenwich.

8 June. The stages of my Progress were set forth which were these: from Greenwich to Westminster, from Westminster to Hampton Court, from Hampton Court to Windsor, from Windsor to Guildford, from Guildford to Oatlands, from Oatlands to Richmond, etc.

Also the Vidame made a great supper for the Duke of Somerset and the Marquis of Northampton with many masques and other conceits.

9 June. The Duke of Somerset, Marquis of Northampton, the Lord Treasurer, the Earl of Bedford and Secretary Petre went to the Bishop of Winchester to know to what he would stick. He made answer that he would obey and set forth all things set forth by me and my Parliament and if he were troubled in conscience he would reveal it to the Council and not reason openly against it.

The first payment by the French men was laid up in the Tower for all chances.

10 June. The books of my proceedings was sent to the Bishop of Winchester to see whether he would set his hand to it or promise to set it forth to the people.

11 June. Order was given for fortifying and supplying Calais for four months and also Sir Harry Palmer and Sir Lee were sent to the frontiers of Scotland to take a view of all the forts there and to report to the Council where they thought best to fortify. Rogers and Atwood were also sent to Alderney to make fortifications there.

12 June. The Marquis de Mayenne came from Scotland in post and went his way into France.

1550

13 June. Commissions were signed to both Sir William Herbert, and 30 others, to entreat of certain matters in Wales, and also instructions to the same on how to behave himself in the presidentship.

14 June. The surveyor of Calais was sent to Calais first to raise the walls of Risebank towards the sand hills and afterwards to make the wall massive again and the round bulwark to be change into a pointed one which should run 26 feet into the sea to beat the sand hills and to raise the mount. Secondly to Newnhambridge to make a high bulwark in the middle with flankers to beat through all the strait and also four sluices to make Calais harbour better. Afterwards he was bid to go to Guines where first he was to take away the four-cornered bulwark to make the outward wall of the keep and to fill the space between the keep and the said outer wall with the aforesaid bulwark and to raise the old keep that it might beat the town. Also he was bid to make Purton's bulwark where it is now round without flankers both pointed and also with six flankers to beat hard to the keep.

Atwood and Lambert were sent to take view of Alderney, Scilly, Jersey, Guernsey and the Isle of Jethou.

The Duke of Somerset, with five others of the Council, went to the Bishop of Winchester who made him this answer: 'I having deliberately seen the Book of Common Prayer, although I would not have made it so myself, yet I find such things in it as satisfy my conscience and therefore both I will execute it myself and also see my other parishioners to do it.' It was subscribed by the aforesaid councillors that they had heard him saying these words.

16 June. The Lord Marquis, Mr Herbert, the Vidame, Hunaudaye, and many other gentlemen went to the Earl of Warwick's where they were honourably received and the next day there ran at the ring a great number of gentlemen.

19 June. I went to Deptford, being asked to supper by the Lord Clinton, where before supper I saw certain men stand upon the end of a boat, without holding anything, and charging at one another until one was cast into the water. At supper Monsieur Vidame and Hunaudaye supped with me. After supper there was a fort made upon a great barge in the Thames which had three walls and a watchtower in the middle. Mr Winter was captain of it with 40 or 50 other soldiers in yellow and black. A galley of yellow colour also belonged to the fort with men and munition in it for the defence of the castle. Wherefore there came four pinnaces with their men dressed handsomely in white; these, intending to give assault to the castle, first drove away the yellow pinnace and afterwards with clods, squibs, canes of fire, darts made for noise and bombards they assaulted the castle and, at length, came with their pieces and burst the outer walls of the castle. They beat those in the castle into the second ward but they issued out and drove away the pinnaces, sinking one of them, out of which all the men in it, being more than 20, leaped out and swam in the Thames. Then came the Admiral of the Navy with three more pinnaces and won the castle by assault and burst the top of it down and took the captain and under-captain. Then the Admiral went forth to take the yellow ship and, at length, came alongside her, took her and also assaulted her top and won it by treaty and so returned home.

20 June. The Mayor of London caused the watches to be increased every night because of the great fights and also one alderman to see good rule kept every night.

22 June. There was a privy search made through all Sussex for all vagabonds, gypsies, conspirators, prophets, ill-players and such like.

ᴥ 1550 ᴦ

24 June. There were certain men in Essex, around Romford, who went about a conspiracy which were taken and the matter prevented.

25 June. Removing to Greenwich.

23 June. Sir John Gates, Sheriff of Essex, went down with letters to see the Bishop of London's injunctions performed, which touched upon the plucking down of superalters, altars and suchlike ceremonies and abuses.

29 June. It was appointed that the Germans should have the Austin Friars church to have their service in for avoiding of all sects of Anabaptists and suchlike.[48]

17 June. The French queen was delivered of a third son called Monsieur d'Angoulême.[49]

13 June. The Emperor departed from Argentina to Augusta.[50]

30 June. John Ponet was made Bishop of Rochester and received his oath.

JULY

5 July. Money was provided to be sent to Ireland for the payment of the soldiers there and also order taken for the dispatch of the strangers in London.

7 July. The Master of Erskine went to Scotland having come from France. The French ambassador also came before me, first

---

[48] Here we see the establishment of a church to serve the exiled Protestant community and Dutch and German merchants. A church for French Protestants was established in Threadneedle Street.

[49] This boy was later to be crowned as Charles IX. Edward noted the date down incorrectly as it should have been the 27th of June.

[50] The Emperor, Charles V, went from Strasbourg to Augsburg.

telling me of the birth of Monsieur d'Angoulême, afterwards declaring that whereas the French king had, for my sake, let the prisoners who had shamefully murdered the cardinal, and were at St Andrew's, go, he desired that all Scots who were prisoners should be released.[51] It was answered that all had been delivered. Then he asked for one called the Archbishop of Glasgow who had, since the peace, come disguised and without passport and so was taken. It was answered that we had no peace with Scotland such that they might pass through our country and the Master of Erskine affirmed the same.

8 July. It was agreed that the 200 that were with me and the 200 [horsemen] with Mr Herbert should be sent into Ireland. Also that the mint should be set to work that it might make £24,000 a year and bear all my charges in Ireland for this year and add £10,000 to my coffers.

9 July. The Earl of Warwick, the Lord Treasurer, Sir William Herbert and Secretary Petre went to the Bishop of Winchester with certain articles signed by me and the Council containing a confession of his fault: the supremacy, the establishing of the holy days, the abolishing of the six articles, and many others whereof the copy is in the Council chest, whereunto he put his hand except for the confession.

10 July. Sir William Herbert and Secretary Petre were sent to him to tell him that I marvelled that he would not put his hand to the confession; to which he made answer that he would not put his hand to the confession because he was innocent and also that the confession was only the preface to the articles.

---

51 Cardinal Beaton had been killed in 1546. John Knox was among this group of prisoners.

1550

11 July. The Bishop of London, Secretary Petre, Mr Cecil[52] and Goodrich were commanded to make certain articles according to the laws and submit them [to the Bishop of Winchester].

12 July. It was appointed that under the shadow of preparing for the same matters £5,000 should be sent to the Protestants to get their good will.[53]

14 July. The Bishop of Winchester denied the articles that the Bishop of London and the others had made.

13 July. Sir John Gates was sent into Essex to stop Lady Mary going away because it was credibly informed that Scepperus was to steal her away to Antwerp, many of her gentlemen were there and Scepperus had been to see the landing places a little before.[54]

16 July. It was appointed that 200 [men] under the Duke of Somerset, 200 under the Lord Privy Seal and 400 under Mr St Leger should be sent to the seacoast.

17 July. It was agreed that on Wednesday next we should go to Windsor and dine at Sion.

18 July. It was thought best that Lord Bowes should still remain in his position and that the Earl of Warwick should remain here and be recompensed.

19 July. The Bishop of Winchester was sequestered from his fruits for three months.

---

52 William Cecil, later Elizabeth I's greatest minister and adviser.
53 This obscure entry probably relates to a sum of money being despatched to Scotland to aid the Protestants north of the border.
54 The Emperor Charles V did send an expedition over to assist Mary in escaping England in July 1550. It was commanded by Cornelius Scepperus (1502-1555), a Flemish admiral and diplomat. The rescue attempt failed when Mary refused to leave behind most of her personal possessions.

20 July. Hooper was made Bishop of Gloucester. The merchants were commanded to put off as much as they could their trips to Flanders as the Emperor had made many strict laws against those who professed the Gospel.

21 July. A muster of the men of Boulogne was made and they were wholly paid what they were owed and for a month to come. Sir John Wallop, Francis Hall and Doctor Cook were appointed commissioners to set the boundaries between me and the French king.

23 July. Removing to Windsor.

22 July. The Secretary Petre and the Lord Chancellor were appointed to go to Lady Mary to cause her to come to Woking or to the court.[55]

25 July. It was appointed that half of the French king's first payment should be bestowed on paying £10,00 to Calais, £9,000 to Ireland, £16,000 to the north, £2,000 to the Admiralty so that every crown might be worth one noble.[56]

27 July. Because of the rumour that Scepperus was coming it was appointed that those in the Admiralty should set my ships in readiness.

26 July. The Duke of Somerset went to establish order in Oxfordshire, Sussex, Wiltshire and Hampshire.

28 July. Lady Mary, after long communication, was content to come to Leighs Priory [in Essex] to the Lord Chancellor and

---

55 On the 22nd of July these two gentlemen were despatched to ask Mary to come to meet her brother but she preferred to maintain contact with him through letters only.

56 ie each crown was to be worth one noble, the latter being six shillings eight pence soon to be six shillings and four pence according to a proclamation dated that December.

then to Hunsdon but she utterly refused to come to the court or Woking at that time.

31 July. The Earl of Southampton died.[57]

14 July. Andrea Doria took the city of Africa from the pirate Dragut who, in the mean time, burnt the city of Genoa.[58]

8 July. The Emperor came to Augsburg.

AUGUST

Mr St Leger was appointed, by my letters patent, to be deputy in Ireland and had his commission, instructions and letters to the nobles of Ireland for the same purpose.

5 August. The same deputy departed from the castle of Windsor.

6 August. The Duke of Somerset departed to Reading to take an order there.

7 August. It was appointed that of the money delivered to me by the French king there would be 100,000 Crowns. Of this £10,000 would be paid at Calais, £15,000 in the north, £2,000 to the Admiralty and £8,000 in Ireland.

8 August. Monsieur Hunaudaye took his leave to depart for Calais and so, upon payment, would be sent home; Trémoille, being sick, went in a horse-litter to Dover.

9 August. The French ambassador came to Windsor to sue for a passport for the Dowager of Scotland which, being granted, she came like a friend. He required 300 horse to pass with 200 keepers but this was not wholly granted and only 200 horse and 150

---

57 Thomas Wriothesley, former Lord Chancellor.
58 This relates to Doria's attack on Mehedia, a city held by the notorious Barbary Corsairs. Edward's dates are incorrect as the first attack was actually launched on the 25th of July and the city did not fall for some considerable time.

keepers were in the company, coming into the realm as should be appointed, passing into France and not returning this way.

11 August. The Vidame of Chartres showed his licence to stay here and a letter written to the same purpose.

10 August. The ambassador of France departed, not a little contented with the gentle answers.

12 August. Removing to Guildford.

13 August. The Parliament was prorogued until the 20th of February next year. Mr Cook, the Master of Requests, and certain other lawyers were appointed to make a short table of the laws and acts that were not wholly unprofitable and to present them to the board.

13 August. The Lord Chancellor fell very sick along with 40 more in his house so that the Lady Mary did not go there at that time.

14 August. There came many warnings from Sir Thomas Chamberlain, ambassador to the Queen of Hungary, that it was their intent to take away the Lady Mary and so to begin an outward war and an inward conspiracy. The queen said that Scepperus was a coward and for fear of one gentleman who came down he did not continue with his enterprise to get my Lady Mary.[59]

16 August. The Earl of Maxwell came down to the northern borders with a strong force to overthrow the Grahams who were a certain family that had submitted to me. But Lord Dacre stood before him with a good band of men and so put him off his purpose, and the gentlemen Grahams skirmished with the said earl slaying certain of his men.

---

59 The Queen of Hungary was Mary, sister of Charles V and widow of Louis of Hungary who had died fighting the Turks. She was also Regent of the Netherlands and was therefore an important figure in English foreign policy.

1550

17 August. The Council appointed that among themselves none of them should speak on any man's behalf for land to be given, for reversion of offices, for leases of manors or extraordinary annuities, except for certain captains who had served at Boulogne, their answer being deferred to Michaelmas next.

18 August. A proclamation was made that, until Michaelmas, all foreigners that sued for pensions should go their way.

20 August. Removing to Woking.

15 August. The second French payment was paid and Hunaudaye and Trémoille were set free.

21 August. £8,000 of the last payment was appointed to be paid to Calais and 5,000 to the north.

24 August. £10,000 was appointed to be occupied to win money to pay next year for expenses and it was promised that the money should double every month.

20 August. Removing to Oatlands.

27 August. Andrea Doria launched a hot assault against the town of Africa, held by the pirate called Dragut Arraiz, but was repulsed by the townsmen.

29 August. The pirate launched a hot assault on Andrea Doria by night and slew the Captain of Tunis with many other notable men.

31 August. Duke Maurice [of Saxony] replied to the Emperor that if the Council were not free then he would not come to it.

SEPTEMBER

2 September. Maclamore in Ireland, once a rebel, surrendered himself to Mr Brabazon and gave pledges.

6 September. Mr Wotton gave up his secretaryship and Mr Cecil took it.[60]

SEPTEMBER 1550 AD, CONTINUED

8 September. Removing to Nonesuch.
15 September. Removing to Oatlands.
22 September. A proclamation was set forth by which it was commanded firstly that no kind of victual, no wax, tallow candles nor any such thing should be carried over except to Calais, putting in sureties to go thither. Secondly, no man should buy or sell the same things again, except brokers, and should not have more than ten quarters of grain at once. Thirdly that all justices should look in their quarters to see what superfluous corn was in every barn and order it to be sold at a reasonable price. Also that one of them should be in every market to see the corn brought in. Furthermore whoever shipped over anything abovementioned for parties beyond the sea or to Scotland after eight days following the publication of this proclamation should forfeit his ship and the goods therein, half going to the lord of the franchise and the other half to the finder thereof. Whosoever bought to sell again after the abovementioned day should forfeit all his goods, farms and leases. One half should go the finder, one half to the king. Whosoever did not bring corn to market as he was appointed should forfeit £10 except if the purveyors took it up or it was sold to his neighbours.

---

60 William Cecil hereby became one of the secretaries of state, a position of enormous influence. He drew up the Council's agendas and oversaw the Council's correspondence and kept his patron, Warwick (later the Duke of Northumberland), informed as to the Council's deliberations.

25 September. Letters were sent out to the Justices of the Peace for the due execution thereof.

18 September. Andrea Doria was repulsed from the town of Africa and lost many of his men and the Captain of Tunis and nevertheless did not raise the siege.

24 September. Order was given for the supplying of Calais.

26 September. Lord Willoughby, Deputy of Calais departed and took his leave of the place.

28 September. The Lord Treasurer was sent to London to give orders for the preservation of the City with the help of the Mayor.

15 September. Whereas the Emperor required a Council they were content to have it if it were free and ordinary, requiring also that every man might be restored to his rights and a general peace proclaimed. They also desired that in the meantime no man might be forced to use the Emperor's fashion of religion.

18 September. The Emperor made answer that the Council should be to the glory of God and maintenance of the empire, at Trent. He knew no title to any of his territories. He desired peace and would have them observe the Interim of the last Council of Trent in the meanwhile.[61] He also wanted that those from Bremen and Hamburg, with their associates, should leave their seditions and obey his decrees.

21 September. George, Duke of Mecklenburg, came to the Protestant city of Magdeburg with 8,000 men of war. The Count of Mansfeld and his brother with 6,000 men and eight guns came to drive him from pillage. But the other, offering

---

[61] The Interim of Augsburg had been imposed on Germany's Protestant princes following their defeat at the hands of Charles V in 1547. It was an aggressive counterattack on Lutheranism by the Holy Roman Emperor and many Protestants subsequently fled Imperial territory.

battle, put the count to flight, took his brother prisoner and slew 3,000 men, as it is reported.

OCTOBER

4 October. Removing to Richmond.

5 October. The Parliament was prorogued until the 20th of January.

6 October. The French king made his entry into Rouen.

10 October. It was agreed that Sir John York, master of one of the mints in the Tower, should make a bargain with me: to make a profit from my silver from the bullion that he himself bought, in return he should pay all my debts to the sum of £120,000 or above and remain accountable for the overplus, paying no more than 6s and 6d the ounce until the exchange in Flanders was equal. Afterwards he should pay 6s and 2d. Also that he should declare all his bargains to anyone who should be appointed to oversee him and leave off when I would. For which I would give him 15,000 in advance and permission to take £8,000 overseas to lower the exchange rate.

16 October. Removing to Westminster.

19 October. Prices for all kinds of grains, butter, cheese and poultry were set by proclamation.

20 October. Some 800 Frenchmen came to Sandingfield and Fiennes Wood and there, on my land, did spoil my subjects who sheltered by the wood.

26 October. The French ambassador came to excuse the aforementioned men saying that they thought that it was not right that the wood should be used by us, being thought of and claimed as theirs and therefore they went there.

24 October. Some 1,000 men were embarked for Calais and

then to Guines, Hammes, Risebank, Newnhambridge, the Causeway and the bulwarks with supplies for the same.

NOVEMBER

19 November. Letters were sent out to every bishop to pluck down the altars.

20 November. There were letters sent out to the gentlemen of every shire for the observation of the last proclamation touching corn commanding them to punish the offenders as none had come to the markets.

29 November. Upon letters written back by the same the proclamation was abolished.

DECEMBER

15 December. Letters were sent out for the taking of certain chaplains of the Lady Mary for saying mass, which she denied.

19 December. Borthwick was sent to the King of Denmark with private instructions for the marriage of Lady Elizabeth to his son.[62]

20 December. It was appointed that a band of horsemen should be divided amongst the nobles, 100 to the Duke of Somerset, 50 each to my Lord Marquis Northampton, the Earl of Warwick, the Lord Privy Seal, Mr Herbert, Mr Treasurer, Lord Marquis Dorset, Earl of Wiltshire, Lord Wentworth, Lord Admiral, Lord Paget, Mr Sadler and Mr Darcy.

21 December. Removing to Greenwich.

26 December. Peace was concluded between the Emperor and the Scots.

---

62 Edward's sister Elizabeth was being offered to Frederick of Denmark, later King Frederick III.

✂ *1551* ✄

Edward VI granting a charter to Bridewell.

ᶜᵒ 1551 ᵍᵒ

JANUARY

6 January. The Earl of Arundel remitted £8,000 which he ought to have paid for certain faults he had committed within the last 12 years.[63]

7 January. It was ordered that because some Frenchmen were conspiring in Ireland, that four ships, four barks, four pinnaces and 12 supply ships should be prepared to take three harbours of which two were on the south side towards France and one was in James Carr's Scot's country and also to break up the aforesaid conspiracies.

10 January. Three ships being sent forth into the Narrow Seas took certain pirates and brought them into England where the most part of them were hanged.

27 January. Monsieur de Lansac came from the French king to request that Cawe Mills, the fishing of the Tweed, Edrington, the Debateable Ground[64] and the Scottish hostages that had been brought here in the days of my father the king should be delivered to the Scots. That the Scots might be allowed to trade as though they were at peace and that all interest of the aforesaid hostages should be delivered to the

---

[63] The charges against Arundel, which led to this fine of £12,000, were never made clear. Arundel seems to have suffered from the enmity of the Earl of Warwick.
[64] An area of disputed land between the rivers Esk and Sark in Northumberland.

1551

Scots. Also that those prisoners who had been bound to pay their ransoms before the peace last concluded should not enjoy the benefit of the peace.

18 January. The Lord Cobham was appointed to be General Lieutenant of Ireland.

30 January. Letters were written to Mr St Leger to tell him to repair to the south of Ireland with his forces.

FEBRUARY

3 February. Mr Croft was ordered to go to Ireland and, along with Rogers and certain workmen, to take the harbours abovementioned and begin some fortifications.

5 February. Many London merchants were spoken to regarding the provision of 40,000 quarters of corn from Denmark.

10 February. Mountford was commanded to go and begin certain preparations for the supply of ships that should go into Ireland.

11 February. Also for provision to be sent to Berwick and the north parts.

16 February. Whalley was examined for persuading many nobles of the realm to make the Duke of Somerset the Protector at the next Parliament and he denied it. The Earl of Rutland, however, affirmed it manifestly.

13 February. The Bishop of Winchester was, after a long trial, deposed from his bishopric.

20 February. Sir William Pickering, knight, was despatched to the French king to answer Monsieur de Lansac and declare that, although I had the right to the aforesaid places yet I was content to forbear them under conditions to be agreed upon by commissioners on both sides and that, for the last article, I agreed to it without condition.

25 February. The Lord Marquis Dorset was appointed to be Warden of the Northern Borders, having three sub-wardens: Lord Ogle and Sir Nicholas Strelley in the east and Lord Conyers in the west. Also Mr Aucher for the charge and supplying of Calais.

28 February. The learned man Bucer died at Cambridge and was buried two days later in St Mary's Church at Cambridge, the whole university with the whole town, to the number of 3,000 persons, bringing him to the grave.[65] Also a very eloquent oration on his death was made by Mr Haddon and a sermon by Dr Parker. After that, Mr Redman made a third sermon. These three sermons made the people lament his death. Last of all, all the learned men of the university made their epitaphs in his praise, laying them on his grave.

MARCH

3 March. Lord Wentworth, the Lord Chamberlain, died at about ten o'clock at night, leaving behind him 16 children.

8 March. Sir John York suffered a great loss of about £2,000 worth of silver through the treason of Englishmen. He had brought it for provision of the mints. Also Judd lost £1,500, also Tresham [Gresham] £500, so the whole came to £4,000.[66]

---

65 This was Martin Bucer, the Protestant exile. He thought highly of Edward, saying 'The king, however, is godly and learned to a miracle; he is well acquainted with Latin, and has a fair knowledge of Greek. He speaks Italian, and is learning French. He is now studying moral philosophy from Cicero and Aristotle, but no study delights him more than that of the Holy Scriptures, of which he daily reads about ten chapters with the greatest attention.'

66 This entry relates to the confiscation of bullion by Flemish authorities in Antwerp following an attempt to have it smuggled out of the Continent.

1551

FEBRUARY

20 February. The Frenchmen brought a fleet of 160 sails into Scotland, laden with provisions of grain, powder and ordnance. Of these 16 great ships perished on Ireland's coast, two laden with artillery and 14 with corn. Also this month the deputy in Ireland punished some of the west lords that were at variance.

MARCH

10 March. Some new fortifications were devised for the defence of Calais so that at Gravelines the water could be let on to my land and up to the six bulwarks to Guines, Hammes and Newnhambridge and that there should be an earth wall eight foot high and six foot wide to keep the water out and to create a marsh around the area of Calais 37 miles long. Also that flankers for the keep at Guines are desired, a three-cornered bulwark at the keep, to keep it. Furthermore, at Newnhambridge there was to be a massive wall on the French side, as was agreed. Besides, at the west jetty, there should be another jetty which should protect those supplying the town from shots fired from the sandhills.

5 March. Mr Aucher had £2,000 in money with which he provided 2,000 quarters of barley and 500 quarters of wheat from Flanders for Calais.

18 March. The Lady Mary, my sister, came to me at Westminster where, after salutations, she was called, along with my Council, into a chamber where it was declared how long I had suffered her mass in hope of her reconciliation but that now, there being no hope, which I perceived from her letters, unless I saw some amendment, I could not bear it. She answered that her soul was God's and that she would not change her faith, nor hide her opinion through contrary doings. It was said that I constrained not her faith but willed her as a subject to obey. And that her example might breed too much inconvenience.[67]

19 March. The Emperor's ambassador came with a short message from his master threatening war if I would not allow his cousin the princess to use her mass. To this no answer was given at this time.

20 March. The bishops of Canterbury, London and Rochester concluded that giving licence to sin was sin; to suffer and wink at it for a time might be borne so all haste possible might be used.

23 March. The Council, having the bishops' answers, seeing that my subjects lacking their sales in Flanders might put the whole realm in danger. Seeing that the Flemings had enough cloth for a year in their hand and were kept far under; the danger of the Papists, the 1,500 quintals of powder I had in Flanders, the harness they had for preparation of the gendarmerie, the goods my merchants had there at the wool fleet, they decided to send an ambassador, Mr Wotton, to the Emperor to deny the matter and persuade the Emperor and thinking that by his going we might win some time for the preparation of a market, conveyance of powder, harness, etc and for the surety of the realm. In the meantime to punish the offenders, first my servants that heard mass, next hers.

---

67 And so continued Edward's, or rather his Council's, persecution of Mary. Although Edward contributed to the campaign by writing 'you, our nearest sister ... wish to break our laws and set them aside deliberately and of your own free will; and, moreover, sustain and encourage others to commit like offence.' Mary fought back with, as the next entry shows, Imperial support. The Council then turned on Mary's household and arrests followed.

1551

22 March. Sir Anthony Browne was sent to the Fleet for hearing mass with Sergeant Morgan. Sir Clement Smith, who had heard mass a year before, was warned.

25 March. The Emperor's ambassador came to have his answer but had none except that someone would go to the Emperor within a month or two to declare this matter.

22 March. Sir William Pickering came with great thanks from the French king.

27 March. Removing to Greenwich.

31 March. A challenge was made by me that I, with 16 of my chamber, should run at base, shoot and run at ring against any 17 of my servants, gentlemen in the court.

Mr Croft arrived in Ireland and went to Waterford, consulting with the deputy on the fortification of the town.

APRIL

1 April. The first day of the challenge, at base, or running, and the king won.

3 April. Monsieur de Lansac came again from the French king to go to Scotland to appoint his commissioners on the Scottish side. These were the French ambassador in Scotland, the bishop, the Master of Erskine, and ….

5 April. Sir Thomas Darcy was made Lord Darcy of Chiche and Lord Chamberlain, for maintenance whereof he was given 100 Marks to his heirs general and 300 to his heirs male.

6 April. I lost the challenge of shooting at rounds and won at rovers.[68]

---

68 This relates to archery. Shooting at rounds being shooting at targets and shooting at rovers being an attempt to hit random targets such as a tree or a gate post. The winning archer selected the next target.

7 April. Commissioners were appointed on my side. Either the Bishop of Lichfield, if he had no objection, or of Norwich, Mr Bowes, Mr Beckwith and Sir Thomas Chaloner.

8 April. Sir John Gates was made Vice-Chamberlain and Captain of the Guard and had £120 worth of land.

9 April. Ponet, Bishop of Rochester, received his oath for the bishopric of Winchester, having 2,000 Marks worth of land given to him for his maintenance.

7 April. A certain Arian of the foreigners, a Dutchman, being excommunicated by the congregation of his countrymen, was, after long deliberation, condemned to the fire.[69]

9 April. The Earl of Wiltshire had 50 more men-at-arms in place of my Lord Marquis of Dorset, now the Warden of the North, and my Lord of Rutland another 50 in place of my Lord Wentworth.

10 April. Mr Wotton had his instructions made so he could go to the Emperor as resident ambassador in place of Mr Morison and to declare this resolution: that if the Emperor would allow my ambassador to worship then I would his. If he would not allow mine to worship, then I would not allow his. Likewise that my sister was my subject and should worship as appointed by Act of Parliament.

It was also decreed that 20,000 pounds in weight should be debased in order to gain £160,000, by which the debt of the realm might be paid, the country defended from any

---

[69] This was Dr George van Parris, from Mainz, a leading exponent of Arianism in London's Dutch and German community. In this context Arians were members of a Unitarian sect which denied the Trinity.

1551

sudden attempt and the coin amended.[70]

11 April. Mr Pickering had his instructions and was despatched to go into France as resident ambassador there in place of Mr Mason who had desired very much to come home. Mr Pickering had instructions to tell the French king of the appointment of my aforesaid commissioners in Scotland.

12 April. The people of Magdeburg, having last January taken part in a conflict with the Duke of Mecklenburg and three other earls, attacked Duke Maurice by boat when the river flooded the country and they slew many of his men and came home safe, bringing a great portion of supplies into the town.

15 April. A conspiracy among the men of Essex who, within three days, were to declare the coming of strangers and so bring people to Chelmsford and would then spoil the rich men's houses if they could. Such woodcock!

16 April. Also a conspiracy of Londoners who thought to rise on May Day against foreigners in the City. Both parties were arrested.

23 April. On this day the French king and Lord Clinton were chosen for the Order of the Garter and it was appointed that the Duke of Somerset, the Marquis of Northampton, the Earl of Wiltshire and the Earl of Warwick should peruse and amend the Order.

---

70 Edward's government was beset by financial problems which originated during the reign of Henry VIII. The debasement of the coinage, when the amount of precious metal in coins was reduced in favour of base metals, had begun in 1542. Between 1542 and 1547 the Crown had made £450,000 profit from the process. The consequences were felt in Edward's reign. The value of sterling fell on the foreign exchanges and debased coins were very unpopular in England. Debasement was halted after this final measure adopted in April 1551.

PART OF APRIL 1551, CONTINUED

24 April. The Lords sat at London and banqueted one another on this day and for three days after in order to show agreement between them after discord had been rumoured and so to look for the punishment of tale-bearers and the apprehending of evil persons.

25 April. A bargain was made with the Fuggers to defer about £60,000 due to be paid in May and August.[71] Firstly, the Fuggers would put it off for 10 percent. Secondly that I should buy 12,000 mark weight at six Shillings the ounce to be delivered to Antwerp and so conveyed over. Thirdly, that I should pay 100,000 Crowns for a very fair jewel of theirs, four rubies marvellous big, one orient an great diamond and one great pearl.[72]

27 April. Mallett, the Lady Mary's chaplain, was arrested and sent to the Tower of London.

30 April. The Lord Marquis of Northampton was appointed to go with the Order and further commission of treaty and that in post, having joined with him in commission the Bishop of Ely, Sir Philip Hoby, Sir William Pickering, Sir John Mason, knights and two other lawyers – Smith that was secretary and Dr Oliver.

---

[71] The Fuggers were the highly successful, and incredibly wealthy, family of bankers originally from Augsburg. They lent money to most of the European monarchies but, at this time, the conditions they imposed on the English Crown were not particularly favourable.

[72] The diamond was known as the 'Three Brothers' and remained in the royal collection of jewels until pawned in 1626.

1551

MAY

2 May. The Earls of Rutland, Worcester and Ormond, the Lords Lisle, Fitzwalter, Braye, Abergavenny and Evre, and many other gentlemen to the number of 30 in all, were appointed to go with my Lord Marquis.

3 May. The challenge of running at ring was performed at which first came the king, 16 footmen, and ten horsemen, in black silk coats pulled out with white silk taffeta; then all lords having three men likewise dressed and all gentlemen, their footmen in white fustian pulled out with black taffeta.[73] The other side came in yellow taffeta. At length the yellow band took it twice in 120 courses and my band hit often, which was counted as nothing, and took never (which seemed very strange) and so the prize was lost by my side. After that a tournament followed between six of my band and six of theirs.

4 May. It was appointed that there should be but four men to wait on every earl that went with my Lord Marquis of Northampton, three on every lord, two on every knight or gentlemen. Also that my Lord Marquis should in his diet be allowed for the loss in his exchange.

5 May. The muster of the gendarmerie was appointed to be on the 1st of June, if possible, or, if not, on the 8th.

6 May. The teston was devalued from 12d to 10d and the groat from 4d to 3d.

9 May. One Stuart, a Scotsman, intending to poison the young Queen of Scotland, and thereby thinking to get favour here, was, after he had been held a while in the Tower and Newgate, delivered on my frontiers at Calais to the French in order to have him punished there as he deserved.

---

73 Running at the ring was an exercise performed on horseback.

10 May. Many lords and knights were sent for in order to furnish the court for the coming of the French ambassador who was bringing the Order of St Michael.

12 May. A proclamation was proclaimed which gave warning to all those who keep many farms, multitudes of sheep above the number limited by the law (ie 2,000), decayed tenements and towns, regraters, forestallers, men that sell dear, those that have plenty enough, those that put plough ground to pasture, carriers overseas of foodstuffs.[74] If they leave not these enormities they shall be strongly punished very quickly so that they should feel the smart of it and to command the execution of laws made for these purposes before.

14 May. One hundred archers were mustered before me with two arrows apiece. They were of the guard and afterwards shot together, and they shot at a board an inch thick which some pierced right through and stuck in the other board. Some pierced it with the heads of their arrows, the boards being very well seasoned timber. So it was ordered that there should be 100 archers and 100 halberdiers on duty, either good wrestlers or casters of the bar, or leapers, runners or tall men of personage.

15 May. Sir Philip Hoby left for France with 10 gentlemen of his own in velvet coats and chains of gold.

16 May. Likewise did the Bishop of Ely depart with a band of well-furnished men.

20 May. A proclamation was made that whosoever found a

---

74 Regraters were middlemen who purchased foodstuffs in order to sell them on again to the retail trade. Forestallers were those who bought up supplies before they reached market in order to sell them on again at a higher price.

Hampton Court.

Greenwich Palace.

seditious bill and did not tear or deface it should be a partaker of the bill and would be punished just as the maker.

21 May. My Lord the Marquis of Northampton was commissioned to deliver the Order of the Garter [to the King of France] and to treat in all things, chiefly the marriage to me of his daughter the Lady Elizabeth.[75] Firstly there was to be a dot of 12,000 Marks a year and the dowry at least 800,000 Crowns. The forfeiture if I did not perform would be 100,000 Crowns at the most. And that this should not impeach the former covenants that had been made with Scotland, and so on.

22 May. He departed.

24 May. An earthquake took place at Croydon and Bletchingley and in much of Surrey but no harm was done.

30 May. Whereas it had been commanded before that £160,000 should be coined with three fine ounces in the pound for discharging of debts, and to get some treasure to be able to alter all, now it was stopped except for 80,000 to discharge my debts and 10,000 mark weight that the Fuggers delivered in the last exchange at four ounces in the pound.

31 May. The musters were deferred until after midsummer.

JUNE

2 June. It was appointed that I should receive those Frenchmen coming here at Westminster, where we made preparations for that purpose and four sets of new vessels were prepared from church stuff such as mitres and golden missals, primers and crosses and relics from Plessay.

---

75 Princess Elizabeth was the eldest daughter of Henry II of France. She was born in 1545.

4 June. Provision was made in Flanders for silver and gold plate and chains to be given to these foreigners.[76]

7 June. A proclamation was set forth that exchanging or rechanging would be punished according to the punishment set forth in King Henry VII's time, duly to be executed.

10 June. Monsieur Maréchal [the Marquis de Fronsac, Seigneur de St André] left the French court at Boulogne and so came hither by water in his galleys and foists.

In this month, and the month before, there was great business at the city of Parma which Duke Horatio[77] had delivered up to the French king. Whereupon the Pope summoned him, saying that he held it in trust for him and that he could not alienate it against the Pope's will. But he did not come on the appointed day for which cause the Pope and the Imperials raised 3,000 men and took a castle on the same side of the river. Also the French king sent Monsieur de Thermes, who had been his general in Scotland, with a great many of his men-at-arms into Italy to help Duke Horatio. Furthermore the Turks made great preparations for the war which some feared would at last burst out.

3 June. I was elected to the Company of St Michael in France by the French king and his Order.

13 June. Agreement between the aforesaid commissioners sent by both parties was made with the Scots about the borders.

---

76 A consignment of church plate was ordered to be despatched to Flanders on 1st of June, probably to pay the Fuggers.

77 Actually this should read Ottavio Farnese, Duke of Parma, brother to Horatio Farnese. Imperial troops had occupied Parma in 1547 but it was claimed by the Pope who rejected the claims of the Farnese. The Farnese called in a French army to support their own claim. Parma thus became a bone of contention between the French and the Papal and Imperial forces.

1551

In this month Rais Dragut, a pirate, escaped Andrew [Andrea] Doria who had trapped him in a creek, by having his galley slaves dig another way into the sea and he took two of Andrea's galleys that lay far into the sea.

14 June. Pardon was given to those Irish lords who would come in before a certain day set by the deputy with advertisement to the deputy to make sharp war on those that would resist and also that my laws should be ministered everywhere.

18 June. Because of my expenses in fortifications at Calais and Berwick which had to be paid it was agreed that besides the debt of the realm, 80,000, 40,000 should be coined with three fine ounces and nine of alloy and 5,000 pounds in weight should be coined to a standard of at least seven fine ounces.

17 June. Superantio [Giacomo Soranzo] came as ambassador from Venice to replace Daniel Barbaro.

16 June. I accepted the Order of St Michael by promise to the French ambassador.

17 June. My Lord Marquis of Northampton went to Nantes with the commissioners and all the noblemen and gentlemen that had gone over the sea with him.

20 June. Upon notice that Scepperus was coming and the rigging of certain ships in Holland, and to show the Frenchmen a pleasant sight when they came, all the navy which lay in Gillingham waters was ordered to be rigged and supplied with ordnance and lie in the river Thames so that if Scepperus came later he might be met with, if not at least the Frenchmen would see the force of my navy.

22 June. The Lady Mary sent letters to the Council, marvelling at the imprisonment of her chaplain Doctor Mallett for saying mass before her household, even though it had been promised to the Emperor's ambassador that she would not be molested in religion and that she and her household could have mass said before them continually.

24 June. The Council answered that because of their duties to their king, country and friends, they were compelled to give her the answer that they would see not only him but also all other mass-sayers and breakers of order sternly punished and that, as for a promise, they would give none to make her free from the punishment of the law in that regard.

18 June. Chatillon came to my Lord Marquis of Northampton and banqueted him twice on the way from Nantes to Chateaubriant, where the king was.

15 June. Mendoza, a gentleman of the king's chamber, was sent to him to conduct him to the court.

19 June. My Lord the Marquis came to Chateaubriant where, half a mile from the castle, he was met by the Comte d'Enghien and Louis de Bourbon with 100 gentlemen and they brought him to the court, booted and spurred, to the French king.

20 June. The French king was invested in his bedchamber with the Order of the Garter and he gave to the Garter a chain worth £200 and a gown decorated with spangles worth £25. The Bishop of Ely made an oration and the Cardinal of Lorraine made an answer.[78]

In the afternoon the Lord Marquis asked the king about the marriage of the Scottish queen which was to have been consummated whose hearing he appointed to the commissioners.

---

78 The Cardinal of Lorraine was Charles de Guise, brother of Mary of Guise, the Dowager Queen of Scotland.

1551

21 June. The cardinals of Lorraine and Chatillon, the Constable and the Duke of Guise were appointed commissioners on the part of France and they absolutely denied the first motion for the Scottish queen saying that they had both taken too much pain and spent too many lives for her, also a conclusion was made for her marriage to the Dauphin. Then my marriage to the Lady Elizabeth, the king's eldest daughter, was proposed to which they most cheerfully gave their assent. So after they agreed that neither party would be bound in conscience or in honour until she was 12 years old and upwards. Then they came to the sum which was first asked at 1,500,000 French *Scutes*, at which they made mock. Afterwards, for *donatio propter nuptias*, they agreed that it should be as great as had been given by the king, my father, to any wife that he had had.[79]

22 June. Our commissioners went down to 1,400,000 Crowns which they refused, then to 1,000,000, which they denied. Then to 800,000 Crowns, which they said they would not agree to.

23 June. Then our commissioners asked what they would offer. First they offered 100,000 Crowns and then 200,000, which they said was the most that had ever been given. Then followed great reasonings and showings of precedent, but they could not come any nearer to agreement.

24 June. They went forward to the penalty if the parties disliked each other after the king's daughter was 12 and upwards, to which the French offered 100,000, 50,000 or

---

79 The *donatio propter nuptias* was a common part of a marriage contract, being, essentially, the settlement bestowed upon the wife in case of the husband's death.

promise. Then that she should be brought at her father's expense three months before she was 12, sufficiently jewelled and stuffed.[80] Then bonds would be delivered alternatively at London and Paris and so forth.

26 June. The Frenchmen delivered their written answers to my commissioners.

JULY

1 July. As certain Flemish ships, 12 sail in all, six being tall men-of-war, and looking for the 18 more men-of-war, going to Dieppe, or so it was thought, to take Monsieur le Maréchal on his way, order was given that six ships, already prepared before, with four pinnaces and a brigantine, should go to conduct him and also to defend us if anything should be attempted against England by carrying away the Lady Mary.

2 July. A brigantine was sent to Dieppe to give knowledge to Monsieur le Maréchal that the Flemings were coming, and the Flemings doffed their caps to this boat. Also the French ambassador was advised. He answered that the thought the Maréchal safe enough when he came into our waters – terming it thus.

2 July. A proclamation was signed for shortening of the fall of the money on the day on which it was proclaimed and it was devised so that it should be in all places of the realm proclaimed within one day.

3 July. Lord Clinton was appointed to meet the French at Gravesend and so convey him to Durham Place where he should stay.

---

80 ie properly outfitted and furnished.

1551

4 July. I was banqueted by Lord Clinton at Deptford where I saw the *Primrose* and the *Mary Willoughby* launched.

The Frenchmen landed at Rye, as some thought through fear of the Flemings lying off the land but chiefly because they saw that our ships could not come out because of the wind.

6 July. Sir Peter Meutas at Dover was commanded to come to Rye to meet Monsieur le Maréchal, and he did so and, after he had delivered his letters, written in my own hand, and made my recommendations, he issued orders for horses and carts for Monsieur le Maréchal and made such provisions as were possible in case of sudden need.

7 July. Monsieur le Maréchal set out from Rye and, on his journey, Mr Culpepper and many other gentlemen and their men, to the number of 1,000, all well-furnished, met him and so brought him to Maidstone that night.

Removing to Westminster.

8 July. Monsieur le Maréchal came to Mr Baker's where he was very well feasted and banqueted.

9 July. He then came to my Lord Cobham's for dinner and, at night, to Gravesend.

Proclamation was made that the shilling should go for 9d and a groat at 3d in all places of the realm at once.[81]

At this time the sweating sickness came into London, and this was more vehement than the old sweating sickness. For if one took cold he died within three hours and if he escaped it

---

[81] This was something of an emergency measure to offset the effects of debasement on the coinage. The Council's calling down of the currency was followed by two further proclamations on the 24th of July and the 16th of August. The measures should be seen in the context of great uncertainty, rumour and frustration regarding the value of the coinage.

held him for nine hours or 10 at the most. Also, if he slept the first six hours, as he would be very desirous to do, then he would rave and would die raving.

11 July. The sickness grew so much for in London 70 died in the liberties on the tenth day and, on this day, 120 and also one of my gentlemen, another of my grooms, fell sick and died. So I removed to Hampton Court with very few with me.

That same night the Maréchal came and was saluted, all my ships being in the Thames, 50 or more, all with shot well furnished and also ordnance fired from the Tower. He was met by the Lord Clinton, Lord Admiral, and 40 gentlemen at Gravesend and so was brought to Durham Place.

13 July. Because of the infection in London he came this day to Richmond where he stayed with a great band of gentlemen, at least 400 men, as it was estimated by many, and where that night he hunted.

14 July. He came to see me at Hampton Court at nine o'clock, having been met by the Duke of Somerset at the wall end. He was conveyed first to me and then, after his master's recommendations and letters, went to his chamber on the queen's side all hanged with cloth of Arras as was the hall and my lodging. He dined with me also. After dinner, and being brought into an inner chamber, he told me he had come not only to deliver the Order but also to declare the great friendship the king, his master, bore me which I should think to be that which a father bore towards his son, or a brother to a brother. And although there had been many persuasions, as he thought, which attempted to dissuade me from the friendship of his master the king, and that witless men made many rumours, yet he trusted I would not believe them.

1551

Furthermore he declared that just as good ministers on the frontiers do great good so too do bad ministers do much harm. For which cause he desired that no innovation should be made to things which had long been so long in controversy by violence but rather by the talk of commissioners. I answered that I thanked him for his Order and also for his love, etc, and that I would show similar love on all points. As for rumours, they were not always to be believed and that I sometimes provided for the worst but never did any harm upon their hearing. For ministers I said I would rather appease controversies with words than do anything by force. So afterwards he was conveyed to Richmond again.

16 July. He came to present the Order of St Michael and so after the accustomed ceremonies, in which he put on the garments and he with Monsieur Gye, also of the Order, we went to the chapel, one on my right side and one on my left. Where, after communion was celebrated, each of them kissed my cheek. Afterwards they dined with me and talked after dinner and saw some entertainment and so went home again.

18 July. A proclamation was made against regraters and forestallers and the words of the Statute were recited with punishment for the offenders. Also letters were sent to all officers and sheriffs for the execution thereof.

19 July. Another proclamation was made for the punishment of those that made rumours about the abasing or enhancement of the coin so that they could make things dear.

The same night Monsieur le Maréchal St André supped with me. After supper we saw a dozen courses and afterwards came and made me ready.

20 July. The next morning he came to see me being equipped and saw my bedchamber and went a hunting with hounds and saw me shoot and saw all my guard shoot together. He dined with me, heard me play on the lute, saw me ride, came to me in my study, supped with me and so departed to Richmond.

19 July. The Scots sent an ambassador here in order to receive the treaty, sealed with the Great Seal of England, which was duly delivered to him. Also I sent Sir Thomas Chaloner, Clerk of my Council, to have their seal to confirm the last treaty made at Norham.

On this day my Lord the Marquis of Northampton and the commissioners who had gone to negotiate the marriage, offered, according to instructions, 600,000 Crowns, afterwards 400,000 *Scutes* and so departed for an hour. Then, seeing that they could get no better, they came to the French with an offer of 200,000 *Scutes*, half to be paid at the marriage, half to be paid six months after that. Then the French agreed that the dot should be but 10,000 Marks of the lawful money of England. Thirdly it was agreed that if I died then she would not have the dot. The French said they were doing this out of friendship and that there was no precedent.

19 July. The Lord Marquis, having received and delivered back the sealed treaty, took his leave, as did all the rest.

At this time there was bickering at Parma between the French and the Papists. Monsieur de Thermes, Pietro Strozzi and Fontanello, with many other gentlemen, to the number of 30, with 1,500 soldiers, entered Parma. Gonzaga with the Emperor's and the Pope's forces lay near the town. The French made sallies and overcame them, slaying the Prince of

Macedonia and Signor Battista, the Pope's nephew.[82]

22 July. Mr Sidney was made one of the four chief gentlemen.

23 July. Monsieur le Maréchal came to me, declaring the king, his master, was pleased with my readiness for this treaty and also how much his master was inclined that way. He presented Monsieur de Boisdauphin, who was to be ambassador here, as my Lord Marquis had presented Mr Pickering on the 19th day.

26 July. Monsieur le Maréchal dined with me and after dinner saw the strength of the English archers. After he had done and upon his departure I gave him a diamond from my finger worth, by estimation, £150 for his pains and for my memory. Then he took his leave.

27 July. He came to me whilst hunting to tell me the news and to show a letter his master had sent him, and copies of Monsieur de Thermes' letter and Marillac's letters, he being ambassador with the Emperor.

28 July. Monsieur le Maréchal came to dinner at Hyde Park where a fair house was made for him and he saw the hunting there.

30 July. He came to the Earl of Warwick's house, staying there one night, and he was well received.

29. He had his reward, being worth £3,000 in gold of current money, Monsieur de Gye had £1,000, Monsieur Chemault had £1,000, Monsieur Morvilliers £500, the secretary £500 and the Bishop of Perigueux £500.

---

82 This report seems to be incorrect as the Prince of Macedonia, or Duke of Acaia, was to be killed in November 1551. Similarly, Giovanni Battista del Monte was also unharmed on this occasion, living on until April 1552.

AUGUST

3 August. Monsieur le Maréchal left for Boulogne having had a certain number of my ships to conduct him thither.

9 August. Twenty-four Lords of the Council met at Richmond to discuss the matter of my sister Mary. They agreed at length that it was not right that it should be tolerated any longer and made an instrument, signed with their hands and sealed, for the record.

11 August. The Lord Marquis, with the most part of his band, came home and delivered the sealed treaty.

12 August. Letters from Rochester, Englefield, Waldegrave, etc, were to come on the seventeenth day but they did not come until another letter was sent to them on the thirteenth day.

14 August. My Lord Marquis' reward was delivered to Paris and was worth £500 to my Lord, £200 to Ely, £150 to Mr Hoby and all the rest a smaller amount.

14 August. Rochester, etc, was commanded not to hear, nor to tolerate, any kind of service but the communion and orders set forth at large by Parliament. Also one letter to my Lady's house from my Council and another to herself from me. It was also appointed that I should come to, and sit at, Council when great matters were being debated or when I would.

This last month, Monsieur de Thermes with 500 Frenchmen came to Parma and entered safely. Afterwards, certain men issued out of the town and were overthrown, and Monsieur Sipier, d'Andelot, Petro Corso and others were taken and some slain. After they fought a skirmish they entered the camp of Gonzaga and spoiled a few tents and then returned.

1551

15 August. Sir Robert Dudley and Barnaby[83] were sworn as two of the six ordinary gentlemen.

This last month the Turkish navy captured a little castle in Sicily.

17 August. Instructions were sent to Sir James Croft [in Ireland] for various purposes a copy of which is in the hands of the Secretary.

18 August. The shilling fell from nine pence to six pence, the groat from three pence to two pence, the twopence to a penny, the penny to a halfpenny, the halfpenny to a farthing, etc.

Monsieur de Thermes and Monsieur Sipier overthrew three squadrons of horsemen three times, took a despatch sent from Don Fernando di Gonzaga to the Pope concerning this war, and another from the Pope to Don Fernando, discomforted four companies of infantry, took Count Camillo di Gonzaga of Castiglione, and slew a Spanish captain.

22 August. Removing to Windsor.

23 August. Rochester, etc, returned, denying that they would deliver the orders for Lady Mary's house in case of displeasing her.

26 August. The Lord Chancellor, Mr Comptroller and the Secretary Petre were sent to perform the task.

27 August. Mr Coverdale was made Bishop of Exeter.

28 August. Rochester, etc, were sent to the Fleet [prison].

The Lord Chancellor, etc, did what they were commanded to do to my sister and her house.

---

83 This was Barnaby Fitzpatrick, an Irish gentleman, the son of the Lord of Upper Ossory and cousin to the Earl of Ormond. He was Edward's friend and companion. Despite popular legend he does not seem to have been Edward's whipping-boy, to be punished by proxy for Edward's misdemeanours.

31 August. Rochester, etc, committed to the Tower.

The Duke of Somerset, seizing certain people who had begun a new conspiracy for destruction of the gentlemen at Wokingham two days ago, executed them with death for their crime.

29 August. Certain pinnaces were prepared in order to see that Lady Mary could not be secretly conveyed overseas. It was also appointed that the Lord Chancellor, the Lord Chamberlain, the Vice-Chamberlain, and Secretary Petre should see by all means whether she used the mass and if she did then the laws should be used against her chaplains. Also that when I came from this Progress to Hampton Court, or Westminster, both my sisters should be with me until further orders were taken for this purpose.

SEPTEMBER

3 September. The French ambassador came to declare that, firstly, how the Emperor wronged many of his master's subjects and vassals, and also arrested his merchants and tried clandestinely to begin a war. For he was besieging Mirandola with forts he had made in the French king's territory. Also he stopped certain French ships from going fishing in Newfoundland. Furthermore the Emperor had sent a dozen ships which bragged they would take the Dowager of Scotland, which thing kept her at Dieppe for a long time. Whereupon his master had taken the wool fleet of Antwerp, conveying it into his country's ports with 10 ships he had sent forth under Baron de la Garde. He was also of the mind to send more help to Piedmont and Mirandola. For this purpose he desired that the dowager might have safe passage on my coasts and might be assisted by my servants on the seacoast should any mischance occur. He was requested to put it in writing. He showed how the Turks' navy, having spoiled a part of Sicily, went to Malta and there took an adjacent isle called Gozo and from there went to Tripoli. In Transylvania, Roustam Bassa commanded an army and had spoiled the land wholly. In Hungary the Turks had made mines under forts in order to get them. Magdeburg was freshly supplied with food and Duke Maurice came that way, it being suspected that he had conspired with those in the city.[84]

4 September. It was answered to the French ambassador that the dowager would be defended from all enemies in my ports, and from tempest, and so on, and thanks were also given for the news.

5 September. The Emperor's ambassador came to request that my sister Mary's officers should be restored to their liberty and that she should have her mass and the Emperor had been promised this. It was answered that, first, I need only answer if I wanted to for he spoke without commission, which was seen by the shortness of the time since the arrest of her officers, of which the Emperor could not have been told. He was requested to no longer raise these issues, in which he had been often answered, without commission. He was told that the Emperor was by this time advertised, although the matter did not pertain to him. Also that I had done nothing but according to a king's office herein, in observing laws that were godly and in punishing the offenders. The promise to the Emperor had not been made as he pretended, as is confirmed by Sir Philip Hoby who was, at that time, the ambassador there.

---

84 Although entrusted with the siege by Charles V, the slippery Duke Maurice of Saxony was by now actively conspiring against the Emperor and preparing for a general revolt against his authority.

6 September. Deliberations touching the coin. Memorandum. That there were many standards. Nine ounces fine a few; eight ounces fine and as bad as four, because although that was fine, yet a shilling was reckoned for two shillings; six ounces, very many; four ounces many also, three ounces £130,000 now of late. Whereupon it was agreed that the teston should be called a sixpence, four with the help of six should make 10 fine, eight fine with the help of nine, being fewer than those of eight, should make 10 ounces fine; the two ounces of alloy should quit the charges of minting; and those of threepence, being but few, should be turned into the standard of four, of farthings and halfpence and pence in order to serve for the poor people because the merchants would not exchange for it and the sum was not great; also to bear the charges because it was thought that few, or none, were left which were nine ounces fine, eight ounces there were none and six ounces were made two ways, one without skill, the other was not fully six but of this kind there were not a few.

9 September. A proclamation was issued about the prices of cattle, of hogs, pigs, beef, oxen, mutton, butter and cheese, that they should be sold at a reasonable price. Not as good cheap as they were when the coin was perfect but within a fifth part of it or thereabouts.

10 September. I removed to Farnham.

12 September. A proclamation was issued about the coin. Whereas it was the case that men melted down the 9d teston for gain continually, and the 6d also, then there should be no person of any kind who should melt it down upon pain to incur the penalty of the laws.

Sir Philip Hoby.

A lady (possibly Lady Mary).

1551

13 September. A letter directed to the Lord Treasurer, the Lord Great Master and the Master of the Horse to have them meet at London for the ordering of my coin and the payment of my debts. Which done they were to return and make a report of their proceedings.

11 September. War was proclaimed in England between the Emperor and the French in these terms: 'Charles, Roi d'Espagne et Duc de Milan' leaving out Emperor.

10 September. Four towns in Piedmont, Chieri and St Damian, which were the Emperor's were taken by French soldiers. Also the Emperor's country there was spoiled and 120 castles or fortresses taken.

A proclamation was made in Paris about [Papal] Bulls saying that no man should go to Rome for them.

Other ships were taken by the Prior of Capua: merchants, to the number of a dozen. The Prior of Capua had 32 galleys.[85]

19 September. The French ambassador also sent the news that the Turks had taken Tripoli.

20 September. Secretary Cecil and Sir Philip Hoby were sent to London to help the Lord Treasurer, etc, in the matter of the bishops of Chichester, Worcester and Durham and in the matter of my sister's men.

18 September. Removing to Windsor.

20 September. The lords at London, having tried all kinds of stamping, both of the purity of nine, eight, six, four and three, proved that the coin might be brought to 11 ounces fine without any loss. For whereas before now the teston was

---

85 Leo Strozzi, Knight of Jerusalem and Prior of Capua, was a capable admiral in French service. He had commanded at the successful siege of St Andrews in Scotland in 1547.

thought to have been corrupted by ill officers and ministers, it was shown that it had the right valuation through eight different kinds of melting. So 400 pounds of sterling money, a teston being but sixpence, made 400 pounds 11 ounces fine of money sterling.

22 September. Whereupon they reported the same and then it was concluded that the teston should be 11 ounces fine, the proportion of the pieces according to the gold, so that five shillings of silver should be worth five of gold.

23 September. Removing to Oatlands.

24 September. Agreed that the stamp of the shilling and sixpence should be with a king on one side, drawn to the shoulders with Parliamentary robes and with a chain of the Order. Five shillings of silver and half-five shillings should be with a king on horseback armed, with a naked sword close to his chest. Also that York's mint and Throckmorton's mint in the Tower should go to work on the fine standard. In the city of York and Canterbury the small money should be made with baser materials. Officers for the same were appointed.

A piece of Berwick's wall fell down because the foundation had been shaken by work on a bulwark.

28 September. The Lord Marquis Dorset, grieved much with the disorder of the marches towards Scotland, surrendered the wardenship thereof to bestow it upon whomever I wanted.

27 September. The wardenship of the north was given to the Earl of Warwick.

Removing to Hampton Court.

28 September. Commissioners were appointed to sit before the bishops of Chichester and Worcester – three lawyers and three civilians.

ᴄᴏ 1551 ᴏᴏ

10 September. The Imperials took the suburbs of Hesdin and burnt them.

26 September. The passport of the Dowager of Scotland was extended for a longer time, until Christmas, and also, if she wished it, she could pass by land quietly into Scotland.

20 September. Monsieur d'Angoulême was born and the Duke of Vendome had a son by his wife the Princess of Navarre.

30 September. The feast of Michaelmas was kept by me in my robes of the Order [of St Michael].

OCTOBER

1 October. The commission for the making of five shillings, half-shillings, groats and sixpences out of 11 ounces fine, and pence and halfpennies and farthings with four ounces fine, was followed and signed.

1 October. There was Rich, Lord Chancellor of England, who sent back a letter for the commission for certain men to sit before the bishops of Chichester and Worcester because only eight signatures were on it.

2 October. I wrote back a letter saying that I marvelled that he could refuse to sign that bill or deliver that letter which I had willed any one about me to write. Also that it would be a great impediment for me to send for all my Council and that I would appear to be in bondage. But it was an oversight and he better not think any more about it.

5 October. Jarnac arrived in haste to declare two things. The first that the queen had delivered a third son, called the Duc d'Angoulême, of which the king prayed me to be godfather. I answered that I was glad of the news and that I thanked him that I should be godfather, which was a token of the goodwill he bore me. Also that I would dispatch news of the accomplishment to Lord Clinton, Lord Admiral of England.

He said that he had come to tell me a second point about the good success of his master's wars. He told me how last month Martin van Rossem captain of 1,000 Imperial horse, with many Hungarians, had entered into Champagne, near Sedan, and the alarm had been raised. The skirmish began to get hot when the French horse, about 200 or 300 men-at-arms, came out and took van Rossem's brother and slew many. Also how in Piedmont, more towns had fallen since the taking of the last four towns: Montechiaro, Saluzzo and the town of Borgo. The Turks had come to Naples and spoiled the country and taken Ostia in the mouth of the Tiber. Also in Sicily they had taken a good harbour and town.

6 October. Jarnac departed, having spent the night before lodged at the court. The bishops of Worcester and Chichester were deposed for contempt.

7 October. Mr Henry Neville, Mr Barnaby, gentlemen of the chamber, Sir William Stafford, Sir Adrian Poynings, Sir John Norton, Sir John Tyrell, knights, and Mr Brooke, were appointed to go with the Lord Admiral.

8 October. Letters were sent out to the captains of the gendarmerie that they should muster on the 8th of November, being the Sunday after All Hallows Day.

11 October. Harry, the Marquis of Dorset, was created Duke of Suffolk; John, Earl of Warwick, was created Duke of Northumberland; William, Earl of Wiltshire, was created Marquis of Winchester; Sir William Herbert was created Earl of Pembroke and Lord of Cardiff. Mr Sidney, Mr Neville, Mr Cheke, all of the Privy Chamber, were made

1551

knights. As was Mr Cecil, one of the two chief secretaries.

13 *October*. A proclamation was signed touching upon the calling in of testons and groats and that those that wanted to come might come to the mint and have a fine silver twelvepence for two testons.

3 *October*. The Prior of Capua left the French king's service and went back to his Order of Knights in Malta, partly because he was displeased with the Marquis de Villars, the Constable's brother in law, partly because Malta was often attacked by the Turks.

7 *October*. Sir Thomas Palmer came to the Earl of Warwick (since then Duke of Northumberland) in order to deliver a chain to him, it being a very fine one with each link weighing one ounce, so that it could be given to Jarnac and he could receive as much in return. Whereupon, in my Lord's garden, he told of a conspiracy. On the last St George's Day, my Lord Somerset (who was then going to the north if the Master of the Horse, Sir William Herbert, had not assured him on his honour that no hurt should come to him) went to raise the people and Lord Grey in order to know who were his friends. Afterwards a plan was made to summon the Earl of Warwick to a banquet with the Marquis of Northampton and many others and to cut off their heads. Also if he found a company around them to set upon them too.[86]

11 *October*. He declared also that Mr Vane had 2,000 men in readiness. Sir Thomas Arundel had assured my Lord that the Tower was safe. Mr Partridge would raise London and take the Great Seal with the apprentices of London. Seymour and

---

86 Here we have the king's account of the fall of Somerset, an event shrouded in mystery and conspiracy. Edward's account is somewhat coloured by what his advisers, or Northumberland, told him.

Sir John Cheke.

1551

Hammond should wait for him and all the horse of the gendarmerie would be slain.

15 October. Removing to Westminster because it was thought that this matter could be dealt with more easily and more securely there, and likewise all other matters.

14 October. The Duke of Somerset was sent for by Secretary Cecil so he could be told that he suspected some ill. Mr Cecil answered that if he were not guilty he might be of good courage; if he were guilty he had nothing to say to him but to lament him. Whereupon the duke sent him a letter of defiance and called Palmer who, after his declaration was denied, was let go.

16 October. This morning none of the conspirators were at Westminster. The first to arrive was the duke who came, later than usual, by himself. After dinner he was arrested. Sir Thomas Palmer was taken on the terrace walking there. Hammond, passing by Mr Vice-Chamberlain's door, was called in by John Peers to have a shooting match, and so was taken. Likewise John Seymour and Davy Seymour were taken too. Arundel was also taken as was Lord Grey, coming out of the country. Vane, sent for twice in the morning by my Lord, fled at the first summons. He said my Lord was not stout and if he could get home he cared for none of them as he was so strong. But afterwards he was found by John Peers under the straw in one of his men's stables at Lambeth. All these went with the duke to the Tower that night except Palmer, Arundel and Vane who were kept in separate rooms here.

17 October. The Duchess of Somerset, Crane and his wife, with the chamber keeper were sent to the Tower for devising these treasons. James Wingfield was too for distributing seditious bills. Also Mr Partridge was arrested and Sir Thomas Holcroft.

18 October. Mr Bannister and Mr Vaughan were also sent to the Tower and so was Mr Stanhope.

19 October. Sir Thomas Palmer confessed that the gendarmerie were to be attacked on the muster day by Mr Vane's 2,000 footmen and my Lord's 100 horsemen along with those of his friends and the idle people which took his side. If he were overthrown he would run through London and cry 'Liberty, Liberty!' to raise the apprentices and, if he could, he would go to the Isle of Wight or to Poole.

22 October. The Dowager of Scotland was driven ashore at Portsmouth by a tempest and so she sent word that she would take advantage of our safe-conduct and go by land and to see me.

26 October. She came from Portsmouth to Mr White's house.

24 October. The Lords sat in the Star Chamber and there declared the matters and the accusations made against the duke, meaning to calm the minds of the people.

25 October. In the beginning of this month certain German princes desired aid of 400,000 Thalers in the cause of religion, should they be driven to ask for it and also they offered the same amount if I entered war for them. Whereupon I called my Lords and considered the matter as appears on a scroll in the board at Westminster and thereupon appointed that Secretary Petre, Sir William Cecil and another Secretary [Wotton] should talk to the messenger to know precise details of the matter and the names of those who would enter the confederacy.[87]

---

[87] The confederacy was an anti-Imperial alliance between the rulers of Saxony, Mecklenburg, Hesse and Brandenburg. These German princes also approached the French king for support.

∽ 1551 ∾

28 October. The dowager came to Sir Richard Cotton's house.

29 October. She went from Sir Richard Cotton's to the Earl of Arundel's for dinner and was brought to Mr Browne's house where she was met by the gentlemen of Sussex.

30 October. She came and was conveyed by the same gentlemen to Guildford where Lord William Howard and the gentlemen of Surrey met her.

Throughout this month the Frenchmen continued to spoil the Emperor's frontiers and in one skirmish at Asti slew 100 [800 crossed out] Spaniards.

31 October. A letter was sent to Sir Arthur Darcy directing him to take charge of the Tower and to discharge Sir John Markham for this reason – that, without telling any of the Council, he allowed the duke to walk abroad and certain letters to be sent and answered between Davy Seymour and Mrs Poynings with many other suspicions.

17 October. Letters about the late conspiracy were sent to all emperors, kings, ambassadors, noblemen, men and chief men in all countries.

31 October. She [the Dowager Queen of Scotland] came to Hampton Court, conveyed by the same lord and the gentlemen above mentioned, and was met two and a half miles from there by the Lord Marquis of Northampton, accompanied by the Earl of Wiltshire, son and heir to the Lord High Treasurer Marquis of Winchester, the Lord Fitzwalter, son to the Earl of Sussex, the Lord Evre, the Lord Braye, the Lord Robert Dudley, the Lord Garret, Sir Nicholas Throckmorton, Sir Edward Rogers and many other gentlemen along with all the Gentlemen Pensioners, men-of-arms, ushers, servers and

William Paulet, Marquis of Winchester.

carvers to the number of 120 gentlemen. And so she was brought to Hampton Court. At the gate of the palace she was met by the Lady Marquis of Northampton, the Countess of Pembroke and many other ladies and gentlewomen to the number of 60. And so she was brought to her lodging on the queen's side, which was all hung with Arras tapestries and so was the hall and all the other lodgings of mine in the house and finely dressed. And this night, and the next day, were spent in dancing and entertainment, as though it were a court, and a great number of gentlemen came here.

26 *October*. Because of this business [the conspiracy] letters were written to defer the musters of gendarmerie until the [blank] day of December.

NOVEMBER

1 *November*. The dowager perused the house at Hampton Court and also saw some deer hunting.

2 *November*. She then went to the Bishop's Palace at London and she stayed there and all her train lodged with her.

3 *November*. The Duke of Suffolk, the Earl of Warwick, the Earl of Wiltshire and many other lords and gentlemen were sent to welcome her and to say, on my behalf, that if she lacked anything she should have it for her better comfort and also that I would see her the following day.

On the 26th of October Crane confessed the most part even as Palmer had done before, and even more besides. How the place where the nobles should have been banqueted and their heads stricken off was Lord Paget's house, and how the Earl of Arundel knew of the matter as well as he did through Stanhope who was a messenger between them. Also some part of how he, feigning himself sick, went to London once last August in order to get friends. Hammond also confessed that he kept watch in his chamber at night. Brend also confessed much of the matter. Lord Strange confessed how the duke urged him to persuade me to marry his third daughter, the Lady Jane, and urged him to be his spy in all matters of my doings and sayings, and to know when some of my Council spoke secretly with me. This he confessed by himself.

4 November. The Duke of Suffolk and the Lord Fitzwalter, the Lord Braye and many other lords and gentlemen accompanied by Suffolk's wife, the Lady Frances, the Lady Margaret [Douglas], the Duchess of Richmond and of Northumberland, the Lady Jane, daughter to the Duke of Suffolk, the marchionesses of Northampton and Winchester, the countesses of Arundel, Bedford, Huntingdon and Rutland, with 100 other ladies and gentlewomen, went to the dowager and brought her through London to Westminster. At the gate she was received by the Duke of Northumberland, the Great Master, the Treasurer, the Comptroller and the Earl of Pembroke with all the servers and carvers and cupbearers to the number of 30. In the hall I met with her along with all the rest of the lords of my Council as well as the Lord Treasurer, the Marquis of Northampton, etc, and from the outer gate up to the presence chamber the guard stood on both sides. The court, the hall and the stairs were full of serving men; the presence chamber, great chamber and her presence chamber was full of gentlemen. And so having brought her to her chamber, I retired to mine. I went to her to dinner. She dined under the same cloth of state as me, at my left hand. By her dined my cousin Frances and my cousin Margaret. By me sat the French ambassador. We were served by two services of servers, cupbearers, carvers and gentlemen. Her *maitre d'hotel* accompanied her servers and my officers with mine. There were two cupboards brought in, one of gold four tiers high, another of solid silver six tiers high. The ladies dined on three courses in her great chamber. After dinner, when she had heard some music, I brought her to the hall and so she went away.

5 *November*. The Duke of Northumberland, the Lord Treasurer, the Lord Marquis of Northampton, the Lord Privy Seal and many others went to see her and to deliver a ring with a diamond and two nags as a token from me.

6 *November*. The Duke of Northumberland came with his band of 100, of which 40 were in black velvet with white and black sleeves, and 60 in cloth. The Earl of Pembroke had his band and 50 more. The Earl of Wiltshire had 58 of his father's band. All the Pensioners, men-of-arms and the equerry, with many ladies, such as my cousin Margaret and the duchesses of Richmond and Northumberland, accompanied the queen to Shoreditch, through Cheapside and Cornhill, and there she was met by the gentlemen of Middlesex, 100 horse, and so she was conveyed out of the realm being met in every shire by gentlemen.

8 *November*. The Earl of Arundel was committed to the Tower with Sir Stradling, St Albin and his men because Crane did more and more confess of him.

7 *November*. A Frenchman was returned to France in order to be delivered to the Frenchmen on the borders because of a murder he had committed at Dieppe after which he had fled here.

14 *November*. Answer was given to those Germans who had required 400,000 Thalers, if so required, for the maintenance of religion. They were told firstly that I was very well inclined to

make peace, amity or a bargain with those I knew were of the same religion (because this messenger had only been sent to find out my inclination and desire to enter into agreement, and not to fully resolve any matters). Secondly I desired to know whether they would be able to get any other strength of any other princes as were able of maintaining the war and would reciprocate to me again if I so desired. And therefore those three princes – Duke Maurice of Saxony, the Duke of Mecklenburg and the Marquis John of Brandenburg – were urged to open the matter with the Duke of Prussia and to all those princes around them and somehow to get the good will of Hamburg, Lübeck, Bremen, etc, to show them an inkling on this matter. Thirdly I would have the matter of religion made more plain lest when war might be made for other quarrels they would say it was for religion. Fourthly, he should come back with more ample commission from the same states to talk of the sum of money and other conditions. This answer was given in case, should I have agreed wholly at first, they might have declared my intent to the Hanse towns and the senates and news would come abroad and I would run into the danger of breaking the league I had made with the Emperor.

16 November. The Lord Admiral took his leave to go to France for the christening of the French king's son.

18 November. Mr Fossey, secretary to Duke Maurice, who was here for the matter specified above [incomplete entry].[88]

20 November. A proclamation was appointed to go forth, although one had gone out before this time, that the set prices for beef, oxen and mutton were meant to continue until November

---

88 Johann Füss, an ambassador from the German Protestant princes, probably worked for the Marquis of Brandenburg and was attempting to secure English support for the 'confederacy' against Charles V.

when Parliament should have abrogated that and certain commissioners were to be appointed to cause graziers to bring livestock to market and sell it at reasonable prices. And that certain overseers should be there to certify the justices' doings.

23 November. The Lord Treasurer [Winchester] was appointed High Steward for the trial of the Duke of Somerset.

At this time Duke Maurice began to show himself to be a friend to the Protestants whereas, before that time, he had appeared to be their enemy.

27 November. The aforementioned proclamation was proclaimed.

17 November. The Earl of Warwick, Mr Harry Sidney, Sir Harry Neville and Sir Harry Gates did challenge all comers at the tilt on the 3rd of January and at the tournament on the 6th of January and this challenge was proclaimed.

28 November. News came that Maximilian, coming out of Spain, had nine of his galleys, with 120 horses and his treasure, seized by the French.

24 November. The Lord Admiral entered France and went to Boulogne.

26 November. The Captain of Portsmouth was commanded to bring the model and the map of the castle so that it might be fortified because the Baron de la Garde had seen it, having an engineer with him, and he had a plan of it.

30 November. Some 22 peers, as nobles, besides the Council, heard Sir Thomas Palmer, Mr Hammond, Mr Crane and Newdigate swear that their confessions were true and that they were saying what they were saying without any compulsion, force, envy or displeasure but as favourably towards the duke as they could swear to in safe conscience.

DECEMBER

1 December. The Duke of Somerset came to stand trial at Westminster Hall. The Lord Treasurer sat as High Steward of England under the cloth of estate on a bench between two posts three steps high. All the Lords, to the number of 27, were present:

Dukes	*Barons*
Suffolk	Abergavenny
Northumberland	Audley
	Wharton
Marquises	Evre
Northampton	Latimer
	Burgh
Earls	Zouche
Derby	Stafford
Bedford	Wentworth
Huntingdon	Darcy
Rutland	Stourton
Bath	Windsor
Sussex	Cromwell
Worcester	Cobham
Pembroke	Braye
Viscounts	
Hereford	

These sat below the bench and heard the matter debated. First, after the indictments were read, of which there were five in number, the learned counsel relayed Palmer's confession to my Lord of Somerset. To which he answered that he never

ᦉ 1551 ᧑

wished to raise the north and declared everything bad which he could think about Palmer. He was afraid of rumours and that moved him to send to Sir William Herbert. It was again replied that the worse Palmer was the more he served his purpose for the planned banquet. First he swore it was untrue and called more witnesses. When Crane's confession was read he wanted him to come in face to face. As for London he meant to do nothing which would hurt any lord but acted for his own defence. As for the gendarmerie, it would have been a mad thing for him to try with his 100 against 900. As to having men in his chamber at Greenwich, confessed to by Partridge, he said that it showed he meant no harm as when he could have done harm he did not do it. As to my Lord Strange's confession: he swore it was untrue, but the Lord Strange took his oath that it was true. He denied Newdigate's, Hammond's and Alexander Seymour's confessions because they were his men.

The lawyers cited that to raise men at his house so as to kill the Duke of Northumberland, was treason by an Act made in the third year of my reign against unlawful assemblies; to devise the death of the lords was a felony; to mind resisting his attachment was a felony; to raise London was treason; and to assault the lords was a felony. He answered that he did not intend to raise London and the witnesses who swore otherwise were not there. His assembling of men was only for his own defence. He had not determined to kill the Duke of Northumberland, the marquis, etc, but only spoke of it and afterwards decided against it and yet seemed to confess he went about their death. The lords went together. The Duke of Northumberland would not agree that any intention to kill him was treason. So the lords acquitted him of treason and condemned him of treason felonious, and so he was sentenced to be hanged. He gave thanks to the lords for their open trial and cried forgiveness of the Duke of Northumberland, the Marquis of Northampton and the Earl of Pembroke for his ill-meaning towards them and pleaded for his wife and children, servants and debts and so departed without the axe of the Tower.[89] The people, knowing not the matter, shouted so loudly half a dozen times that from the hall door it could be heard plainly at Charing Cross and rumours went out that he had been found innocent of all.

2 *December.* The peace concluded by the Lord Marquis was ratified by me before the ambassador and delivered to him signed and sealed.

3 *December.* The duke told certain lords who were in the Tower that he had hired Berteville to kill them which thing, upon being questioned, Berteville confessed as did Hammond who also knew of it.[90]

7 *December.* I saw the musters of the new band of men-of-arms, 100 of my Lord Treasurer's, 100 of Northumberland, 100 of Northampton, 50 of Huntingdon, 50 of Rutland, 120 of Pembroke, 50 of Darcy, 50 of Cobham, 100 of Sir Thomas Cheyney and 180 of the Pensioners and their bands, with the old men-of-arms all well-armed men some with feathers, staves and plumes of their colours, some with sleeves and half coats of mail, some with bards and staves, etc. The horses were all fair

---

89 If the axe was turned away from the prisoner it generally signified that there had been an acquittal.

90 Berteville, the French mercenary who had proved so useful in 1547, later had his debts paid off by Edward's Council, suggesting that he had supplied perjured evidence to convict Somerset.

and great and the least one of them would not have been sold for less than £20. There were none under 14 hands, most being 14 and a half, and almost all were horses. With their guidon going before them they passed twice around St James's field, going right round it, and so departed.

15 December. Certain devices for laws were delivered to my learned Council to write, as according to the schedule.

18 December. It was appointed that I should have six chaplains ordinary of which two were to be always present and four always absent preaching. One year two in Wales, two in Lancashire and Derby; next year two in the marches of Scotland, two in Yorkshire; the third year two in Devonshire, two in Hampshire; the fourth year two in Norfolk, Suffolk and Essex and two in Kent, Surrey, etc. These six would be Bill, Harley, Estcourt [crossed out], Perne, Grindal and Bradford [crossed out].

20 December. The Bishop of Durham was committed to the Tower for having concealed a treason which he had been told of in writing and not having disclosed it until the party exposed him.[91]

21 December. Richard Lord Rich, Chancellor of England, considering his sickness, delivered his seal to the Lord Treasurer, the Lord Great Master and the Lord Chamberlain and Parliament which had been sent by him for that purpose during the time of his sickness.

5 December. The Lord Admiral came to the French king and afterwards was sent to the queen and so conducted to his chamber.

---

91 The elderly Cuthbert Tunstall was here being punished for being a Somerset sympathiser.

6 December. The Lord Admiral christened the French king's child and called him by the king's command Edward Alexander. All that day there was music, dancing and playing with triumph in the court. But the Lord Admiral was sick with a double ague. Yet he presented Barnaby to the French king who took him to his chamber.

7 December. The treaty was delivered to the Lord Admiral and the French king read it in an open audience at mass with the ratification of it. The Lord Admiral took his leave of the French king and returned to Paris very sick.

The same day the French king showed the Lord Admiral letters that had come from Parma about how the French had taken two castles from the Imperials and that, in the defence of one, the Prince of Macedonia had been slain on the walls and was buried in state at Parma.

22 December. The Great Seal of England was delivered to the Bishop of Ely who was to be keeper of it during Lord Rich's sickness.

The band of 100 men-of-arms, which Lord Somerset had previously had, was appointed to go to the Duke of Suffolk.

23 December. Removing to Greenwich.

24 December. I began to keep holy this Christmas and continued until Twelfth Night.[92]

26 December. Sir Anthony St Leger was banished from my chamber until he had answered matters laid against him by the Bishop of Dublin, and had the articles delivered to him.

28 December. The Lord Admiral came to Greenwich

---

92 There were many masques and balls at court that Christmas; Edward acted in a number of plays and was involved in re-writing some of them.

~ 1551 ~

30 December. A commission was drawn up for the Bishop of Ely, the Lord Privy Seal, Sir John Gates, Sir William Petre, Sir Robert Bowes and Sir William Mildmay to call in my debts.[93]

---

[93] This so-called Revenue Commission was charged with recovering money for the Crown in an attempt to boost royal revenue as debasement of the coinage could no longer be relied upon. Subsequently further commissions were established to find additional ways of improving royal finances.

∽ 1552 ∾

Thomas Cranmer, Bishop of Canterbury.

∽ 1552 ∾

JANUARY

1 January. Orders were issued to the chandlers of London for the selling of tallow candles which before some had refused to do and some were punished with imprisonment.

3 January. The challenge which had been made last month was fulfilled.

The challengers were:	Defendants:
The Earl of Warwick	Lord William Howard
Sir Harry Sidney	Lord Fitzwalter
Sir Harry Neville	Lord Ambrose Dudley
Sir Harry Gates	Lord Robert Dudley
	Lord FitzWarren
	Sir George Howard
	Sir Will Stafford
	Sir John Perrot
	Mr Norris
	Mr Digby
	Mr Warcopp
	Mr Courtney
	Mr Knollys
	Lord Braye
	Mr Paston
	Mr Carey
	Sir Anthony Browne
	Mr Drury

These, 18 in all, ran six courses each at tilt against the challengers and accomplished their course right well, and so departed again.

5 *January*. Sir Richard Cotton and Mr Braye were sent to Guines to take a view of Calais and Guines and the area around and, with the advice of the captains and engineers, to devise some amendments. After which they would make me a report and upon my answer would go further into the matter.

4 *January*. It was appointed that if Hull was taken from Mr Stanhope then I should not be charged with its expenses but that the town would bear them and should have £40 a year to keep the castle in repair.[94]

2 *January*. I received letters out of Ireland copied in the Secretary's hand. Following which the earldom of Thomond was given by me to O'Brien's heirs, whose father was dead, and would have it for the term of life to Donough, Baron of Ibrachan, and his male heirs. Also letters of thanks were written to the earls of Desmond and Clanricard and to the Baron of Dungannon.

3 *January*. The Emperor's ambassador requested me several times to let my sister Mary have her mass which, with no little argument with him, was denied him.

6 *January*. The aforesaid challengers came to the tournament and the aforesaid defendants came in afterwards along with two more of them – Mr Tyrell and Mr Robert Hopton. They fought right well and so the challenge was accomplished. The same night there was a play in which there was a talk between Riches

---

94 The municipal government therefore became responsible for maintaining the city's defences, the government contributing revenue from Crown lands as recompense. Stanhope, it may be recalled, was in the Tower.

and Youth and which one of them was better. After some pretty reasonings there came in six champions on either side:

On Youth's side came:	On Riches' side:
My Lord Fitzwalter	My Lord FitzWarren
My Lord Ambrose Dudley	Mr Robert Stafford
Sir Anthony Browne	Mr Courtney
Sir William Cobham	Digby
Mr Carey	Hopton
Warcopp	Hungerford

All these fought two against two at barriers in the hall. Then two came in dressed like Germans and two came in dressed like friars, but the Germans would not allow them to pass until they had fought. The friars were Mr Drury and Thomas Cobham. After this followed two masques, one of men and one of women. Then a banquet of 120 dishes. This was the end of Christmas.

7 January. I went to Deptford to dine there and to end the Christmas festival.

8. Following a certain disagreement between Lord Willoughby and Sir Andrew Dudley, Captain of Guines, over their jurisdiction, the Lord Willoughby was sent for to come over with the intention of ceasing the controversy and that order might be taken.

12 January. A commission was granted to the Earl of Bedford and to Mr Vice-Chamberlain and certain others to call in those debts that were owing to me and those which would be owing to me when the day comes.

1552

17 January. There was a tilting match between six gentlemen on either side:

On one side:	On the other side:
The Earl of Warwick	The Lord Ambrose
The Lord Robert Dudley	The Lord Fitzwalter
Mr Sidney	Sir Francis Knollys
Mr Neville	Sir Anthony Browne
Mr Gates	Sir John Perrot
Anthony Digby	Mr Courtney

The first won by four broken lances.

18 January. The French ambassador suggested that we should lay waste the Scottish part of the Debateable Ground as they had done ours. It was answered, firstly, that Lord Conyers who had made the agreement only made it so that it should stand with his superior's pleasure. Whereupon, the same agreement was disliked because the Scottish part was much harder to overcome, word was sent to hold the matter. Nevertheless the Lord Maxwell did, upon malice to the English Debateable Ground, overrun them. Whereupon it was now concluded that if the Scots would agree to it, the ground shall be divided. If not then the Scots should waste their Debateables and we ours, commanding them by proclamation to depart.

On this day the Steelyard[95] provided their answer to a

---

95 The Hanse merchants of northern Germany based their activities at the Steelyard in London. The site of the merchants' guildhall is now Cannon Street station.

John Russell, Earl of Bedford.

1552

certain complaint which the Merchant Adventurers had levelled against them.

19 January. The Bishop of Ely, *custos sigilli*, was made Chancellor because as *custos sigilli* he could execute nothing that should be done in the Parliament but could only seal ordinary things.

21 January. Removing to Westminster.

22 January. The Duke of Somerset had his head cut off upon Tower Hill between eight and nine o'clock in the morning.[96]

16 January. Sir William Pickering delivered a token to the Lady Elizabeth [Princess of France] – a fair diamond.

18 January. The Duke of Northumberland, having under him 100 men-of-arms and 100 lighthorse, gave up the keeping of 50 men-of-arms to his son the Earl of Warwick.

23 January. The sessions of Parliament began.

24 January. John Gresham was sent over to Flanders to show the Fuggers, to whom I owed money, that I would defer it or, if I paid it, I would pay it in English money to make them keep up their French crowns with which I was minded to pay them.

25 January. The Steelyard's answer was delivered to certain of my learned Council so they could look at it and oversee it.

27 January. Sir Ralph Vane was condemned of felony in treason, answering like a ruffian.

Paris arrived with horses and showed me how the French king had sent me six horses with docked tails, two Turkish horses, an Arab horse, two jennets, a stirring horse and two little mules and he showed them to me.

---

96 Thus Edward's uncle was executed before Parliament opened the following day. Edward had signed the death warrant.

29 January. Sir Thomas Arundel was also convicted of felony in treason after much argument – the matter having been brought to trial at seven o'clock in the morning of the 28th day at noon the inquest went together and shut themselves up together in a house without meat or drink because they could not agree. And so on for all that day and all that night but on this 29th day they convicted him.

FEBRUARY

2 February. A King of Arms was created for Ireland and whose name was Ulster and his province was all Ireland and he was the first one for Ireland and the fourth King of Arms. He was the first Herald of Ireland.

The Emperor borrowed £1,000,000 last month in Flanders and this month too.

6 February. It was appointed that Sir Philip Hoby should go to the Regent [of the Netherlands] upon pretence of settling some quarrels among merchants and he should take with him £63,000 in French crowns to Antwerp in Flanders to pay the debts that I owed to the Schetz and their family. It was intended he might despatch both duties at the same time.

8 February. Sir Miles Partridge was condemned of felony in the Duke of Somerset's matter as he was one of the conspirators.

8 February. Fifty men-of-arms were appointed to Mr Sadler.

9 February. John Beaumont, Master of the Rolls, was put into prison for forging a false deed of certain lands and leases from Charles Brandon, Duke of Suffolk, to Lady Anne Powis.[97]

---

[97] Beaumont was to confess to his fraud and corrupt actions in June 1552.

1552

10 February. A commission was granted to 32 people to examine, correct and set out ecclesiastical laws. These were the persons' names:

The Bishops	Civilians
Canterbury	Mr Secretary Petre
Ely	Mr Secretary Cecil
London	Mr Traheron
Winchester	Mr Reed
Exeter	Mr Cook
Bath	May, Dean of St Paul's
Gloucester	Skinner
Rochester	Mr Lyell [originally left blank]

The Divines	Lawyers
Taylor of Lincoln	Justice Bromley
Taylor of Hadleigh	Justice Hales
Mr Cox, almoner	Gosnold
Sir John Cheke	Goodrich
Sir Anthony Cooke	Stamford
Petrus Martyr	Caryll
Johannes à Lasco[98]	Lucas
Parker of Cambridge	Gawdy

---

98 The famous Polish Protestant reformer had arrived in England in the summer of 1548.

10 February. Sir Philip Hoby departed with somewhat more crowns than 53,500 or so and had authority to borrow 10,000 Flemish Pounds at 7 in the hundred for six months in the name of Lazarus Tucker. He was to ensure that it was in bullion that was brought over with him. He was also to carry 3,000 mark weight upon a licence the Emperor had granted to the Schetz and which they gave to me. After that he was to depart for Bruges where the Regent was and there he would declare to her the griefs of my subjects.

11 February. John Gresham delivered armour composed of 1,100 pairs of corselets and cavalry harnesses, very fair.

14 February. It was appointed that the *Jesus of Lübeck*, a ship of 800 tons, and the *Mary Gonston*, of 600 tons, should be hired out for £1,000 to merchantmen for one voyage. At the end of the voyage to the Levant they would answer for the tackling if the ship, the ordnance and munition and they would give it back in the same condition as they took it. Certain other of my worst ships were appointed to be sold.

9 February. A proclamation was made in Paris that the bands of the Dauphin, the Duke of Vendome, the Count d'Enghien, the Constable of France, the Duke of Guise and of Aumale, the Count of Sancerre, the Maréchal St André, Monsieur de Jarnac and Monsieur Tavannes should assemble at Troyes in Champagne on the 15th of March to resist the Emperor. Also that the king in person would go there with 200 gentlemen of his household and 400 archers of his guard.

16 February. The French king sent his secretary, de l'Aubespine, to declare this voyage to Mr Pickering and to desire him to go with him and be a witness of his doings.

The Tower

Westminster.

19 February. Whereupon it was appointed that he should have 2,000 Crowns for his furnishment, besides his diet, and Barnaby 800.

20 February. The Countess of Pembroke died.[99]

18 February. The Merchant Adventurers sent in their reply to the Steelyard's answer.

23 February. A decree was made by the board [the Council] that upon knowledge and information on their charters they had found that they [the Steelyard] were no sufficient corporation. Secondly that their number, names and nation were unknown. Thirdly that when they had forfeited their liberties King Edward IV had restored them on the condition that they should colour no strangers' goods, which they had done.[100] Also that whereas in the beginning they had not shipped more than eight cloths, afterwards 100, afterwards 1,000, after that 6,000 and now in their names 14,000 cloths were shipped in one year and but 1,100 by all the other strangers. For these considerations sentence was given that they had forfeited their liberties and were in like case with other strangers.

28 February. Ambassadors from Hamburg and Lübeck came to speak on behalf of the Steelyard merchants.

29 February. A Fleming wanted to search the *Falcon* for Frenchmen. The *Falcon* turned, opened fire, boarded the Fleming and captured it.

Payment of £63,500 Flemish was made to the Fuggers by Sir Philip Hoby except £6,000 which he borrowed in French crowns.

---

99 She was Catherine Parr's sister.

100 The probable sense of this passage is that the merchants were accused of having passed foreign goods off as domestic goods.

MARCH

2 March. The Lord Abergavenny was arrested for striking the Earl of Oxford in the chamber of presence.

The answer for the ambassadors of the Steelyard was given to the Lord Chancellor, the two secretaries, Sir Robert Bowes, Sir John Baker, Judge Montagu, Griffith Solicitor, Gosnold, Goodrich and Brooke.

3 March. It was agreed that for better despatch of certain things the Council, with some others joined to them, should look over the penal laws and put some of them into execution. Others should answer suitors. Others should oversee my revenues and the order of them as well as the superfluous and the payments heretofore made. Others should have commission for taking away superfluous bulwarks.

1 March. An order was given for the defence of the merchants and to send four barks and two pinnaces to sea.

4 March. The Earl of Westmoreland, the Lord Wharton, the Lord Conyers, Sir Thomas Palmer and Sir Thomas Chaloner were appointed in commission to meet the Scottish ambassadors for the equal division of those lands called the Debateable Grounds.

6 March. The French ambassador declared to the Duke of Northumberland how the French king had sent him a letter of credit. After delivery of this letter had been made he declared how Duke Maurice of Saxony, the Duke of Mecklenburg, the Marquis of Brandenburg, the Count of Mansfeld, and many other German princes, had made a league with his master which was both offensive and defensive. The French were to go to Strasbourg with 3,000 footmen and 8,000 horsemen and the Germans were to meet them there on the 25th of the month

1552

with 15,000 footmen and 5,000 horsemen. Also the city of Strasbourg had promised them supplies and he declared how the King of France would send ambassadors to me to have me in the same league. Also that the Marquis of Brandenburg and Count of Mansfeld had been secretly conveyed to the French king's presence and had again departed to raise men and he though that they would be in the field by this time.[101]

10 March. He declared the same thing to me in the same manner.

9 March. There was consultation about the markets and it was agreed that it was most necessary to have a mart [market] in England for the enriching of the same, to make it more famous, to be less in danger from other men and to make all things better cheap and more plentiful. The time was thought good to have it now because of the wars between the French king and the Emperor. The places which were though best were Hull for the east parts and Southampton for the south parts of England as is shown by two bills in my study. London was thought no ill place but it was appointed to begin with the other two.

11 March. The bills put up to the Parliament were overseen and certain of them were thought meet to pass and to be read. Others, to avoid tediousness, were to be omitted and no more bills were to be taken.

15 March. Those who had been appointed commissioners for the requests or for the execution of penal laws or for overseeing of the courts received their commissions from my hand.

---

[101] A meeting which led to a treaty signed at Chambord and the despatch of 30,000 Frenchmen into southern Germany in March.

18 March. It was appointed that for the payment of £14,000 at the end of April there should be made an anticipation of the subsidy of London and of the lords of my Council and this should go near to pay the sum with good provision.

20 March. The French ambassador brought me a letter of credit from his master and thereupon delivered to me the articles of the league between the Germans and him, desiring me to take part in the same league. These articles I have also in my study.

23 March. The merchants of England, having been long delayed, now departed, in all about 60 sail, the wool fleet and all, to Antwerp. They were countermanded because of the [disruption of the] market but it was too late.

24 March. Forasmuch as the exchange was shifted by the Emperor to Lyons the merchants of Antwerp were very afraid. And so that the market would not be without an exchange, liberty was given to the merchants to exchange and rechange money for money.

26 March. Harry Dudley was sent to the sea with four ships and two barks to defend the merchants who were being robbed daily before and as soon as he came to the sea he took two pirate ships and brought them to Dover.

28 March. I did deny, after a sort, the request to enter into war as is shown by the copy of my answer in the study.

29 March. To the intent that the ambassador might better understand my meaning, I sent Mr Hoby and Mr Mason to him to declare to him my intentions more fully.

31 March. The commissioners for the Debateable Grounds on the Scottish side did refuse to meet unless a certain castle or pile might first be razed. Whereupon letters were sent to halt our commissioners from the meeting until they had further word.

1552

10 March. Duke Maurice mustered all his own men at Arnstadt in Saxony and the Count of Mansfeld for the defence of his country and chiefly for fear of the Bohemians. The young Landgrave Reiffenberg and others mustered in Hesse.

14 March. The Marquis Albert of Brandenburg mustered his men two leagues from Erfurt and afterwards entered the same, receiving 20,000 Florins as a gift from the inhabitants. He borrowed 60,000 Florins from them and so came to Schweinfurt where Duke Maurice and all the German princes were assembled.

APRIL

2 April. I fell sick with the measles and the smallpox.

4 April. Duke Maurice came to Augsburg with his army and the town was immediately surrendered to him and delivered into his hands.[102] There he changed certain officers, restored their preachers and made the town more free.

5 April. The Constable with the French army came to Metz and within two days it was surrendered to him. Here he found great provision of food and he determined to make it the staple of victual for his journey.[103]

8 April. He came to a fort in which there was an abbey called Gorze and that fort suffered 80 cannon shot until at length there came a parley but the Frenchmen took it, won it by assault, slew all save for 15 with the captain, whom they hanged.

---

102 The fall of Augsburg was a bitter blow to Charles V. The campaign was going against the Imperial forces and Charles would soon be forced to flee over the Brenner Pass to Villach.

103 ie he decided to make Metz his supply depot for the coming campaign.

9 April. He [the Constable] took a fort called Marange and razed it.

12 April. The French king came to Nancy to go to the army and there he found the duchess and the young Duke of Lorraine.

13 April. The Maréchal St André with 200 men-of-arms and 2,000 footmen carried away the young duke, accompanied by a few of his old men, towards France and to join the Dauphin who was at Rheims, to the no little discontention of his mother, the duchess. He also fortified many towns in Lorraine and put French garrisons in them.

14 April. He departed from Nancy to the army, which was at Metz.

7 April. Monsieur Senarpont overthrew the Captain of St Omer, having with him 600 footmen and 200 horsemen.

15 April. The Parliament broke up because I was sick and as I was not able to go out as much as before I signed a bill containing the names of the acts which I would pass, which bill was read in the house.

16 April. I also gave commission to the Lord Chancellor, two archbishops, two bishops, two dukes, two marquises, two earls and two barons to wholly dissolve this Parliament.

18 April. The Earl of Pembroke surrendered his mastership of the horse, which I bestowed on the Earl of Warwick.

19 April. Also he left 50 of his men-of-arms of which 25 were given to Sir Philip Hoby and 25 to Sir John Gates.

21 April. It was agreed that commissions should go out in order to take note of the superfluous church plate for my use and to see how it has been embezzled.

The French ambassador desired that because it was dangerous to carry supplies from Boulogne to Ardres by land, that I would give license to carry them by sea to Calais and so from Calais to Ardres through my land.

22 April. Lord Paget was degraded from the Order of the Garter for some of his offences and chiefly because he was no gentleman of blood, neither on his father's side nor on his mother's side.

Sir Anthony St Leger, who had been accused of various brawling matters by the Bishop of Dublin was again taken into the Privy Chamber and sat among the knights of the Order.

23 April. Answer was given to the French ambassador that I could not accomplish his desire because it went against my league with the Emperor.

24 April. The Order of the Garter was wholly altered as appears in the new statutes. Sir Andrew Dudley and the Earl of Westmoreland were elected.

26 April. Monsieur de Courrières came from the Regent [of the Netherlands] to desire that her fleet might occasionally take safe haven in my harbours. Also he said he had come to give order for redressing all our merchants' complaints.

25 April. Whereas it was appointed that the £14,000 I owed on the last of April should be paid by an anticipation of the subsidy of London and of the Lords, because to exchange the same overseas would be to lose a sixth part of the money I had sent over. A halt was therefore made and the payment was appointed to be made out of 20,000 Flemish Pounds which I took up there at 14 per centum and so there remained £6,000 to be paid there on the last day of May.

30 April. Removing to Greenwich.

28 April. The charges of the mints were diminished £1,400 and there was left £600.

William, First Lord Paget.

1552

18 April. King Ferdinand, his son Maximilian and Albert the Duke of Bavaria came to Linz to negotiate with Duke Maurice for a peace, where Maurice declared his griefs.

16 April. Duke Maurice's men received a setback at Ulm whereupon Marquis Albert despoiled the country and gave them a day to answer.

31 April. A debt of £14,000 was paid to the Fuggers.

MAY

1 May. The Steelyard men received their answer which was to confirm the former judgment of my Council.

2 May. A letter was sent to the Fuggers from my Council to this effect: that I had paid 63,000 Flemish Pounds in February and £14,000 in April, which came to 87,000 Flemish,[104] which was a fair sum of money to be paid in one year especially in this busy world where money is most necessary for princes. Besides this it was thought that money should not give him as much pleasure now as perhaps it would another time. Upon these considerations they had advised me to pay just 5,000 of the 45,000 I now owed and so to put the rest according to the old interest rate of 14 per cent with which they desired him to take patience.

4 May. Monsieur de Courrières received his answer which was that I had long ago given the order that all Flemish ships should not be molested in my havens, as was shown because Frenchmen chasing Flemings into my harbours could not get them because of the rescue they had. But that I thought it not convenient to have more ships to come into my harbours than

---

104 Edward has made an error as the sum should read 77,000.

I could well rule and control. Also a note of some complaints by my subjects was delivered to him.

10 May. Letters were sent to my ambassadors that they should suggest to the princes of Germany, to the Emperor and to the French king that if this treaty came to any effect or end then I might be advised of the same.

Commission was given to Sir John Gates, Sir Robert Bowes, the Chancellor of the Court of Augmentations, Sir Walter Mildmay and Sir Richard Cotton to sell some part of the chantry lands and of the houses in order to pay my debts which were at least £251,000 sterling.

Taylor, Dean of Lincoln, was made Bishop of Lincoln.

Hooper, Bishop of Gloucester, was made Bishop of Worcester and Gloucester.

Scory, Bishop of Rochester, was made Bishop of Chichester.

Sir Robert Bowes was appointed to be Master of the Rolls.

7 May. Command was given to the treasurers that nothing of the subsidy should be disbursed without a warrant from the Council and likewise for our Lady Day revenues.

14 May. The Baron of the Exchequer was made Chief Justice upon the resignation made by Justice Lyster. The Attorney became Chief Baron. The Solicitor General became Attorney. The Solicitor of the Augmentation, Gosnold, became General Solicitor and no more solicitors to be in the Augmentations Court. Also eight sergeants of the law were to be appointed before the coming Michaelmas: Gawdy, Stamford, Caryll [and the rest are missing].

16 May. The muster was made of all the men-of-arms, except 50 of Mr Sadler, 25 of Mr Vice-Chamberlain and 25 of Sir Philip Hoby, and also of all the Pensioners.

1552

17 May. The Progress was fixed to be from Portchester[105] to Poole in Dorsetshire and so through Salisbury homewards to Windsor.

18 May. It was ordered that money should be cried down in Ireland after a payment of money next midsummer. In the meantime the thing was to be kept secret and close. Also that Pirry, the mint master, taking with him Mr Brabazon, Chief Treasurer of the realm, should go to the mines and see what profit might be made from the ore that the Germans had dug in a silver mine and to see if it would be worthwhile continuing. If not, to stop and to discharge all the Germans.[106]

Also that 500 of the 2,000 soldiers there should be sent back as well as those who might go to serve the French king or the Emperor, leaving sufficient at home. No fortifications to be made as yet for those places which were unfortified and many other articles were concluded for Ireland.

20 May. Sir Richard Wingfield, John Rogers and Sir Andrew Dudley were appointed to view the state of Portsmouth and to bring back their opinions on the fortifying of it.

4 May. The French king, having passed the straits of Lorraine, reached Saverne four miles from Strasbourg and was supplied by the countryside but denied passage through their town.

21 May. Answer came from the Fuggers that he was content to defer £30,000, part of the £45,000, and likewise for the August payment, just so long as he might be paid £20,000 as soon as possible.

22 May. It was appointed that as there was much disorder along the marches on the Scotland side, both in useless

---

105 The king means Portsmouth.
106 This concerns a company of German miners working in Wexford.

fortification of some places and the negligent looking after of other forts, the Duke of Northumberland, General Warden thereof, should go down and view it and order it and return home with speed. Also a payment of £10,000 was to go before him.

23 May. It was appointed that these bands of men-of-arms should go with me on this Progress:

Lord Treasurer	30	Lord Admiral	15
Lord Great Master	25	Lord Darcy	30
Lord Privy Seal	30	Lord Cobham	20
Duke of Suffolk	25	Lord Warden	20
Earl of Warwick	25	Mr Vice-Chamberlain	15
Earl of Rutland	15	Mr Sadler	10
Earl of Huntingdon	25	Mr Sidney	10
Earl of Pembroke	50		

26 May. It was appointed that Thomas Gresham should be paid out of the money that came of my debts £7,000, which was to pay £6,800 on the last of the month, which he received the same night.

28 May. The same Thomas Gresham had £9,000 paid to him towards the payment of the £26,000 which the Fuggers required to be paid at the Easter Fair. For he had taken by exchange from hence some £5,000 and £10,000 he had borrowed from the Schetz and £10,000 from Lazarus Tucker. So there was in the whole £25,000 of which £14,000 was paid on the last of April, so there remains £11,000 and £9,000 which I know made over by exchange, which made £20,000 to pay the Fuggers with.

1552

30 May. I received notice from Mr Pickering that the King of France had gone from Saverne to Arromaches, which was surrendered to him, and from there to Limbourg and so towards Spires. His army was to be about 20,000 footmen and 8,000 well-appointed horsemen, besides rascals.[107] He had with him 50 pieces of artillery of which there were 26 cannon and six organs and a great number of boats. From Limbourg - partly doubting Duke Maurice's word and partly through lack of victuals, and also because he had word that the Regent's army, guided by the Count of Egmont, Monsieur de Rie, Martin van Rossem and the Duke of Holstein, to the number of 16,000 footmen and 6,000 horsemen, had invaded Champagne and fortified Stenay - he retired homewards until he came to Struthof and there commanded that all unprofitable carriages and men should depart to Chalons and he sent for the Admiral to come to him with 6,000 Swiss, 400 Frenchmen, 1,500 horsemen and 30 pieces of ordnance. It was thought that he was meaning to do some enterprise around Luxembourg or to recover Stenay which the Regent had fortified. There died on this journey 2,000 men through want of good victuals. For eight days they had but bread and water and they had marched 60 Dutch miles at least and they had gone through many a pass very painfully and with difficulty.

19 May. On this day Duke Maurice, coming from Augsburg in great haste, came to the first passage, called the Clouse, which the Emperor had caused to be heavily fortified and supplied. A passage had been cut artificially through a hill on the way to Innsbruck and there was a strong bulwark made hard by it

---

107 Rascals meaning the stragglers and camp followers of an army.

Sir Thomas Gresham (1519(?)-1579).

which he won, after a long fight, within half an hour by assault and took and slew all that were within it. And that night he marched through that hill [tunnel] into a plain where he looked to see 12 companies of his enemy's Landsknechts. But they retired to the second pass and yet many of them were both slain and taken. And so that night he lodged in the plain at the entry to the second pass where there were five forts and one castle, the ordnance of which slew some of Duke Maurice's men.

20 *May.* This morning the Duke of Mecklenburg with 3,000 footmen, built a bridge over a river five miles beneath a sluice and came and gave assault behind the sluice while Duke Maurice gave assault in the face. The countrymen of the Tyrol, for hate of the Spaniards, helped Duke Maurice so that the five forts were won by assault and the castle surrendered upon the condition that the garrison could depart if they would not serve the Emperor for three months afterwards. In this enterprise he slew or took 3,500 persons and 23 pieces of artillery and 240,000 *Scutes*. The Emperor, hearing of this, departed Innsbruck by night and covered 40 miles. He killed two of his horses and rode continually every night first to the Brenner Pass and afterwards, for doubt of the Cardinal of Ferrara's army, turned to Villach in Carinthia on the 30th of May and waiting for the Duke of Alva who should come to him with 2,000 Spaniards and 3,000 Italians coming from Parma. Also the Emperor delivered Duke Frederick from captivity and sent him through Bohemia and into Saxony to raise a force against his nephew Duke Maurice.

22 *May.* Duke Maurice, after Hall and some other towns around Innsbruck in the Tyrol had surrendered, came to Innsbruck and there caused all the stuff to be brought to the

market place and confiscated all that pertained to the Imperialists. The rest he suffered the townspeople to enjoy. He took there 50 pieces of ordnance which he conveyed to Augsburg, for that town he had fortified it and turned it into his supply depot.

JUNE

2 June. Sir John Williams, who had been committed to the Fleet [prison] for disobeying a command given to him for not paying any pensions without telling my Council, was delivered out of prison upon his submission.

4 June. Beaumont, Master of the Rolls, confessed his offences and how he had brought land with my money when in his office of wards, had lent it and had kept from me sums to the value of £9,000 and above for more than a year, and £11,000 in obligations. About how he had, as a judge in Chancery, between the Duke of Suffolk and the Lady Powis, taken her title and went about to get it into his hands, paying a sum of money and letting her have a farm or manor of his and causing an indenture to be made with the forged signature of the old duke upon it and went about to make 12 men perjured. Also how he had concealed the felony of a man for the sum of £200 which he stole from him and took the money to his own hand. For these considerations he surrendered into my hands all his offices, lands and goods movable and unmovable, toward the payment of this debt and of the fines due on these particular faults done by him.

6 June. The Lord Paget, Chancellor of the Duchy of Lancaster, confessed how he, without commission, had sold away my lands and timber woods; how he had taken great fines

1552

off my lands for his particular profit and advantage, never giving any for my use or commodity; how he made leases in reversion for more than 21 years. For these crimes and others similar to those given before, he surrendered his office and submitted himself to those fines that I or my Council would appoint to be levied on his goods and lands.

7 June. Whalley, Receiver of Yorkshire, confessed how he had lent my money out for gain and profit; how he had paid one year's revenue over with the arrearages of the last; how he had brought my own land with my own money; how in his accounts he had made many false suggestions; how, at the time of the fall of the money, he had borrowed some sums of money and had profit on it afterwards, by which he gained £500 at once, the whole sum being £2,000 and above. For these and such like considerations he surrendered his office and submitted to fines which I or my Council should assign him to be levied on his goods and his lands.

8 June. The Lords of the Council sat at the Guildhall in London, where, in the presence of 1,000 people, they declared to the Mayor and the brethren their slothfulness in suffering the unreasonable prices of things, and to craftsmen their wilfulness, etc, telling them that if they did not amend [their behaviour] following this admonition, I was wholly determined to call in their liberties as confiscate and to appoint officers that should do their duty.

10 June. It was appointed that the Lord Grey of Wilton should be pardoned of his offences and delivered out of the Tower.

Whereas Sir Philip Hoby should have gone to Calais with Sir Richard Cotton and William Barnes, auditor, it was appointed that Sir Anthony St Leger, Sir Richard Cotton and

Thomas Mildmay should go there taking with them £10,000 to be received from the Exchequer.

Whereas it was agreed that a payment of £5,000 should now be made to Ireland, and then the money to be cried down, it was appointed that 3,000 pounds weight [of silver] which I had in the Tower should be sent there and coined at three denar. fine and that the coin should be cried down immediately.

Also... play should be shifted to the porter's lodge.[108]

12 June. Because Pirry was waiting here for the bullion, William Williams, assay master, was put in his place to view the mines with Mr Brabazon or whoever the deputy should appoint.

13 June. Bannister and Crane were delivered out of the Tower because the first had made a large confession and the second because there was little against him.

16 June. The Lord Paget was brought into the Star Chamber and there declared his submission effectuously by word of mouth and delivered it in writing. Beaumont, who had before made his confession in writing, began to deny it again but, after being called before my Council, he confessed it again and acknowledged a fine of his lands and signed an obligation to surrender all his goods.

17 June. Monsieur de Courrières took his leave.

2 June. The French king took the castle of Rodemanche.

3 June. Certain of the Regent's horsemen came and set upon the king's baggage and slew some of the carters but, at length, they were compelled to retire with some loss of Frenchmen. The French king took Mount Saint Jean.

---

[108] This entry was crossed out and then inked in once again, making part of it unreadable. It probably refers to a dramatist called Cowper being held in the Tower.

1552

4 *June*. The French king came to Damvillers, which was a strong town, and besieged it, making three breaches in the wall.

12 *June*. The town surrendered to him with the captain. He found in it 2,500 footmen, 200 horsemen, 63 great brass pieces, 300 harquebus a croc, a lot of supplies and much munitions, as he did write to his ambassador.

19 *June*. It was appointed that the Bishop of Durham's matter should wait until the end of the Progress.

20 *June*. In the Star Chamber Beaumont confessed to those faults he had put his hand to after a little sticking upon the matter.

23 *June*. It was agreed that the bands of men appointed to Mr Sidney, Mr Vice-Chamberlain, Mr Hoby and Mr Sadler should not be furnished but left off.

25 *June*. It was agreed that none of my Council should move me in any suit of land for forfeits above £20, for reversions of leases, or any other extraordinary suits, until the state of my revenues is further known.

15 *June*. The French king came to a town called Yvoix standing on the river Meuse which gave him many hot skirmishes.

18 *June*. The French king began his bombardment of the walls.

14 *June*. The townsmen of Montmédy gave a hot skirmish to the French and slew Monsieur de Toge's brother and many other gentlemen of the camp.

12 *June*. The Prince of Salerno, who had been with the French king in order to negotiate matters touching upon Naples, was dispatched with his answer: that the French king would aid him with 13,000 footmen and 1,500 horsemen, in the pay of France, to recover and conquer the kingdom of

Naples, and that he should marry, as some said, the French king's sister, Madame Marguerite. The reason why this prince rebelled against the Emperor was partly the uncourteous handling of the Viceroy of Naples, partly ambition.

18 June. The Flemings made an invasion into Champagne insomuch that the Dauphin was almost captured and the queen, staying at Chalons, sent some of her stuff towards Paris.

12 June. Also another company [of Flemings] took the town of Guise and despoiled the country there too.

22 June. Monsieur de Thais was sent for so he could raise the *arriere-bande* and the legionaries of Picardy and Champagne to recover Guise and invade Flanders.

27 June. Removing to Hampton Court.

30 June. It was appointed that the Steelyard should have this answer: that those cloths which they had bought to carry over, to the sum of 2,000 cloths and odd, should be carried at their old custom, so they were carried within six weeks. Likewise all commodities they brought in until Our Lady Day[109] in next Lent. In all other matters the old decree was to stand until by further communication the matter should be ended and concluded.

The Lord Paget was licensed to stay at London and thereabouts until Michaelmas because he had no provision in his country.

26 June. Certain of the heralds – Lancaster and Portcullis – were arrested for having counterfeited the Clarenceux seal in order to get money from the giving of arms.

23 June. The French king had many skirmishes with the townsmen [of Yvoix] but two main ones – one in which they

---

109 25 March.

slew the French lighthorse lying in a village by the town and the other when they entered the camp and pulled down the tents. The two skirmishes were against the Count of Mansfeld, governor of the town, and of the Duchy of Luxembourg, and his 300 lighthorse. But understanding through the treason of four priests the weakest part of the town this so frightened the townsmen and the Flemish soldiers that by threatenings they compelled their captain, the count, to yield himself and the gentlemen prisoners. The common soldiers were allowed to depart with white wands in their hands. The town was well-fortified, supplied and furnished.

24 June. The town of Montmédy surrendered to the French king which before had given him a hot skirmish.

JULY

4 July. Sir John Gates, Vice-Chamberlain, was made Chancellor of the Duchy of Lancaster.

7 July. Removing to Oatlands.

5 July. The Emperor's ambassador delivered the Regent's letter which was to the following effect: that whereas I was bound by a treaty with the Emperor made in the year 1542 at Utrecht, that if a man did invade the Low Countries I should help [the Emperor] with 5,000 footmen or 700 Crowns a day for four months and make war on him within a month after the request was made, and now the French king had invaded Luxembourg he desired me to follow the effect of the treaty.

7 July. The names of the commissioners were added to and made more, both in the debts, the surveying of the courts, the penal laws, etc, and because my Lord Chamberlain, my Lord

Privy Seal, Mr Vice-Chamberlain and Mr Secretary Petre went with me on this Progress.

8 July. It was appointed that 50 pounds of gold should be coined after the new standard to carry about this Progress, which makes £1,500 sterling.

9 July. The Chancellor of the Augmentations was willed to cease his commission, given him in the third year of our reign.

3 July. Monsieur de Bossu, Grand Esquire to the Emperor, was made General of the army in the Low Countries and Monsieur de Praet [was given command of] the horsemen.

10 July. It was appointed here that if the Emperor's ambassador requested any more help or aid then this answer should be sent to him by two of my Council: that during this Progress time my Council was dispersed; I would work by their advice and he must wait until the matter was concluded and their opinions heard. Also I had committed the treaty to be considered by some learned men, etc. And if another time he would press me [for an answer] then answer was to be made that I trusted the Emperor would not wish me in these young years, having felt them so long, to enter into them; how I had sworn amity with the French king which I could not break; and therefore, if the Emperor thought it right, I would be a mediator for a peace between them, but not otherwise. And if he did press [us to obey] the treaty, lastly to conclude that the treaty my father had made did not bind me, being against the profit of the realm and country; and to desire that a new treaty be made between me and the Emperor which (being allied to the Emperor in the last wars) he answered that he marvelled what we meant for we (said the Emperor) are bound and not you. Also the Emperor had refused to fulfil it many times both

◈ 1552 ◈

in not letting horse, armour, munition, etc, pass, which were provided by me for the wars, and also in not sending aid during the foraging of the low country of Calais.

12 July. A letter was written to Sir Peter Meutas, Captain of the Isle of Guernsey, both to command him that divine service should be used there as it is in England and also that he take heed that the church plate should not be stolen away but should be kept safe until further order be given.

9 July. The French king came to the town of Avesnes in Hainault where, after he had viewed the town, he left it and besieged a place called Tirloc [Trélon]. But the bailiff of the town, perceiving his departure gave the onset of his rearward[110] with 2,000 footmen and 500 horsemen and slew 500 Frenchmen. After this, and the winning of certain places of little strength, the French king returned to France and divided his army up among some good towns to rest them because many were sick of the flux and other such diseases; he intended soon to increase his power and so to go forward with his enterprise.

12 July. Frederick, Duke of Saxony, was released from his imprisonment and sent to his own country by the Emperor, to the great rejoicing of all the Protestants.

5 July. The Emperor declared that he, and the King of the Romans also, would accept none of those articles to which Duke Maurice had agreed. The copy of them remains with the Secretary Cecil.

Marquis Albert of Brandenburg did great harm in the country of Franconia, burning all the towns and villages around Nurnberg and compelling them to pay 200,000

---

110 ie the garrison of Avesnes launched an attack against the French king's rearguard.

Thalers, 10 pieces of the fairest pieces of ordnance and 150 quintals of powder to the princes of his league. After that he went to Frankfurt to distress certain soldiers gathered there for the Emperor.

15 July. Removing to Guildford.

21 July. Removing to Petworth.

23 July. Mr Wotton and Mr Hoby gave answer to the Emperor's ambassador touching upon the aid he had required according to the first article [mentioned] above.

24 July. Because the number of bands going with me on this Progress made the train great, it was thought good that they should be sent home except for 150 only who were picked out from all the bands. This was because the train was thought to be nearly 4,000 horse which was enough to eat up the country for there was little meadow or hay along the way that I would go.

25 July. Removing to Cowdray, Sir Anthony Browne's house.

27 July. Removing to Halnaker.

30 July. Whereas it had been devised before that the new fort of Berwick should be made with four bulwarks and that, to make two of them, the town would be left open on the enemy's side for some time, which thing was both dangerous and negligent, it was agreed that the wall should stand and that two slaughterhouses were to be made to scour the outer curtains, a great rampart to be made within the wall, a great ditch within that, another wall within that with two other slaughterhouses and a rampart within that again.

26 July. The Flemings entered into the country of Therouanne in great numbers whereupon 500 French men-of-arms arose and gave battle to the Flemings, overthrew them and slew 1,435 of them of which 150 were horsemen.

1552

31 July. It was appointed upon my Lord of Northumberland's request that he should give half his fee to Lord Wharton and make him his deputy warden there.

AUGUST

2 August. Removing to Warblington.

2 August. The Duke of Guise was sent into Lorraine to be the French king's lieutenant there.

4 August. Removing to Waltham.

8 August. Removing to Portsmouth.

9 August. In the morning I went to Chaderton's bulwark and also viewed the town. In the afternoon I went to see the storehouse and there took a boat and went to the wooden tower and from there to Hasleford. After viewing these things it was devised that two forts should be made at the entry to the harbour, one where Ridley's tower stands, upon the neck that makes the Camber, the other upon a little neck standing on the other side of the haven where an old bulwark of wood once stood. This was devised for the strength of the harbour. It was meant that the one on the town side should be stronger and larger.

10 August. Harry Dudley, who was at Portsmouth with a warlike company of 140 good soldiers, was sent to Guines with his men because the Frenchmen had assembled along those frontiers in great numbers.

Eodie. Removing to Titchfield, the Earl of Southampton's house.

14 August. Removing to Southampton.

16 August. The French ambassador came to declare how the French king meant to send one that was his lieutenant in the civil law at Paris to say which of our merchants' matters have been adjudged on their side, which they were against, and for what consideration.

16 August. Removing to Beaulieu.

The French ambassador brought news of how the city of Siena had been taken by the French side on St James's Day by one that was called Count Perigliano and other Italian soldiers; [how it had fallen through] the treason of some within the town and all the garrison of the town, being Spaniards, were either taken or slain. Also how Marshal Brissac had recovered Saluzzo and taken Verucca. Also how Villebon had taken Turnhout and Montreuil in the Low Countries.

18 August. Removing to Christchurch.

21 August. Removing to Woodlands.

In this month, after long business, Duke Maurice and the Emperor agreed upon a peace. But Marquis Albert of Brandenburg would not consent to it and so went away with his army to Spires and Worms, Cologne and Treves, taking large sums of money from all the cities he passed through but chiefly from the clergy.[111] Almost all of Duke Maurice's soldiers, perceiving that Marquis Albert would not enter into any peace, went into the Marquis' service, among which were principally the Count of Mansfeld, Baron Heideck and a colonel of 3,000 footmen and 1,000 horsemen called Reiffenberg. So that of the 7,000 which should have been sent into Hungary against the Turks, there remained but 3,000. Also the Duke of Württemberg secretly let 2,500 of the best soldiers in Germany go over to the Marquis Albert. So that his power was now very great.

---

111 Albert was attempting to establish himself in southern Germany, overrunning a number of free cities and imperial territories.

ᓚᕙ 1552 ᓛᕗ

Also this month the Emperor having departed from Villach came to Innsbruck and so on to Munich and to Augsburg, accompanied by 8,000 Spaniards and Italians and a little band of a few ragged Germans. Also this month the Turks won the city of Timesoara in Transylvania and gave a battle to the Christians in which Count Pallavicino was slain along with 7,000 Italians and Spaniards. Also this month the Turkish navy took the Cardinal of Trent's two brothers, and seven galleys, and pursued 39 others. Also this month the Turkish navy landed at Terracina in the kingdom of Naples. So the Prince of Salerno set forward with 4,000 Gascons and 6,000 Italians and the Count Pitigliano brought to his aid 5,000 men from those who were at the enterprise of Siena. Also the Marshal Brissac won a town in Piedmont called Busca.

24 August. Removing to Salisbury.

26 August. Upon my Lord of Northumberland's return out of the north it was appointed, for the better strengthening of the marches, that no one man should hold two offices and that therefore Mr Strelley, Captain of Berwick, should leave the wardenship of the east marches to the Lord Evre. And upon the Lord Conyers' resignation the captainship of the castle of Carlisle was appointed to Sir Grey and the wardenship of the west marches to Sir Richard Musgrave.

27 August. Sir Richard Cotton was made Comptroller of the Household.

28 August. Removing to Wilton.

30 August. Sir Anthony Aucher was appointed to be Marshal of Calais and Sir Edward Grimpston Comptroller of Calais.

22 August. The Emperor, being at Augsburg, banished two preachers (Protestants) out of Augsburg under pretence that they had preached seditiously and left Mecardus, the chief preacher, and six other Protestant preachers in the town, giving the magistrates leave to choose others in the place of those who had been banished.

29 August. The Emperor caused eight Protestant citizens of the town to be banished as they, going to the fair at Linz, took Marquis Albert's side whilst pretending that they would not abide his [the Emperor's] presence.

SEPTEMBER

2 September. Removing to Mottisfont, my Lord Sandy's house.

5 September. Removing to Winchester.

7 September. From there to Basing, My Lord Treasurer's house.

10 September. And so to Donnington Castle next to the town of Newbury.

12 September. And so to Reading.

15 September. And so to Windsor.

16 September. Stuckley, being lately arrived out of France, declared how the French king, being wholly persuaded that he [Stuckley] would never return again to England because he came away without leave upon the arrest of the Duke of Somerset, his old master, declared to him his intent that upon a peace being made with the Emperor, he meant to besiege Calais and thought he would surely win it by the way of the Sandhills, for having Risebank, both to famish the town and also to beat the market place.[112] He asked for Stuckley's opinion. When

---

112 Thomas Stuckley was a mercenary and adventurer who had supported Somerset. He fled to France and agreed to return to England as a French agent. However, he elected to inform the authorities of his spying mission, only to be subsequently lodged in the Tower for his efforts.

1552

Stuckley had answered he thought it impossible then he told him that he meant to land in England near Falmouth and said that the bulwarks might easily be won and that the people were papistical. Also that Monsieur de Guise should enter England from the Scottish side with the aid of the Scots.

19 September. After long reasoning it was determined and a letter was sent in all haste to Mr Morison willing him to declare to the Emperor that I, having pity, as all other Christian princes should have, on the invasion of Christendom by the Turks, would willingly join the Emperor and the other states of the empire, if the Emperor could bring to pass some league against the Turks and his confederates, but not to be known by the French king. He [Morison] was only to say that he had no more commission but if the Emperor were to send a man into England, he should know more. This was done with the intention of getting some friends. The reasonings are in my desk.[113]

21 September. A letter was sent, only to test Stuckley's truth, to Mr Pickering to know whether Stuckley had declared any of this matter to him.

Barnaby was sent for to come home.

23 September. The Lord Grey was chosen as Deputy of Calais in Lord Willoughby's place, who was thought unmeet [unsuitable] for it.

24 September. Sir Nicholas Wentworth was discharged of the portership of Calais and one Cotton was put into it. In consideration of his age, the said Sir Nicholas Wentworth had a pension of £100.

---

113 This desk, which could be locked, is described in an inventory of Edward's goods as being of black velvet garnished with plates of copper and gilt.

26 September. Letters were sent for the discharge of the men-of-arms the Michaelmas after next.

27 September. The young lords' table was taken away and the masters' of request and the sergeant of arms' and some other extraordinary allowances.

26 September. The Duke of Northumberland, the Marquis of Northampton, the Lord Chamberlain, Mr Secretary Petre and Mr Secretary Cecil ended a matter at Eton College between the master and the fellows and also brought order for the amendment of certain superstitious statutes.

28 September. Removing to Hampton Court.

29 September. Two lawyers came from the French king to declare what things had passed with the Englishmen in the king's Privy Council, what was against them and why and what was now in doing and with what urgency. For which, when they had eloquently declared this, they were referred to London where Mr Secretary Petre, Mr Wotton and Mr Thomas Smith should speak to them. Where the griefs of our merchants were then declared to them, which came to the sum of £50,000 and upwards. To which they gave little answer but that they would make a report of this when they got home because they had no commission as yet but only that of declaring to us the causes of things done.

On the first day of this month the Emperor departed from Augsburg towards Ulm and thanking the citizens for steadfastly sticking to him in these parlous times he passed by them to Strasbourg accompanied by only 4,000 Spaniards, 5,000 Italians, 12,000 Germans and 2,000 horsemen. He thanked also them of Strasbourg for the goodwill they bore him that they would not let the French king come into their town. He went to

1552

Wissenbourg and then to Spires and reached there on the 23rd of this month. Of which thing the French king was advertised and he summoned an army to Metz and went towards it himself, sent a payment of three months to the Marquis Albert and the Rhinegrave and his band, also willing him to stop the Emperor's passage to the Low Countries and to fight with him.

27 September. The matter of the Debateable Ground was agreed upon according to the last instructions.

6 September. Duke Maurice, with 4,000 footmen and 1,000 horsemen, arrived at Vienna to fight the Turks.

21 September. Marquis Hans of Brandenburg came to join the Emperor's army with 13,000 footmen and 1,500 horsemen and many German soldiers increased his army wonderfully. For he refused none.

OCTOBER

3 October. Because I had a payment of £48,000 to be paid in December and as yet had but £14,000 beyond the sea to pay it with, the merchants loaned me £40,000 to be paid by them on the last day of December and to be repaid by me again on the last day of March. The manner of levying this loan was off the cloths at the rate of 20 Shillings off a cloth. For they carried out at this shipping 40,000 broadcloths. This grant was confirmed on the 4th day of this month by an assembled company of 300 Merchant Adventurers.

2 October. The bulwarks of earth and boards in Essex, which had a continual garrison of soldiers in them, were discharged by which £500 was presently saved and, hereafter, £700 more.

4 October. The Duke of Alva and the Marquis of Marignano set out with a great part of the Emperor's army, having all the

Sir Thomas Smith.

1552

Italians and Spaniards with them, towards Treves where the Marquis Albert had set [posted] ten companies of lance knights [landsknechts] to defend it and he remained with the rest of his army at Landau next to Spires.

6 October. Because Sir Andrew Dudley, Captain of Guines, had indebted himself very much during his service at Guines, and also because it should seem injurious to the Lord Willoughby that for the contention between him and Sir Andrew Dudley he should be put out of his office, it was therefore agreed that the Lord William Howard should be Deputy of Calais and the Lord Grey Captain of Guines.

Also it was appointed that Sir Nicholas Strelley should be captain of the new fort at Berwick, that Alexander Brett should be porter and that one Rokesby should be marshal.

7 October. Upon receipt of letters written from Mr Pickering saying that Stuckley had not declared [anything] to him all the time he had been in France, not one word touching upon the communication specified and declared above, and also how Mr Pickering thought and certainly advertised that Stuckley never heard the French king speak any such word, nor was ever in credit with him or the Constable save once when he became an interpreter between the Constable and certain English pioneers. So he was committed to the Tower. Also the French ambassador was advised how we had committed him to prison for having unduly slandered the king our good brother (as other such renegades daily do the same). This was told him to make him suspicious of the English renegades who are there. A like letter was sent again to Mr Pickering.

8 October. The Seigneur de Villandry came in haste from the French king with this message. Firstly that although Mr Sidney's and Mr Winter's matters were justly condemned yet the French king (because they were both my servants and one of them about me) was content to *gratuito* give back Mr Sidney his ship with all the goods in her and Mr Winter his ship and all his goods. Which offer was refused saying we required nothing *gratuito* but only justice and expedition. Also Villandry declared that the king, his master, wished that an agreement might be made between the ordinances and the customs of France in maritime affairs. To which it was answered that our ordinances were nothing but the civil law and certain very old additions by the realm, that we thought it reasonable not to be bound to any other law than their old laws, which had been of long time continued and no fault found with them. Also Villandry brought forth two new proclamations which for things to come were very profitable for England, for which he was given a letter of thanks to the king his master. He required also the pardon and release from imprisonment of certain Frenchmen taken on the seacoast. It was shown to him that they were pirates, how some of them should, by justice, be punished and some by clemency pardoned. And with this despatch he departed.

10 October. Removing to Westminster.

11 October. Horne, Dean of Durham, declared a secret conspiracy by the Earl of Westmoreland in the year of the arrest of the Duke of Somerset. How he would have taken treasure out of Middleham and would have robbed his mother and sold £200 of land to please the people who would have made a proclamation for the bringing up [improvement] of the coin because he saw them grudge at the fall. He was commanded to keep this matter secret.

1552

6 *October.* Mr Morison, ambassador with the Emperor, declared to the Emperor the matter about the Turks above specified. His answer was that he thanked us for our gentle offer and would cause the Regent to send a man for the same purpose to know our further meaning in that regard.

11 *October.* Mr Pickering declared to the French king, being then at Rheims, Stuckley's matter, confession and the cause of his imprisonment. He, after protestation of his own good meaning in the amity, and of Stuckley's ingratitude towards him, lewdness and ill-demeanour, thanked us much for this so gentle an uttering of the matter and that we would not be led by false rumours and tales.

15 *October.* Bishop Tunstall of Durham was deprived of his bishopric.

This month Monsieur de Rie, Martin Rossem and an army of Flemings razed and despoiled many towns and villages (such as Noyon, Roye, Chauny, Nesles, Folembray, a newly-built house of the king, etc) between the river Somme and the Oise. This while the French king had assembled his men of war in Lorraine, sent the Constable to the army which lay four leagues from Verdun and the Duke of Guise with 7,000 men to Metz and the Maréchal St André to Metz. The French king therefore sent the Admiral of France to help the Duke of Vendome against that army. At this time a great plague reigned in sundry parts of France of which many men died.

20 *October.* A man of the Earl of Tyrone's was committed to the Tower because he had made an untrue suggestion and complaint against the deputy and the whole Council of Ireland. Also he had voiced some bad rumours in Ireland about how the Duke of Northumberland and the Earl of Pembroke had

fallen out and were one against the other in the field.

17 October. The Flemings, and the Englishmen who took their side, assaulted Hamleteu [Ambleteuse] by night. The Englishmen were on the walls, and some of the Flemings also, but by the cowardice of a great part of the Flemings the enterprise was lost and many men were slain. The number of Flemings was 4,000 and the number of men with Hamleteu was 400. The captain of this enterprise was Monsieur de Vendeville, Captain of Gravelines.

6 October. Monsieur de Bossu entered Treves with a Flemish army numbering 12,000 footmen and 2,500 Burgundian horsemen, without any resistance because the squadrons left there by Marquis Albert had departed. Thereupon the Duke of Alva and the Marquis of Marignano marched towards Metz. The Emperor himself, and the Marquis Hans of Brandenburg, having with him the rest of his army, departed from Landau on the 9th day of this month towards Metz. Monsieur de Bossu and his army joined with him at a place called Zweibrucken or Deux-Ponts.

23 October. It was agreed that because the state of Ireland could not be known without the deputy's presence, that he should, in this dead time of the year, leave the governance of the realm to the Council there for the time being and bring with him the whole estate of the realm. Whereby such order might be taken as the superfluous charge might be avoided, and also the realm kept in quietness and the revenue of the land better and more profitably gathered.

25 October. Whereas one George Paris, an Irishman, who had been a practiser [negotiator] between the Earl of Desmond and other Irish lords and the French king, did now, being weary

1552

of that matter, try means to come home and to have his old lands in Ireland again. His pardon was granted to him and a letter written to him from my Council in which he was promised to be considered and helped.

There fell in this month great contention among the Scots. For the Carrs slew the Lord of Buccleuch in a fight in Edinburgh and has soon as they had done so they associated themselves to Lord Home and all his kin. But the governor thereupon summoned an army to go against them. But at length, because the Dowager of Scotland favoured the Carrs and Homes, and so did all the French faction, and the French king also having sent for 5,000 Scottish footmen and 500 horsemen for his aid in these wars, so the governor agreed that the 5,000 footmen, under the command of the Earl of Cassilis, and 500 lighthorsemen, of which the Carrs and the Homes should be captains, should go in all haste into France. There the French king would have them serve until Christmas or Candlemas (2nd of February) at the latest. And thus he trusted to be rid of his mortal enemies.

27 October. The Scots, hearing that George Paris was asking for pardon, committed him to prison in Stirling Castle.

25 October. Monsieur de Rie, having burnt land 18 leagues in length and three leagues in breadth, having burnt, pillaged, sacked and razed the fair towns of Noyon, Roye, Nesles and Chauny, the king's new house at Folembray, and infinite other towns, bulwarks and gentlemen's houses in Champagne and Picardy, returned to Flanders.

23 October. The Emperor came in person with his army, which was reckoned to be 45,000 footmen, according to rumour, and 7,000 horsemen, to the town of Metz. The Duke of Alva, with a good band, went to view the town, upon which issued forth the soldiers of the town and slew about 2,000 of his men and kept him in play until the main force of the camp came down, which caused them to retire with loss. On the French side the Duke of Nemours was hurt in the thigh. The Duke of Guise was in the town as captain and there were many other great lords with him such as the Prince of Roch-sur-Yon, the Duke of Nemours, the Vidame of Chartres, Piero Strozzi, Monsieur Chatillon and many other gentlemen.

NOVEMBER

5 November. Monsieur de Villandry returned to declare how the king, his master, again offered to deliver back the four ships against which judgement had been passed. He said that the king would appoint men to hear our merchants at Paris, and these would be men of the best sort. He also said how the king, his master, meant to amend the ordinance of which amendments he had brought many articles.

7 November. These articles were delivered to be considered by the secretaries.

9 November. Certain men were thought to be sought out by several commissions, ie whether I had had been justly answered about the plate, lead, iron, etc that belonged to the abbeys. Whether I was justly answered about the profit from the alum, copper, fustians, etc, which had been appointed to be sold. And suchlike articles.

12 November. Monsieur de Villandry received an answer on the first article as he had done before – how I meant not by taking freely so few to prejudice the rest. For hearing of our merchants' matters at Paris by an inferior council we thought

ᔓ 1552 ᔒ

too dilatory after these long suits and also unreasonable because the inferior council could do nothing (even though there was cause) which had been judged before by the higher council. And as for the new ordinances, we liked them in effect as little as their old and desired none other than the old, accustomed ones which have been used in France of late time and are still continued between England and the Low Countries. Finally, we desired no more words, but deeds.

4 November. The Duke d'Aumale, being left in Lorraine, both to stop supplies to the Emperor and to collect up the stragglers of the army, with a band of 400 men-of-arms, which is 1,200 horse and 800 lighthorse, hearing how the Marquis Albert began to take the Emperor's side, first sent some lighthorse to view what they could. That vanguard fell upon a troop of 500 horsemen who drove them back until they came upon the duke's person. Whereupon the skirmish grew so great that the marquis, with 12,000 footmen and 1,000 horsemen, came to his men's help. An so the duke's side was discomfited, the duke himself was taken and hurt in many places. Monsieur de Rohan was also slain and many other gentlemen slain or taken. The fight was near Toul into which fort escaped a great part of the lighthorse.

6 November. Heding [Hesdin] town and castle was taken by Monsieur de Rie. The castle was reckoned too well stored of all things and surrendered either through cowardice or treason. The battery was very small and not suitable. The most was that the captain, Monsieur Genlis, was killed by one of the first shots of the cannon and his lieutenant with him. In this month, Fernando Gonzaga besieged St Martin's in Piedmont.

18 November. A commission was granted to Sir Richard Cotton, Sir John Gates, Sir Robert Bowes and Sir Walter Mildmay to examine the account of fall of money by the two proclamations.

20 November. The Lord Ogle, leaving the wardenship of the middle marches, because my Lord Evre's land lay there, he [Lord Evre] was made Deputy Warden there with the fee of 600 Marks and Sir Thomas Dacre of the east [west] marches with a fee of 500 Marks.

24 November. Thomas Gresham came from Antwerp to declare how Monsieur de Longin, treasurer to the Emperor of Flanders, was sent to him by the Regent with a certain packet of letters which the Burgundians had taken around Boulogne. These were from the Dowager of Scotland and the effect of them was how she had committed George Paris, the Irishman, to prison because she had heard of his meaning to return to England. How she had found the pardon he had and some other writings, and how she had sent O'Connor's son into Ireland to comfort the lords of Ireland. Also he showed certain instructions, dated 1548, upon the Admiral's [Thomas Seymour's] fall, given to a gentlemen who came here, that if there were any heir to the Admiral's faction then he should do his utmost to raise an uproar.

29 November. Sir Harry Knollys was sent in post into Ireland with a letter to halt the deputy if he met him in Ireland because of this business, and that he should make it seem that he was staying for his own affairs and prolong his going from week to week, in case it was perceived. Also he had with him certain articles concerning the whole state of the realm which the deputy was willed to answer.

1552

30 November. A letter of thanks was written to the Regent and sent to Mr Chamberlain to deliver to her for the gentle overture made to Thomas Gresham by the treasurer, Longin. He was also desired to use gentle words in the delivery of the letters, wishing for further amity. And, for recompense of her overture, to tell her of the French king's request for 5,000 Scottish footmen and 500 horsemen, and also how he takes up £100,000 by exchange at Lübeck, which might mean something, next spring.

28 November. The Lord Paget was put to his fine of £6,000 and £2,000 diminished, to pay it within the space of x years on days specified.

END

The king's diary here ends. His fatal illness seems to have begun following a bout of flu in February 1553. In February he was visited by his sister, Mary. In early April he received the Lord Mayor of London and on the 11th of April he went by water from Westminster to Greenwich. Rumours of his death began to circulate. In late May, John Saunders of Reading was sentenced to have his ears cut off at market day for having spread such rumours. The king had improved a little in early May, the French ambassadors reporting back that he would soon hold an audience with them, which he did on the 17th. Meanwhile Northumberland was busy preparing Lady Jane Grey for the throne following her marriage to his son Lord Guildford Dudley, a union solemnised at Durham Place, Northumberland's town house, on 21st of May. In early June the king, still wracked by fevers and progressively weaker, met Thomas Gresham but on the 16th of June the French ambassador wrote back to Paris saying there was no further hope.

Edward's illness has been the subject of much conjecture through the centuries but he appears to have been suffering from an acute form of broncopneumonia which developed out of a chest infection. It proved fatal. The king died in the evening of the 6th of July and the 'boy of wondrous promise' passed away. Lady Jane Grey was proclaimed queen in London on the 10th of July. Nine days later, Mary, Edward's sister, assumed the throne and thus restored the throne to the children of Henry VIII.

Letters from Edward VI

King Edward VI.

To Queen Catherine
from Hunsdon, 12th of May 1546

Pardon my rude style in writing to you, most illustrious queen and beloved Mother, and receive my hearty thanks for your loving kindness to me and my sister. Yet, dearest Mother, the only true consolation is from Heaven, and the only real love is the love of God. Preserve, therefore, I pray you, my dear sister Mary from all the wiles and enchantments of the evil one and beseech her to attend no longer to foreign dances and merriments which do not become a most Christian princess. And so, putting my trust in God for you to take this exhortation in good part, I commend you to his most gracious keeping.

From Hunsdon, this 12th of May, Edward the Prince

⊷ LETTERS ⊶

To Barnaby Fitzpatrick
from Westminster, 25th of January 1552

To our well-beloved servant Barnaby Fitzpatrick, one of the Gentlemen of our Privy Chamber

We have received your letters of the 28th of December, whereby we perceive your constancy, both in avoiding all kinds of vices, and also in following all things of activity, or otherwise, that be honest and meet for a gentleman, of the which we are no little glad, nothing doubting your continuance therein. We understand also by certain letters that you have sent to the Earl of Pembroke and Mr Vice-Chamberlain that you have a lack of mules and that you desire to have sent to you some of ours. Whereupon we have considered that our mules, being old and lame, will do you but little service and at least less than good ones bought there. For which cause we have willed Bartholomew Campagne to deliver 300 Crowns to you, by exchange, for the buying of your two mules, over and besides your former allowance.

Here we have little news at present, but only that the challenge that you heard of before your going was very well accomplished. At tilt 18 defenders came, at tournament, 20. At the barriers they fought eight against eight to Twelfth Night. This last Christmas has been very well and merrily past. Afterwards there was run at tilt, six to six, which was very well run.

Also, because of Lord Rich's sickness, the Bishop of Ely was made Chancellor of England during Parliament.

Of late here there has been such a tide as has overflowed all rivers and marshes. All the Isle of Dogs, all Plumsted marsh, all

Sheppey, Foulness in Essex, and all the sea coast was quite drowned. We hear that it has done no less harm in Flanders, Holland and Zealand, but much more. For there have been towns and cities drowned.

We are advertised out of Germany that Duke Maurice has turned from the Emperor and he, with the Protestants, raises men to deliver the old Duke of Saxony and the Landsgrave out of prison.

The cause of our slowness in writing this letter has been the lack of messengers, or else we would have written before now.

Now shortly we will prove how you have profited in the French tongue for within a while we will write to you in French. Thus we make an end, wishing you as much good as we do ourselves.

I have since received your letters of the 19th, assuring you that I am the gladder the more often I hear from you.

❧ LETTERS ☙

To Barnaby Fitzpatrick, from Greenwich, 3rd of May 1552

We have received your letters of the 2nd and 15th of April, whereby we perceive you were at Nancy, ready to go with Mr Pickering to the French camp. And, with the intent that you might be better instructed how to use yourself in these wars, we have thought good to advertise you of our pleasure therein. First, we would wish you, as much as conveniently, to be in the French king's presence, or at least in some part of his army where you shall perceive much business to be, and that for two causes: one is because you may have more experience in the wars, and see things which might stand you in good stead another day; the other is, because you might be more profitable in the language. Our ambassador, who may not wear armour, cannot well come to these places of danger, nor seem so to serve the French king as you may who we sent there for that purpose. It shall be best for you therefore, as much as you may, to be with the French king and so you shall be more acceptable to him and do yourself much good. We doubt not also that you shall not fail to advertise us of such things as you shall see done there, as you have well begun in your last letters, for thereby we shall judge by your diligence in learning and seeing things that be there done. We shall not be wearied with often advertising, nor with reciting of particular things. And to the intent that we shall see how you profit in the French tongue, we would write to you again therein. We have been a little troubled with the smallpox, which has stopped us writing hereto; but now we have shaken that quite away. Thus fare you well.

To Barnaby Fitzpatrick, from Windsor, 24th of September 1552

After our right hearty recommendations to you this shall be to signify to you how that, as well as upon consideration of your long absence from us, one whole year almost being expired, and also for some other causes, which you shall perfectlier know when you come here, we have thought good to call you home again at present with as much expedition as you can conveniently make at your ease. And for that purpose you, or Mr Pickering for you (if you think so good), shall declare to the French king that, where you have waited on his majesty for this year past, and now considering the dead time for wars draws near, you are determined to repair homewards to your country, to visit your friends, declaring that, for your part, you will, at any other time, when he shall have need, with leave of your master, serve him with all that you can make, and with other good words, requiring his majesty's good leave for the same purpose. Which, when you have it, you shall repair to our presence with as much haste as you can conveniently make.

For occurrences here we leave them out because you will soon be here, save only that we, since our last letter, dated at Chichester, we have seen our towns of Salisbury and Winchester, Newbury and Reading, and so returned to the castle in good health.

Further, for sickness, I hear of no place where any sweat or plague has reigned, but only in Bristol and in the country near about. Some suspected that it be among a few in the town of Poole in Dorset, but I think rather not. For I was within three miles of it and less, and yet no man feared it. And thus God have you in his keeping.

King Henry VIII on his deathbed points to his heir, Edward.

PRINCIPAL PERSONALITIES

Abergavenny, Baron: Henry Neville
Angoulême, Monsieur d': later Henry III of France.
Arundel, (twelfth) Earl of: Henry FitzAlan.
Bath and Wells, Bishop of: William Barlow.
Beaudesert, Baron Paget of: William Paget.
Bedford, Earl of: John Russell.
Canterbury, Archbishop of: Thomas Cranmer.
Capua, Prior of: Leo Strozzi.
Chancellor, Lord: Richard Rich (1547-1552), Thomas Goodrich (1552-1553)
Chichester, Bishop of: George Day (to October 1551), John Scory.
Clinton, Lord: Edward Fiennes.
Cobham, Lord: George Brooke.
Constable of France: Anne de Montmorency.
Derby, Earl of: Edward Stanley.
Dorset, Marquis of: Henry Grey (also Duke of Suffolk).
Dowager Queen of Scotland: Mary of Guise.
Dublin, Bishop of: George Browne.
Durham, Bishop of: Cuthbert Tunstall.
Earl Marshal: Edward Seymour (to 1551) then John Dudley.
Ely, Bishop of: Thomas Goodrich.
Emperor, Holy Roman: Charles V.
Essex, Earl of: see Northampton, Marquis of.
Exeter, Bishop of: Miles Coverdale.

PRINCIPAL PERSONALITIES

Fitzwalter, Lord: Thomas Radcliffe.
FitzWarren, Lord: John Bourchier.
Glasgow, Archbishop of: Alexander Gordon.
Gloucester, Bishop of: John Hooper.
Hereford, Bishop of: John Harley.
Hereford, Viscount: Walter Devreux.
Hertford, Earl of: Edward Seymour.
Huntingdon, Earl of: Francis Hastings.
Huntly, Earl of: George Gordon.
Lady Mary: Mary Tudor.
Lincoln, Bishop of: John Taylor.
Lisle, Lord: John Dudley (son of the Earl of Warwick).
London, Bishop of: Nicholas Ridley.
Lord Chancellor: Sir Richard Rich.
Lord High Admiral: Thomas Seymour (1547-1549), John Dudley (1549-1550), Edward Clinton (1550-1553).
Master of the Household: William Paulet (to 1550) then John Dudley.
Northampton, Marquis of: William Parr.
Northumberland, Duke of: John Dudley (see also Warwick, Earl of).
Norwich, Bishop of: Thomas Thirlby.
Oxford, Earl of: John de Vere.
Parham, Baron Willoughby of: William Willoughby.
Pembroke, Earl of: William Herbert.
Rochester, Bishop of: John Ponet.
Rutland, Earl of: Henry Manners.
Shrewsbury, Earl of: Francis Talbot.
Solicitor General: Edward Griffin then John Gosnold.
Southampton, Earl of: Thomas Wriothesley.

Strange, Lord: Henry Stanley.
Sudeley, Baron: Thomas Seymour.
Suffolk, Duke of: Charles (first duke) or Henry (second duke) Brandon. Later Henry Grey.
Sussex, Earl of: Henry Radcliffe.
Vice-Chamberlain: Sir John Gates.
Warwick, Earl of; John Dudley (see also Northumberland, Duke of).
Westmoreland, Earl of: Henry Neville.
Wiltshire, Earl of: see Winchester, Marquis of.
Winchester, Bishop of: Stephen Gardiner then John Ponet.
Winchester, Marquis of: William Paulet.
Worcester, Bishop of: Nicholas Heath then John Hooper.

Listening through the lens

CHRISTOPHER NUPEN

Listening through the lens

KAHN & AVERILL • LONDON

Published by Kahn & Averill
2-10 Plantation Road
Amersham, Buckinghamshire, HP6 6HJ
United Kingdom

www.kahnandaverill.co.uk

First published in hardback in 2019 by Kahn & Averill
Copyright © 2019 by Christopher Nupen

DVD Copyright © 2004 & 2019 by Allegro Films

The right of Christopher Nupen to be identified as the author of this work has been asserted by him in accordance with the Copyright, Design, and Patents Act 1988

All rights reserved

A CIP record of this book is available from the British Library

Cover and text design by Økvik Design

Typeset by Pindar Creative, Aylesbury
www.pindarcreative.co.uk

Printed in Great Britain by Halstan UK, Amersham
www.halstan.co.uk

This book is sold subject to the condition that it shall not, by way of trade or otherwise, be lent, resold, hired out, or otherwise circulated without the publisher's prior consent in any form of binding or cover other than that in which it is published and without a similar condition including this condition being imposed on the subsequent purchaser

ISBN 978-0-9957574-2-4

For Caroline

Contents

Foreword by Vladimir Ashkenazy

1	**Angels**	3
2	**Sparkling eyes and ruby lips** The mahogany box, black shellac, white and gold	7
3	**Beniamino Gigli and Tito Gobbi** Italian Opera comes to South Africa, Christoforo 'per ricordo cordiale'	11
4	**Sadler's Wells Theatre Ballet** Kenneth MacMillan and Margaret Hill, a world premiere in Johannesburg, an unexpected romance	13
5	**Lotte Lehmann** PART ONE The Vienna State Opera, the greatest adventure	21
	Lotte Lehmann PART TWO Lotte Lehmann, Frances Holden – Adieu	30
6	**Eiulf Peter Nupen** A most unusual fellow, my one-eyed father	37
7	**The Charing Cross Road** Len Williams, John Williams, the Spanish Guitar Centre, the coal cellar, some Woolly Monkeys	43
8	**BBC Radio** PART ONE Public Service Broadcasting, BBC Features Department	49
	BBC Radio PART TWO Louis MacNeice, a tragedy, Connemara	52
	BBC Radio PART THREE Count Guido Chigi Saracini, the Piazza del Campo in Siena, the high shelf in London	55
9	**Accademia Chigiana – Siena** The Siena tapes, the Mulliner Rolls-Royce and the two-seater Austin 7	61
10	**Evesham** The training course, the barber shop, *High Festival in Siena*	67

11	Diana Baikie PART 1 The blue silk blouse, an impassioned indiscretion	73
12	Andrés Segovia PART 1 Siena revisited, *Andrés Segovia and the Revival of the Guitar*, attachment to the music department of BBC TV	77
13	BBC television A truly gifted film editor, a talented Australian cameraman, enter Peter Heelas and David Findlay	81
14	Double Concerto A piano duo, a trio allegro con brio, the first silent cameras, *Double concerto*	85
15	Isaac Stern An interlude, a devilish plan, *Isaac Stern and the London Symphony Orchestra*	91
16	Daniel Barenboim Flying sparks, some colourful expletives, the elegant blue suit, *Mozart for New Year's Eve*, Beethoven's birthday, a gift for structure, heady days	95
17	Andrés Segovia PART TWO A synthesis of the forest, passion and conviction, the Costa del Sol, the keys to the Alhambra, *Segovia at Los Olivos* and *The Song of the Guitar*	101
18	Jacqueline du Pré Surprises and smiles, *The Ghost*, a new dimension, lifting the spirit, the impossible burden, the interview, a deeply revealing testament	109
19	Diana Baikie PART 2 The summer that never came	119
20	Vladimir Ashkenazy Scriabin, Iceland, the resignation, the birth of Allegro Films, *The Vital Juices are Russian*	125
21	The Trout South Bank Summer Music, a different orientation, fishing worries, still swimming happily	131
22	Pinchas Zukerman. Here to make music A new exuberance, a new trio, *The Ghost*, the English Chamber Orchestra, the Hercules Hall protest, the Zukerman sound, the sugarplum	135
23	Itzhak Perlman. I know I played every note! A curious confusion, who was who, duos with Pinchas, 'a wonderful piece of history'	141

24	**Origins** The Bored Child, secondary schools, petty restrictions, the Priest and the Priest's wife, the clock tower, the Rector, 'Wild with all regret'	145
25	**Michael Nupen** The accident, the triple first, politics, a murder, Respighi, A *Dream of Italy*, *We Want the Light*, the legacy	155
26	**Hayat – Nieves de Madariaga** Franco, Van Gogh, Tchaikovsky, Hayat remembers, the blessed telephone lines	163
27	**Huw Wheldon** A happy coincidence, Chicago, the 81st floor	167
28	**Nathan Mironovich Milstein. Master of invention** Honesty, the painful finger, the Paganini ploy, images and light	171
29	**Manfred Gräter, Sten Andersson, Gidon Kremer, Niccolo Paganini, José Montes Baquer** The IMZ Congress, a tall elegant fellow, the German translation, the virus of perfectionism, the Paganini Institute, dancing with Hasso	175
30	**Gigi – Alice Sommer. Sage, Saint, Mavin** Seeing into the life of things	185
31	**Len Selby. Doctor to the Stars** A man of a different order	189
32	**Evgeny Igorevich Kissin** The BBC Promenade Concert, the Albert Hall Encores, Jankev Glatshteyn 'Mozart'	193
33	**Karim Said** Charisma and persuasion, a passion for Beethoven, *Karim's Journey*	199
34	**Daniil Trifonov** The Wigmore Hall Debut Recital, the philosophy, Judith Ramirez, a small boat on the ocean, the swimming pool, *The Magics of Music*	205
35	**Caroline and Matthew Percival** The generous gesture, close to the soul, the Mallorcan adventure, *Chapeau Matthieu!*	209
36	**Why?**	215
	DVD Contents & Filmography	218

Foreword

It is not easy to find the right words to describe Christopher Nupen's genuine understanding of how important great music and its greatest interpreters are to mankind. His commitment to bringing these spiritual essentials to as many people as possible, in the most clearly narrated and understandable manner, is beyond description.

I have collaborated with Christopher to the best of my abilities for more than 50 years and I consider it a great privilege to know him and to have worked with him.

Christopher is a man of great professional expertise, great passion and wonderful humour. This book reflects these qualities in a most captivating way.

Vladimir Ashkenazy
Pura, May 2019

Acknowledgements

The publisher would like to thank the following people without whose help this book would not have been published:
Christopher and Caroline Nupen and Matthew Percival for all their advice and contributions.
Sidney Buckland for editing and proof reading the book and for all her help and guidance.
Vladimir Ashkenazy for contributing the Foreword.
To all our production team especially Astrid Griffiths of Økvik Design for the complete book design, Sue Barham at Pindar Creative for the typesetting, and Halstan UK for the printing.

The publisher would like to thank the following for their kind permission to reproduce the following photographs:
Foreword and plate 22 © Stefan Gregorowius
Plates 6 and 7 © The Lotte Meitner Graf Archive
Plate 9 Allegro Films
Plates 10, 11, 13 and 23 © Christopher Nupen
Plates 12 and 26 © David Findlay
Plate 14 © Reg Wilson
Plate 15 © Karl Kummels by kind permission of Ingrid Kummels
Plate 19 © BAFTA
Plate 21 © John R Rifkin
Plate 24 © Caroline Nupen
Plate 25 © Matthew Percival

Though every effort has been made to trace copyright holders, the publisher will be pleased to hear from anyone not acknowledged here.

1

Angels

●

Angel is the term used in the theatre and film worlds to describe shadowy figures who invest money in speculative artistic enterprises. They remain in the shadows – until one materializes and we discover just how apt is the term.

Angels usually provide money but in my case they have given me gifts of much greater value than any which money could ever buy. I here offer thanks and pay tribute to some of them, in order of appearance.

Eiulf Peter Nupen, who gave me life and courage and taught me that nothing is impossible.

'Always do the decent thing. Your heart and mind will breathe more easily.'

Claire Meikle Nupen, who carried me inside her for nine months and taught me to know and to love the magics of music – singing endlessly to her unborn child.

'If you are kind to people, you will have a happier life.'

Kitty Oldroyd, who tried so hard, so generously, so untiringly – but unsuccessfully – to teach me how to work and all the while with a most remarkably sustained kindness and understanding, right to the last day of my prep-schooling.

'He has the ability to become a fine scholar and a fine man but he MUST learn the meaning of WORK!'

Fanie Gouws, who brought my ability to speak Afrikaans to a level that earned me a 96% result in my final school oral exam and who taught me to listen for what Risë Stevens called the heart-tugging quality in the voice of Lotte Lehmann. Fanie's care and guidance prepared me for the most far-reaching encounter of my life in music.

Lotte Lehmann, who felt that I might have something to say, who fired the will to try and make something of it and advised me to join the BBC – the most important single gift in the whole of my career.
 'You are **verking** in a bank? **Zat** is completely **UN**possible!'

John Williams the guitarist, through whom I met and made friends with some of the most gifted musicians in the world, bringing about a speed of change that was dizzying: Andrés Segovia, Jacqueline du Pré, Vladimir Ashkenazy, Daniel Barenboim and through him Pinchas Zukerman, Zubin Mehta, and Itzhak Perlman.

Laurence Gilliam, who gave me the chance to make my first radio programme in the face of serious opposition from all concerned at the BBC.
 'If this programme is a failure, I will add it to my list of failures.'

Huw Wheldon who gave me the opportunity to make my first film and who – addressing the assembled dignitaries of the PBS Network in Chicago – said, with true Wheldonian generosity of spirit,
 'Nupen and I, we are the ones who made it.'

Hans Keller, who invited me to work with him on the making of a radio programme about Arnold Schoenberg and from whom I learned so much about broadcasting. The same Hans Keller who said of my first film when it came along,
 'I see that somebody has at last found answers to all the traditionally insoluble problems of putting music on television. The structure is impeccable. This achievement is remarkable in a first film.'

Andrés Segovia, who trusted me to make a radio programme with him when I had made only one before and then allowed me to make a television film with him when I had made only one of those before – an adventurous and courageous spirit if ever there was one.

'I give you green light to go ahead but be careful not to get in economic difficulties by excess of enthusiasm.'

Diana Anne Wishart Baikie Nupen, who taught me the raptures of young love, who had the purest of hearts, who shared everything with me for fifteen years, who taught me to respect the natural world which she loved so much and which she left too soon. Of the summer that never came for her she said,

'The summer is coming and I am not ready for it.'

Denis Forman, who gave me the opportunity to make a 13-part series called *Barenboim on Beethoven* when I really had neither the knowledge nor the experience needed and who later arranged the broadcast of our film *Carmen* on the main commercial channel, the ITV Network. He then moved 'The News at Ten' to 9.30 pm, so that our film should not finish too late – and this for a film which had already been rejected by the BBC.

'Christopher, I am afraid you will always be more of a Van Gogh than a Picasso, when it comes to money.'

Manfred Gräter, who was our first international supporter when Allegro Films became fully independent and without whom we would simply not have survived. Manfred and WDR became our best supporters for more than 40 years. In response to me one day he exclaimed, '*Mein Gott!* Everything you DO is so interesting!'

Rudolf Sailer, who challenged us to make *Elegies for the Deaths of Three Spanish Poets* – the most difficult thing we had ever attempted – and who supported us through three consecutive failures. With his encouragement the film went on to win three international prizes.

'Mr Nupen, you are not committed to success, you know, you are committed to giving us the best you can with your talent and our money.'

Jeremy Isaacs, who gave me the longest retrospective ever devoted to the work of a single director on UK television at the time, and who, when it was over, described it as Channel Four's biggest success of the year, overall.

'Christopher Nupen pioneered a style of filming music and music making for television in which his excellence has rarely been equalled and never excelled. Of that genre he is the undoubted master.'

Dr. Leonard Selby, who tried so valiantly to look after my health for more than fifty years.

'We do not understand your metabolism. We are forced to the conclusion that you are a nervous, creative type, doomed to suffer, and Western medicine cannot help you.'

Caroline Percival Nupen, who, through her natural grace and her earthy wisdom, pulled me out of the darkest shadow I have ever been in. Following that reprieve we have together weathered all the storms that the world has thrown at us along the road and come out still smiling after 36 years.

2

Take a pair of sparkling eyes
And a pair of ruby lips

I was seven years old when I heard those words for the first time – words carried on wings of just-right music – and the first thing that struck me was the speed, the way in which it soared so high, so fast, trailing clouds of glory in its wake. It was a strange encounter, outside the range of all past experience, arresting and even imperiously demanding.

How is it possible for a seven-year-old with no musical education, to be so captivated by the flight of a rising musical line, apparently leading straight to heaven, and accompanied by indelible images of sparkling eyes and ruby lips? The internal response is as mysterious as the magic of music itself.

That fusion of words and music marked the start of something that continues to this day and I have a suspicion that there was another seminal discovery in that determining moment. I seem to have been searching, ever since, for smiling eyes, smiling lips and the winning ways of femininity.

That brief encounter may also have been the origin of a deep-seated conviction that the mirror of the soul is better seen in the lips and the smile than in the eyes. The eyes are more adept at concealment, especially if they have been endowed by nature with the gift of beauty – a benediction so much prized but so potentially double-edged.

If my life in music did not start with those sparkling eyes then I have to guess at the origins, so tantalisingly beyond the reach of memory. The most likely guess is my mother listening endlessly to Enrico Caruso and Beniamino Gigli when I was still inside her. Or perhaps my father, playing Norwegian folk-fiddle in his youth, leaving its imprint in the genes. Or the deep impression made by my father lying flat on the floor with his eyes closed, between two English Setters who adored him, Roy (a king of dogs) and his son Spotty, all three of them listening to Caruso singing *Vesti la giubba* from Pagliacci. This ritual was always preceded by the injunction: 'Silence will now be enjoined, or sanctions will be applied.'

I loved all three of them very dearly and I was impressed. I can still hear those sounds and I understood that they represented something important. These rich memories draw their special power and their mystery from music. These are the seeds from which my radio programmes, and later my television films grew but there was much more to come along the way.

On one dark and rainy day when I was about 13, my father decided that we should acquire one of the newfangled radio-gramophones, housed in a single wooden cabinet. He took the whole family to the main purveyor of such marvels in Johannesburg – Polliack's, it was called. We were there presented with an imposing mahogany beast of which the top was ceremoniously lifted to reveal a gramophone turntable. This was demonstrated with a flourish and my eyes fell on a black shellac disc with a white label carrying gold lettering – the HMV Archive Series.

The combination of black, white and gold struck me forcibly. I had never seen such colour resonances before and it stimulated an excited alertness, but the real magic was yet to come. The shop assistant set the machinery in motion and the monster emitted sounds unheard in my world before: the quartet, *Bella figlia dell'amore*, from *Rigoletto* with Amelita Galli-Curci, Beniamino Gigli, Louise Homer and Giuseppe de Luca. The need to buy the disc became as urgent as the need to buy the gramophone. I said so, and my father agreed to buy both.

I next remember sitting on the living room floor with my knees tucked under my chin, so close to the mahogany magic box that I seemed to be trying to get inside it, and listening to 'I remember that it happened in the moonlight and I remember that it happened with you.' Wonderful images emerged. I heard a gentle, silver voice, quietly calling. I saw a purple-silver moon in the starriest of skies since time began. All of this was promising but *La bella figlia dell'amore* remained at the centre of my universe and the gods were preparing to extend its dominion.

3

Beniamino Gigli and Tito Gobbi

Gigli's unforgettable bel-canto on the white-label disc followed me wherever I went. I sang everywhere possible, especially in the bath and my parents did not object. I had singing lessons, my voice improved, I sang the solos at school. I visited record shops and collected operatic recordings to play on the mahogany box. Then, out of the blue, the fates conspired to bring an Italian opera company to Johannesburg for the first time in its short history; the same Johannesburg that my father kept reminding me was still a mining camp, financially, culturally, socially and ethically – despite its golden riches and its pretensions.

The two stars of the visiting company were Beniamino Gigli and Tito Gobbi, two of the biggest names in Italian opera at the time. My first opera, at the age of seventeen, was *La Traviata* with Beniamino Gigli as Alfredo and his daughter Rina as Violetta. I entered a new and wondrous world. I heard and saw things the likes of which I had never seen or heard before. Once again I was lifted above the earth.

A few nights after *Traviata* I heard Tito Gobbi sing Scarpia in *Tosca*. It was a different kind of revelation, with a character and an aura that took us to an entirely opposite world – about as far from *La Traviata* as anything on earth. First, the sound of that unique voice, totally arresting, whatever it sang – but then, and greater by far, the shock of its being harnessed to the expression of appalling evil, personified and writ large. I shuddered at both the visual and aural power that engulfed me.

Gobbi was dramatically dressed and made up, all in black with waist-high shiny black boots and a fearsome eagle nose. The effect was frightening, diametrically opposed to what radiated from Gigli in *Traviata*.

In two evenings I had been carried from total immersion in a love reinforced in its impact by the tragedy of death, to a representation of pure evil and unbridled violence – also ending in death. It affected me deeply and for many days. Nobody near me could understand why I was quite so upset. My discovery of the magics of music advanced a great deal more rapidly and went infinitely further than would have been possible without the visit of those singing Italians.

These confounding experiences were soon followed by a happy, unexpected and unforgettable encounter. My father took it upon himself to present me to Mabel Schlesinger, mother of the impresario who was promoting the opera season. She was the widow of the millionaire, I.W. Schlesinger, who had been a major force in the development of South Africa in the early pioneering days and for whom my Norwegian grandfather had built the railways in the Transvaal. As a result there had been some fairly close contact with the family and Mrs Schlesinger knew that I was known for my boy soprano solos. My mother impressed on me that, despite her considerable wealth, Mrs Schlesinger had never forgotten her humble origins and had a warm heart. I was lucky again. My father asked Mrs Schlesinger to introduce me to Gigli and Gobbi and this amazing event actually happened. Both the great singers were welcoming and generous. Both were kind to me. On being told that I had been a well-known boy singer Gigli pinched my cheek and called me his colleague. They each gave me signed photographs with the inscription, *Christoforo, per ricordo cordiale*. I have called myself Christoforo on all possible occasions, ever since.

The unfathomable workings of fate had set me on a happy path. That unlikely Italian encounter, at the end of Africa, prepared me for something much more dramatic and enduring that the gods would find for me further down the road.

Sadler's Wells Theatre Ballet

Kenneth MacMillan and Margaret Hill, Alfred Rodrigues, London, the merchant bank, Deborah and Kenneth Macmillan

•

In the burgeoning cultural life of Johannesburg the next great happening was the arrival of the Sadler's Wells Theatre Ballet in 1954.

They brought *Coppelia*, *Façade* (Ashton), *Les Rendezvous* (Ashton), *Beauty and the Beast* (Cranko), *Pineapple Poll* (Cranko), *The Lady and the Fool* (Cranko), *The Rake's Progress* (de Valois), *Les Sylphides* (Fokine), *Carte Blanche* (Gore), *La Fête Étrange* (Howard) and three ballets by Alfred Rodrigues: *Ile des Sirènes*, *Blood Wedding* and *Café des Sports*, which had its world première in Johannesburg.

My parents bought tickets for each new production and a new world opened up and flowered before my eyes. I had never seen anything remotely like it. Once again, I was, of course, carried away.

One evening, about half way through the season, I found a backstage pass door. I developed a gift for discoveries of that kind that was to prove very fruitful over the next few years and in several different cities. Access was easy. There were no serious security guards in 1954.

Backstage I ran about like a lost dog, bounding with enthusiasm, thanking everybody I laid eyes on and telling them how fine they were. They were wonderfully welcoming, smiling and pleased to hear what I had to say. I guess that that is not surprising in view of my message, but its greater importance lay in that it built my confidence. It was the beginning of my discovery that my identification with artists and their inspiring doings, plus my apparent understanding of their artistic concerns and the artistic temperament, won their trust. Those things were to become essential ingredients in the films that I was to make in the years to come.

One evening, I saw an invitation, pinned to the stage door notice board. It extended an invitation to the entire company to a Braaivleis (South African expression for barbecue) at a private home. I made a note of the time and the address and, when the date arrived, I borrowed my mother's car, parked it a little way down the road, and ambled quietly in through the front gate. Nobody challenged me. The world was different in 1954, especially the privileged world of white South Africans in their sunny land.

As I went in I saw three people sitting on the grass around a small fire, quite noticeably apart from the rest. One of them looked like Rachmaninov. The other two looked sensitive and refined. I approached, tentatively and, despite their unmistakable shyness, they accepted my intrusion, presumably because of my backstage effusions.

I was attracted by their good looks, their quiet charm and an unmistakable air of vulnerability. I asked for their names: Rachmaninov turned out to be Alfred Rodrigues, choreographer of the ballet, *Café des Sports*, which we had seen that evening. The other two were Margaret Hill and Kenneth MacMillan. Margaret Hill had danced in *Café des Sports*. She was gloriously pretty and her looks projected convincingly, well beyond the footlights. I found, to my delight, that her looks were echoed in her personality. She was instantly appealing, with her modesty playing a leading role in the alchemy. It was the beginning of my discovery that the vulnerable are almost always more appealing than the people who make themselves important in the world.

Maggie Hill cared passionately about dancing and her shyness did not blunt her critical faculties. At one moment she told Alfred Rodrigues that some of the arm movements in *Café des Sports* were superfluous and made no choreographic point. Rodrigues put up a half-hearted defence and she pointed out that in addition to its pointlessness, the movement was sexually suggestive and inappropriate in the context. If it was to remain, she said, it would have to be re-named the *pas de wank*. That was the first time that I had heard a woman refer to masturbation in mixed company, without a trace of embarrassment or inhibition, and it came from someone so manifestly shy. The effect was instant – the attraction notched up. I felt I had found some very real people.

On stage I was even more impressed by Kenneth MacMillan who seemed to me to be the most expressive dancer in the company. There was a striking ease about him, a surprising looseness in his movements with seemingly elastic legs and wonderfully arched feet. I was particularly captivated by his portrayal of the unhappy Moondog in John Cranko's *The Lady and the Fool*. Entirely believable and immensely touching, his portrayal had a lamenting, suspended elegance which left an indelible image in the mind – a pinnacle of artistic expression. I told him that he had left a curious impression of fluidity with me. He said a hesitant thank you which seemed to cost him dear – he was so clearly, so painfully shy and yet he communicated warmth.

I was attracted to all three of them and stayed with them for the rest of the evening. We were not short of things to talk about and we talked as though we had been friends for years. I had never encountered anything quite like this – a readiness to communicate internal conviction cloaked in external reticence.

Social behaviour in South Africa at that time was defensive, to say the least, so this was new to me. There were too many partisan frontiers in the country at the time: English-Afrikaans, Black-White, Jew-Gentile, African-Indian and more. I had discovered that the easiest going were the indigenous African people because of their nature and doubtless because they had so little to lose. I learned a lot from seeing my grandfather's relationship with the thousand Zulus who built the railways in the Transvaal under his guidance, but the inequalities worried me – from the age of seven.

It was impossible, at that time, to look directly at a Zulu or a Swazi or a Xhosa in the street without receiving a smile of recognition in return – and this despite the prejudice and the oppression. Their behaviour was so different from that of the Whites that they gave a quality to my youth which has left an enduring impression on me. I found my new friends from London as welcoming as the Zulus and

I enjoyed that.

Sitting around the fire with them, I was also impressed by the ease, the lack of inhibition and the enjoyment, with which they talked about sex. It seemed so right, so natural, so healthy and so dramatically opposite from what I had encountered at school and university. I said so and we laughed about it.

Kenneth told me that he wanted to become a choreographer and I begged him not to give up dancing because he was so marvellously good at it. How wrong I was. Nineteen-year-old South Africans have an endless capacity for rushing in where angels fear to tread. How was I to know that he was to become one of the finest choreographers of his time – some say the greatest.

When the party was drawing to a close and there was talk of their having to go to the bus which had brought them there, I offered to drive them back to their hotel. They accepted. At the hotel, we went on talking in the lobby until late. I was hungry for every echo of the theatre that I could lay my ears on and they loved to talk about the company and their fellows. I revelled in their tales, the liveliness of the telling and the attractiveness of their personalities. At one point Alfred Rodrigues, who was married to one of the dancers in the company, Julia Farron, and looked convincingly heterosexual to me, lured me into a dark corner, half behind a door, pinned me to the wall and kissed me on the mouth. It did not phase me at all, precisely because of their openness, their ease and the sanity in their attitudes to sex but the lack of response was a touch disappointing to him.

I explained that I was a naive South African boy with no education in the ways of the world and simply too limited, too inhibited by my background and too dedicated to running after girls to be able to respond. We laughed, and I remember feeling as though some great weight had been lifted from the world. The difficult was suddenly made easy.

I could see that Kenneth and Maggie were close but I had not the faintest idea that they had both an emotional and a sexual relationship. Had I done so, what followed would never have happened.

The party finally ran out of steam and I offered to accompany Maggie to her room. We took the staircase because there were too many in the lobby waiting for the lift. As we turned the second corner, out of sight of the foyer, I jumped in front of her and had a very strange experience. I saw the whole scene as if from a distance. I could see drama in the fact that I was looking down and she was looking up – wide-eyed and not a little apprehensive. I was suddenly aware that looking up is infinitely more charged than looking down. We kissed and I was bowled over by the discovery that the shy girl was anything but shy in that breathtaking moment. I felt the most powerful attraction that I had ever experienced and a deep sense of respect for what struck me as generosity on her part, a personal, open-hearted, sexual generosity from a young woman who was so manifestly unsure of herself – strange contrast. I had no idea until that moment that such things existed and I have never forgotten it.

I was smothered with love that night – the happiest night that my nineteen years had so far granted me. As far as I can remember, we did not sleep at all. As the dawn began to appear I remember Maggie giggling, much as Vivienne Leigh had done as Scarlett O'Hara in that unforgettable morning-after scene in her sumptuous morning-after bed. 'Just wait till I tell Peggy' she said. 'Seven times in one night!' Peggy van Praagh was the assistant director of the Sadler's Wells Ballet, much respected, much loved and in charge of the tour. I have not forgotten Maggie's words, nor her warmth, nor my affection for her. Many years later she took her own life, putting an end to the vulnerability which I had seen so clearly.

Shortly after those memorable encounters, the company left Johannesburg and that might have been the end of a happy story but the fates had two more surprising twists in store for me.

I was studying law at Cape Town University and not enjoying it at all. My father was a lawyer and had said to me, 'If you do not know what you want to do, study law, because it will be good training for you, but try to find a better profession because, in this one, you are dealing all the time with thieves, liars, bandits and rogues and, in the end, that takes its toll.' I asked him to find me a vacation job to enable me to buy a hi-fi set to take with me to my university residence. The idea of high fidelity in sound was new in the world and very attractive to someone who was constantly being amazed by new discoveries in music.

My father found me a job in a merchant bank that was entirely populated by Englishmen. The management was uncomfortable about that fact – in an increasingly Nationalist South Africa. They were looking for a well-known local name to add to the executive staff and my father's name was one of the best known in the land. He had been one of South Africa's most popular sporting heroes, playing test cricket for South Africa for many years and written about in the papers on most weekends. The merchant bank required me to study in London for four years. I confess that I heard only as far as the word London and accepted the invitation. I set sail for the UK, with my mother and my brother, on the MS Jagersfontein of the Holland-Afrika line. We arrived in Southampton on the 24th of July 1954.

The only people that I knew in London were Maggie and Kenneth and the ballet company and so I spent most of my free time with them. This meant lots of free tickets – more happy days, and more learning experience.

Maggie and Kenneth were living together but I had no idea that they had a sexual relationship. I thought that Kenneth was gay. When I discovered the truth I was seriously disturbed and I felt I had to apologize to him. It turned out to be surprisingly easy to do so, precisely because they were so sane about sex. That too left a big impression on me. Talking to Kenneth I found the situation was even more complicated than I had guessed. I learned that Maggie had had a very unhappy marriage and had suffered serious physical violence. She had been close to suicide and Kenneth had rescued her. If I remember correctly the relationship began when they were on a ship which took the company to Australia. I had known nothing about all of this, much less that it had become a relationship of such complexity, but, from Kenneth's telling of it, I began to realize that they needed each other and clung to each other for very deep reasons. I already loved both of them and I was profoundly touched and distressed.

Kenneth said that I had done no harm. He said that he had watched it all with amusement and understood it. Happily, my encounter with Maggie had been youthful, innocent, open and giving on both sides – but it was absolutely wrong when I discovered the depth of her relationship with Kenneth. In London we stopped the intimacy but stayed friends and I grew closer and closer to Kenneth. He did not like being seen as gay and his sensitivity and vulnerability caused him immense suffering. I felt that my easy-going South African-ness was a comfort to him. We laughed a lot and went to the cinema on Sundays – usually the three of us, but sometimes with other dancers as well. I particularly remember Pirmin Trecu, partly because of his unusual, exotic looks which perfectly matched his exotic name. I treasure those days. But everything changes in this world and our lives took us in different directions.

Some years later, I was surprised to find Kenneth on the corner of New Cavendish Street and Harley Street. I asked, 'What on earth are you doing in this part of the world?' He answered, 'I have been talking to a psychiatrist.' I asked, 'What about?' He answered, 'About you.' I suddenly saw things that I had not seen before. I was deeply disturbed.

Kenneth had never told me that the affection had penetrated so deep, despite the warmth and closeness of our friendship – more evidence of his vulnerability. For a second time I seriously regretted my ignorance and my naiveté. I was full of hurt for someone who had become such a close and dear friend and whom I so much admired as an artist. We talked for a while but what we talked about has entirely disappeared from my memory. I did not know what to say. All I remember is that I covered my face. We embraced and parted without managing to say anything meaningful. We saw less and less of each other after that although we talked on the telephone occasionally.

Later, Kenneth met and married Deborah Williams, painter, sculptor and a woman of exceptional character, intelligence, determination and perception. There is no doubt that Deborah saved Kenneth both physically and mentally, becoming an integral and essential part of the true greatness which Kenneth MacMillan achieved.

5

Lotte Lehmann

PART ONE

*Poet of Nature, thou hast wept to know
That things depart which never may return:
Childhood and youth, friendship and love's first glow,
Have fled like sweet dreams, leaving thee to mourn.*

Percy Bysshe Shelley (To Wordsworth)

•

Love's first glow found me – unheralded – in Vienna, when I was 21 years old. It was borne of the most unlikely sequence of chance events; so much so that it is difficult to resist the temptation to think that whatever gods there may be were giving a helping hand.

My arrival in London with my mother and my brother sparked high excitement and bounding hopes. I scoured the newspapers for musical events that might offer something of the magic with which Beniamino Gigli and Tito Gobbi had so memorably flooded me. The echoes of those operatic evenings in Johannesburg remained strong and crystal clear but the experiences had been too fleeting for a hedonistic youth spoiled by white South African privilege, sunshine, liberty, and an upbringing based on the belief that nothing is impossible – nothing is beyond the reach of diligent application and intelligent reckoning.

Soon after our arrival at the Park Lane Hotel, in Piccadilly, I found a newspaper announcement declaring, in bold type, that the Stuttgart Opera would present a fully staged performance of *Fidelio* in the Royal Festival Hall with Gré Brouwenstijn as Leonore. My mother booked tickets and the three of us went to the Royal Festival Hall. As we were buying the programme a slip of paper fell out of it. I picked it up and saw that it was an invitation to apply for tickets for the reopening of the Vienna State Opera on the fifth of November 1955 – more than a year ahead. It was trumpeted as the biggest musical event in Europe since the start of the 1939 war. It had taken the Viennese ten years from the end of that war to rebuild their national treasure – a touching story for those interested in how much art can mean to people, both individually and collectively.

The call was clear and imperious. I had to go to Vienna in November of the following year. But there were some serious obstacles to be overcome and the first was cost. I do not like to look down on the action in a theatre. I feel that it diminishes the characters. I prefer to sit in the stalls, on eye level, and as close as possible to the exotic creatures who make the magic. But the stalls were wildly beyond the reach of a junior trainee in a merchant bank.

Further research revealed that the stalls circle boxes offered six seats, the one at the back with somewhat muffled audio and limited vision. The price of this seat at the back was possible, if crippling, but it meant that even if I went to Vienna and stayed a week I could afford to go to the opera only once. To add to the problem, I found that I could not get a seat for either of the first two nights. – *Fidelio* and *Don Giovanni*. Was it worth it for *Die Frau Ohne Schatten* by Richard Strauss, whose music did not speak to me as Beethoven, Schubert, Mozart and Brahms did? The answer was a tentative but resounding, yes!

Air travel was way beyond my means but, fortunately, the railways offered a possibility – third class in the overnight train on wooden seats with no padding anywhere in sight.

A further problem was the question of dress. Full evening dress was *de rigueur* – white tie and tails – but fortunately I was saved again by my guardian gods. My father had toured the United Kingdom in 1924, with the South African cricket side and, when it was over, decided to remain in London for a holiday. He was a wizard bridge player and, by a process which he never revealed and which I wish I could now discover, he found himself playing bridge in London's premier gambling club, Crockford's, for one pound a hundred. A pound a hundred in 1924! That was something truly dramatic, and frightening to all but the very rich – or the stoutest of hearts. My one eyed Norwegian father, Eiulf Peter Nupen, was not rich but he was exceedingly brave. He was also exceedingly good at playing bridge. During three consecutive days he was dealt cards of such richness as he had never seen before. The cards kept tumbling out like manna from heaven. He won himself enough money to buy two lounge suits from Ward, reputed to be the best tailor in Savile Row, plus a suit of tails which some young men still wore to parties and balls in London in those days. And so, on the 5th November 1955, Guy Fawkes night in the British Isles and opening night at the newly refurbished Vienna State Opera, I left London with the famous tails rolled up in a rucksack, tucked behind my feet for security as I travelled third class in the overnight train, with a firework pageant passing by and the wooden seat not yet troubling my fortunately still athletic bottom. I had embarked on the biggest adventure of my life so far – and I knew it.

When I arrived in Vienna I went straight to the Hotel Regina, unpacked my rucksack, hung up my tails in the bathroom, ran hot water into the bath to generate steam which I had been taught could do wonders for creased garments, and rushed out into the triangular place in front of the hotel, jumping in the air and shouting at the cold to keep it from freezing my bones. Every breath hung quivering in the air.

I was in the home of Beethoven and Schubert and all the generations which had so loved them. I felt that I was surrounded by the shades of those people and that I was somehow touching history. The ghosts of Vienna's glorious musical past were omnipresent. I walked, and walked, and walked, drinking in Vienna and drunk with the drinking of it.

On the next morning the newspapers were full of reports of the first night at the Opera, with dozens of photographs of the two guests of honour, Bruno Walter and Lotte Lehmann. I was already an admirer of both, having been introduced to their recordings by one of the only three masters during my school years who were kind to me: a dear fellow called Fanie Gouws who taught me Afrikaans with amazing success and whom I have tried unsuccessfully to find ever since. I would like to thank him for opening some of the great gates of heaven for me but I guess that, by now, he has left the world of opera forever.

In Vienna on the 7th of November I donned my father's tails, left my coat in the hotel in order not to be encumbered and, I suppose, to show off a little to the Viennese. In 1955 there was no more elegant or flattering dress for a presentable young male with an athletic figure. I strode through the cold with my blood on fire.

I knew, from the London newspapers, that most of the princesses in Europe would be at the Opera and I was silly enough to believe that I might just, somehow, meet one of them. I arrived at the Opera House and entered a champagne-bubbling haven of warmth, looking everywhere for princesses. What I thought I might see is no longer clear to me. But no person labelled princess appeared and so I drank champagne and went in search of box number 10 and my long-reserved back seat.

I found box number one and moved on, full of excitement. Box 9 appeared and I promptly entered the following door, unaware that the boxes on that side were numbered 1, 3, 5, 7, 9, 11 with the even numbered boxes on the other side of the stalls. I had chosen the wrong box – although I did not yet know it – and the box was empty. I took my back seat and waited with mounting hope that the other ticket holders had forgotten, or left this earth. Nobody came! A hush announced the imminent arrival of the conductor, Karl Böhm, and I moved quickly to the front row.

The door to the box suddenly opened and I saw an astonishing looking woman. She had silver hair taken straight back and high from a noble forehead. She had a sumptuous silver fur coat which reached to within centimeters of the floor. In its silveriness it was like some sort of vision. I could scarce believe my eyes but I recognized the woman inside it immediately from the newspaper photographs of the first night and managed to offer the gorgeously superfluous intelligence, 'You are Lotte Lehmann!'. The reply was instant and decidedly characteristic in its directness. 'Yes, and when you have recovered from your surprise, young man, can I please go to my seat'.

There was not much room in the box and so some embarrassed

manoeuvering ensued, until order was restored. Madame Lehmann and her two friends then occupied the three front seats and I went, sadly, to the back. Nobody else came and during the applause for Karl Böhm's entrance I slid quietly into the seat behind Madame Lehmann. I still had not realized that I was in Madame Lehmann's guest of honour box.

The Empress in Strauss's *Woman Without a Shadow*, was sung by Leonie Rysanek and repeatedly, during the first act, Madame Lehmann said quietly to herself, responding to Rysanek's voice, '*Schöne Stimme, Schöne Stimme*.' (Beautiful voice, beautiful voice). I have to confess that what little mind I had in those days was much more sharply focused on Lotte Lehmann than on Richard Strauss or his woman without a shadow and so, come the interval, I had to do something worthy of the occasion.

I heard, as if from some distant planet, my voice saying, 'Madame Lehmann, I came to Vienna looking for a princess but I have found something better. I have found myself in a box at the reopening of the Vienna State Opera with one of the greatest singers that this house has ever known and one of the greatest operatic artists that has ever lived. My visit to Vienna has already given me more than I could have dared to hope for.'

I did not, at that moment, know that the Marschallin in *Der Rosenkavalier*, with whom Lotte Lehmann will be forever identified, was often referred to in Vienna as the Princess and, although I did not yet know it, I had actually found the princess that I had been so fervently seeking. Nor did I know that this encounter would change my life – entirely.

Some conversation ensued and then a sudden question. 'Where are you staying?'

'The Hotel Regina.'

'Enjoy your stay in Vienna.'

At 8:30 on the following morning a signed photograph of Madame Lotte Lehmann arrived bearing the words, 'To C.P. Nupen, my charming neighbor in box 11.'

I realized, for the first time, that I had sat in the wrong box and that I had chosen the box of the legendary guest of honour of the first night. I thank the gods for that extraordinarily generous gesture. To this day, the moment when I first read those words remains with me, as if it had happened yesterday. I have never forgotten the visual impression or the wave of excitement that it generated: a physical feeling that started low-down and bounded up to the top of my chest, so aptly described by that wonderful writer, Eric Sams, as 'the leaping salmon in the breast'. The photograph was accompanied by an invitation to lunch at the Hotel Sacher with Madame Lehmann and her friend of the previous evening, the New York art dealer, Betty Mont.

Betty Mont was born in Vienna and was as Viennese a woman as any that one could possibly imagine. I knew little of the world in those days but, from reading about its musical history, I already had a certain idea about Vienna and my impression of Betty as the archetypal Viennese woman fitted like a glove. Subsequent events would strengthen that impression.

Betty Mont skillfully fed the relationship which she saw developing between the Diva and the stage-struck youth. The lunch conversation was lively. Lotte Lehmann was the liveliest person I had ever met. She was so open and easy with me that I managed, somehow, to respond. I felt at home and I felt warmth. She asked about my background and I gave her tales of Africa. They seemed to entertain her. Oh, what moments. I will be sorry if I keep them only until the end of my life.

She asked, 'What do you do?'

'I studied law for two years but didn't like it and I am now a trainee in a merchant bank.'

Madame Lehmann exploded, 'You are **verking** in a **bank**? **Zat** is completely **UN**pozibil.'

A friendship developed – despite the 46-year age difference – which soon flew higher than anything I had previously experienced. It seemed to be based on some sort of natural chemistry. How naturalness could appear to be its most distinguishing characteristic is beyond all understanding. We enjoyed each other with ease and without reservation. I was bewitched by the most generous personality that I had ever encountered.

I wrote a letter which tried to be poetic and, by gentle inference, a timid love letter. All that I can remember of it is that it began with

'Liebe Lotte (may I call you Liebe Lotte?)' and that it contained an imagined description of her winging her way back to California in a freezing night sky, under a winter moon, in a silver, high altitude aeroplane, quietly shining to the quiet moon. The last phrase was borrowed, unacknowledged, from Samuel Taylor Coleridge – remembered from schooldays. Everything about Lotte Lehmann seemed to call for poetry.

When I got back to London I missed her and I missed the magic. Small wonder, for a youth who had hardly experienced anything at all up to that time other than colonial laziness under the African sun and a few fleeting but deeply seductive moments with Beniamino Gigli, Tito Gobbi, Kenneth MacMillan and Maggie Hill.

Some two years later I was still living in London and still working at the merchant bank, 6,000 miles away from what was supposed to be my home and still corresponding regularly with my Liebe Lotte. Suddenly there came a further intervention from the gods. It came in the form of Mrs Emmie Tillett, of the London concert artists' agency, Ibbs and Tillett. She invited Madame Lehmann to give masterclasses in London's famous Wigmore Hall in 1957 with Ivor Newton as accompanist.

The masterclasses were held in the afternoons and so I took a holiday from the bank. I sat with Betty Mont in the front row (seat A14); just fifteen inches from the stage, close to the singers and close to Madame Lehmann. Lotte's stage presence was arresting and dramatic, even when she was doing nothing. I remembered having read that she had been famous for holding the attention of an entire audience, while doing nothing at all. I remembered also having read that Toscanini had called her the greatest artist in the world, not the greatest singer, but the greatest living artist, overall.

The Wigmore Hall was sold out each time and afterwards, on eight evenings, I had supper with Lotte and Betty in their capacious royal suite at the Hyde Park Hotel. Naturally the suite was on the north side of the hotel, facing directly onto Hyde Park and so we dined in what appeared to be the countryside – in the middle of London. That made yet another indelible impression.

Eight suppers in two weeks and lunch with them three times.

At supper there were always just the three of us. At the lunches there were always distinguished guests. The first were Otto Klemperer and his daughter Lotte, so named in affectionate tribute to Lotte Lehmann and some turbulent times when she was a beginner at the Hamburg State Opera and Klemperer had pursued her with a near violent passion that was never requited. The second lunch was with Walter Legge and Ivor Newton and the third with Neville Cardus and Ivor Newton.

Cardus invited me to lunch at his club in the following week and when I got there, offered to train me to follow in his footsteps as a critic. I replied that I felt unequal to the task for three reasons: firstly a shortage of talent, secondly a shortage of musical education and thirdly, because I felt, even then, that I was more of a promoter than a critic. That sentiment came, at least in part, from one of my mother's prime exhortations, 'Be a giver, not a taker. Be kind to people and you will have a happier life.' I have tried to stay true to that. But if I had known then what I know now about the glorious qualities of Cardus's writing, I would have tried to salvage at least something from that highly unusual and very generous offer. I am saddened that I did not.

After the masterclasses Lotte, Betty and I were transported from the Wigmore Hall to the Hyde Park Hotel in a limousine provided by Mrs Tillett, and with Lotte in the spirit of post-performance largesse which I have seen so often in the great performers. She entertained us hugely and made us laugh repeatedly. That is how she was, always giving, keenly observing and commenting on everything: the trees, the greenness of Hyde Park (she was a painter, among other things) and the dozens of *péripatéticiennes* who used to line Park Lane in 1957. 'What are all these virgins doing here?' she asked.

She saw things differently from the way that others saw them. She often challenged me to think again. She helped me to believe in what Schubert called the highest in art. She made me feel that life could be good, at a time when I had begun to be questioning of the whole sorry scheme of things.

She was kind to me. She was extraordinarily generous to me, but those are not the key elements. She was natural and honest with me in a way that I had not thought possible. I felt that I loved her and somehow managed to say so in a timid way.

The first time that we made love she said to me, 'My face is old. Would you like me to turn off the light?' I replied that I loved her face, and I really meant it. Every time my eyes landed on that face it felt like coming home. I had never experienced that before. I remembered some words of William Butler Yeats that had once made a great impression on me: 'And loved the sorrows of your changing face.' I quoted the whole poem to her. She was surprised, she liked it and responded with, 'When, one day, you think you are in love, and you make love to your girl, don't switch off the light , and look in her eyes at the moment of climax. Then you will know if you are in love.'

These are moments which cannot be described in words alone. The best evocation that I know is contained in the sounds which Lotte made when she sang the last two lines of Mozart's song, *Die Verschweigung*, (Discretion) – inimitable, indescribable, pure, supercharged, unforgettable, heart-tugging Lehmann.

> In diesen schwülen Sommertagen
> Hat er ihr oftmals zugesehn,
> Und er ist jung, und sie ist schön:
> Ich will nichts weiter sagen.
>
> In these sultry summer days
> He gazed at her, long and often
> And he is young and she is beautiful:
> I will say no more.

PART TWO
Lotte Lehmann and Frances Holden
Adieu

When I made my life-changing mistake in 1955 and sat in the wrong box at the Vienna State Opera, I knew that Lotte Lehmann was thought of as one of the greatest singers that had ever lived but I knew only a very few recordings. My ignorance makes me feel decidedly foolish but, in retrospect, I see that it helped a great deal. I was more natural with her than I could ever have been had I known of the almost unmatched public and critical adulation. My ignorance also enabled her to be more natural with me. Against all the odds and because of her abiding honesty, our relationship seemed amazingly free of the weight of the world.

At our suppers Lotte had me riveted. She recounted high-level adventures and often with some enlivening ironic or critical twist in her commentary. She had a great memory for details. These included the tale of her encounter with Hermann Göring and her letter refusing his offer to make her a leading artist of the Third Reich, a letter which eventually found its way to Hitler and threw him into a frenzy of rage. She feared that it might have cost the Third Reich a rug since Hitler was reputed to have chewed through the carpet in some of his finest rages. We laughed. She loved to laugh. It was a defining characteristic. We talked about what I should do with my life. Those discussions were to have profound consequences for me.

Her masterclasses at the Wigmore Hall became the talk of the musical fraternity. I was present at all of them and always sat in the front row with Betty Mont. At the end of one of the classes an astonishing thing happened. Here is an account of it by the actor and author Robert Speaight in *The Tablet* dated October 12th 1957:

> At the end of the afternoon, there came one of the most electrifying moments I have ever experienced in theatre or concert-hall. [Madame Lehmann] was demonstrating the ironic gaiety with which the Marschallin should bid Octavian goodbye.
> Suddenly, from the rather dingy stage of the Wigmore Hall, a sound went up that did not come from either of the very promising pupils of the Opera School. In a second we realised what had happened: Mme. Lehmann had forgotten

that she had no voice! The applause went on for about a minute while she brushed aside the moment of oblivion with a good-humoured wave of the hand.

What Mr Speaight did not know was why and how that happened.

On the previous day Lotte had given me a photograph of herself taken, a few days earlier, by Lotte Meitner-Graf in her Bond Street studio. Lotte had written out, on the photograph, on a deliberately wavy stave, the notes but not the words of the Marschallin's great sigh of impending separation from her youthful lover, Octavian ('Quinquin'). *Heut, oder Morgen, oder den übernächsten Tag.* Today, or tomorrow or the day after, her lover would leave her for a younger woman.

As the line approached, Lotte turned from her pupil and glanced at me and Betty in the front row. She turned back at her pupil. Then it happened, she suddenly gave tone to those words and I had never in my life heard such sounds. Mr Speaight's account of it, aside from the impact on him personally, is a pale shadow of what actually happened.

The sounds that Lotte uttered came from another world and quite literally shook and shocked me. It was the tremendous volume which seemed to make the very walls shake. But there was something else, something visceral in the quality of the sound that I had never heard before. She sang *Heut, oder Morgen oder den übernächsten Tag* and looked at me, trembling, in the front row. I must have had the widest eyes she had ever seen. It stirred something inside me, something physical, something real that I had not met before. I was totally floored. I was still on edge when the class ended.

In his biography (Capra Press,1988), Beaumont Glass writes, 'At 69 the Marschallin off-stage, seems to have lost little of her charm. A susceptible Quinquin longed to come into her life.' Glass then quotes lines from a letter which Lotte had written about me to her friend and patron Frances Holden on 2 October 1957, ten days before that high moment in the Wigmore Hall, a letter which I did not see until 38 years later.

I can't understand it – especially since I am very cold to him and always tell him that he is a crazy fool. It flatters me – naturally… . It would be nice to find some pleasure in flirting with such a handsome boy, but I only think it ridiculous.

The reference to coldness was a camouflage. Nobody, except Betty Mont, knew that we were already lovers. Apart from Betty, I said not one word about it to anyone for more than forty years. I felt that no living soul could ever begin to understand how honest, how innocent, how warm and how beautiful all of it had been. It was the finest and most elevated thing that had ever happened to me, and I would have allowed nothing to cheapen it.

Looking at it now, more than 60 years later, I feel that the story merits a place in the world and I want to tell it. I feel hugely privileged to have been accepted so warmly and without reservation by so great a spirit: a telling testimony to the rare qualities of an exceptional and unafraid human being.

Of all the stories that she told in those magical evenings the one that had the most to say of her astonishing being was her late-night account of her farewell recital in Town Hall, New York, on the 16th of February 1951. Her trained memory and her gift for expression bringing every moment of it vividly to life.

She had made up her mind to retire a few days earlier but told nobody. She sang the first half of the programme and it confirmed her conviction that she should retire before the world tired of her. 'I wanted to go when they would feel regret and not relief', she said. And so, at the end of the first half, she released a bombshell that would not be forgotten by anyone present:

> I didn't announce it before because I don't like to celebrate my own funeral, but this is my farewell recital in New York.
>
> *Vigorous protests erupted in the hall.*
>
> Thank you. I hoped you would protest. But please don't argue. I think you know that the Marschallin in *Rosenkavalier* has always been one of my favourite parts. This Marschallin is a very wise woman. She looks into the mirror and she says: 'It is time!' So I, as a singer, look into the mirror and I say, 'It is time!'
>
> *A shout from the audience; 'Oh no!'*
>
> Oh yes! I have made up my mind. These have been very, very happy years which I have sung for you. Town Hall has always been a kind of home to me, a home which now reluctantly and sadly, I have to abandon.

She thanked several people, and, most fulsomely, her accompanist of many years, Paul Ulanowsky. She ended with this:

> Last but not least I come to thank you, my public, and there I am a little at a loss what to say … . You have always given to me more than I gave you. Let me explain what I mean. When I came home after a recital I always had a feeling of deep dissatisfaction. I know so much better what perfection means, perfection which always was a goal for me and never attained. There were always so many limitations, vocal limitations, limitations in my technique, in my expressive power. So I have sometimes failed you. But you as a public have been perfect. You were kind and understanding. You gave me your enthusiasm, you gave me everything, and you gave me your heart … So when I say goodbye to you I say goodbye not to a public but I say goodbye as though to a very beloved person, and I will cherish the memory as long as I live. You have given me much inspiration, you were the wings on which I soared, and if sometimes it was possible for me to take you with me on my flight into beauty and into a better world, then perhaps I have achieved a fraction of what I wanted to give you.

She sang the second half to thunderous applause and came back on stage for an encore: Schubert's *An Die Musik*. When she had to sing the line *Du holde Kunst, ich danke dir*, (Holy art, I thank you) she could not do it. She covered her face to hide her tears and left the stage without a word. Many in the audience were crying with her.

Appreciation of the courage behind her retirement increases with the knowledge that Lotte Lehmann had been over-generous throughout her career and consequently was in financial straits. Having had to leave Germany and Vienna had cost her a great deal, as had the hundreds of parcels that she had sent to friends, relatives and acquaintances after the war. She was rescued by her great friend Frances Holden, a professor of psychology at New York University and a specialist in the study of genius in the performing arts. Frances had been an admirer for many years and when Lotte's husband Otto Krause died, she came up with an idea which in its generosity gloriously matched the largesse of the Lehmann spirit. She retired from the university and bought a house in Santa Barbara for them to share. She proposed that Lotte should teach aspiring young singers at the budding Music Academy of the West which had sprung from a Lehmann idea.

Frances chose a site with great possibilities both for developing the house itself and for the several acres of sloping land that dropped away in front of it to the ocean. Together they turned it into a famously beautiful and happy place, named it Orplid after the dream island in Hugo Wolf's *Gesang Weylas*, extended it so that each had their own part and they lived there for the rest of their lives.

> You are Orplid, my land!
> The distance shimmers;
> the sea mist dampens your sunny shore
> and bathes the cheeks of the gods.

When Lotte died, on the 26th of August 1976, I wrote to Frances to acknowledge the importance of what she had done for Lotte and for the world and to thank her for it. Frances wrote back with an unprecedented warmth and said that she had decided to put some of my letters to Lotte in the Lehmann archives at UCLA. That was the beginning of a friendship that was to grow, and continue to grow, right up to the time she died.

Some years later I was in New York making a film with Itzhak Perlman and I heard that Frances was failing. I needed to go and say goodbye. I wanted, before the opportunity would be forever lost, to see the house Orplid, which I knew, from Lotte herself, was so full of evidence of her creativity, both inside and out; paintings, sculptures, glass mosaics, ceramics, fountains, many unmistakable reminders of that energetic artistic spirit. I could ill afford the cost of going there but I knew that, if she would see me, I *had* to go.

I telephoned Santa Barbara and asked Frances whether I could take her to dinner. 'No,' she said. 'Come and stay the night and we will have supper here.' I flew to Los Angeles and then in a small plane to Santa Barbara. I arrived just in time for supper. We talked about Lotte, about loss, about music and about philosophy. We did not talk about psychology.

Frances had been told, some years earlier, that she had two operable cancers. The diagnoses were accompanied, as usual, with urgent recommendations for surgery. Frances elected not to have the surgery. I was told that she had said, 'I will die of my cancers when the time comes. That is the natural way.' At the time of my visit she was

96, wizened, and ready to leave this world.

I had to leave very early on the following morning to go back to New York and did not expect her to be awake. But Frances Holden was awake, sitting, huddled and tiny, in her living room, with walls full of Lehmann paintings, a white shawl around her shoulders and waiting for me. I had the impression that she was much smaller than she had been when she was that pioneering professor of psychology.

I said, 'I am sorry that my visit has been so short but you know why I came and you know also how important it was for me to come.'

'Go to my study. You will find two letters on my desk written by Lotte from London about you. If you want to take them you may do so.'

I went there. I read them. There were several surprises. One of them asked the question, 'Tell me how it is *humanly possible* that this boy can be so much in love with me, a woman of almost 70. I honestly don't understand.' (She was, in fact, 67 at the time).

I returned to the living room fearing that I could not find adequate words. I did not need any. Frances silenced me with a kindly, understanding gesture. A tiny figure, full of wisdom but clearly failing, she lifted her head to look me straight in the eyes and, with a gaze that I have not forgotten, she said,

'I see what Lotte saw in you.'

> Thou in the grave shall rest – yet till the phantoms flee
> Which that house and heath and garden made dear to thee erewhile
> Thy remembrance, and repentance, and deep musings are not free
> From the music of two voices and the light of one sweet smile.
>
> Percy Bysshe Shelley

Eiulf Peter Nupen

Gurskøy, Peter Cornelius, the mountain railway, some Zulus, the test match, Jack Hobbs, Wally Hammond

•

My father, Eiulf Peter Nupen, was a most unusual fellow, to say the very least – and for me a most lovable one.

He was born on Nupen farm on the island of Gurskøy near Ålesund in Norway, on 1 January 1902. At the age of seven he hit two hammers together and a metal splinter flew into his left eye. All attempts to save the eye failed and he endured three months of agony. Finally he was shipped to London where his eye was removed and he was given a glass eye made by the famous firm, Hamblin. The people who treated him were kind to him and felt for him in his agony. He was grateful for it and I believe that that was the beginning of his life-long attachment to the best things in English culture.

His father, Peter Cornelius was one of the builders of the railway which links Bergen and Myrdal, the railway that gains the greatest height in the shortest trajectory – or so it did at that time. The rock face is too steep for the railway to do the usual doubling back on itself and so, instead, it starts by going left at the steepest manageable angle, for a certain distance, where it then stops. When it arrives at its left limit, the points behind it are changed, linking it to a new branch line, which rises to the right. The train then shunts in reverse until it reaches the altered points after which it finds itself climbing, still in reverse, to the right and again at the steepest manageable angle.

This procedure, forward left – stop – backwards right – stop – forward left, continues until the train arrives at the top of the mountain where the mid-day trains stop for lunch for the benefit of the travellers and tourists – a fine, hospitable Norwegian gesture, as is the stone memorial to Scott which stands imposingly at the top.

The South African millionaire, I.W. Schlesinger, who was planning to plant tens of thousands of orange trees in the Transvaal, needed railways to transport the fruits of his labour to the port at Mozambique and thence by ship to the rest of the world. He heard of the Bergen-Myrdal railway achievement and invited my grandfather to South Africa to build the Transvaal railways. Peter Cornelius accepted the invitation, employing thousands of Zulus with whom he developed a most impressive working and personal relationship. He was much loved and much respected by a people famous for their battles and yet among the most smiling on the face of the earth. Those Zulus enriched the Transvaal, enriched Mr Schlesinger, enriched South Africa, enriched my family and, in time, enriched me in my formative years. I believe that I would never have had the courage to do what I have done and what all the television big shots, including Huw Wheldon, said could not be done, if I had not been the son of Eiulf Peter and grown-up among the Zulus. Together they taught me to see things differently and to believe that all things are possible.

Among the Zulus three hugely colourful characters, who enriched my life immensely, remain bright in the memory, Kamzaan Nwalo, Johannes Ramoshane and Ellen who taught me Zulu children's games, always smiling.

I remember walking along the Natal/Zululand beach on the edge of the Indian Ocean with Johannes and seeing a 'Whites Only' sign. Johannes said 'I can't go there. What happens if Koos comes?' Koos was the pejorative term for the Afrikaner police.

I said, 'If Koos comes, you leave him to me. I will explain that I have health problems and you are my protector.' We continued on our way.

We came to a new sign, 'Coloureds Only.' Johannes said, 'We can't go there.' I gave the same response.

Further along we found a sign, 'Blacks Only.' Johannes said, 'You can't go there.' I gave the same response, yet again.

Johannes thought about this for a while and then stopped dead in his tracks. 'You know, they think they so clever. They think they know everything. Meantime – they backward.'

If Koos had heard these words he would doubtless have arrested him on the spot and perhaps attacked him physically as well.

A little further along I asked Johannes if he ever went into the sea.

'No'

'Why?'

'The trouble with the water is there's no place to hold it.'

It turned out that he had once been on an employer's boat which had sunk and he came close to drowning.

The Zulus, the Xhosas and the Swazis of my youth knew how to brighten the world and the effect was heightened by awareness of the miseries imposed on them.

Peter Cornelius could see that the Transvaal, in its pioneering years, provided no adequate facilities for the education of his son and so, by some unlikely process – since he spoke no English – Eiulf ended up living with the headmaster of King Edward VII School in Johannesburg, not as a boarder – there were no boarders – but as the house guest of the headmaster, Desmond Davis, a gifted English educationist of the first rank, who later became my godfather. My father owed many things to Desmond Davis in the colourful life that he was to lead.

As the personal guest of his headmaster Eiulf rapidly acquired high mastery of the English language – but not only that, he and Mr. Davis spoke Latin at breakfast and in my father's final Latin exam he scored 98%.

Eiulf Peter Nupen also became Victor Ludorum and Head Boy. While still at school he played cricket for the Transvaal at the age of 16 – as a batsman, not a bowler, and with only one eye. When he left school he continued to play cricket for the Transvaal and played his first test match for South Africa in 1921. He was known as 'Buster' Nupen when he was 19.

At home he never said a single word about his sporting achievements, except on one notable occasion. In response to my question 'What do you feel when you start to bowl to someone?' his answer came swiftly: 'I'm going to get this bugger out if it's the last thing I do.'

I was shocked. I had never heard my gentle giant say an aggressive word about anybody. He was a hero and, in many ways, his life was easy. In sporting South Africa most people in the land admired him and followed his exploits in the newspapers. He was so very gifted in so many ways that he was in a position always to be kind and generous. I never saw a more convincing demonstration of *noblesse oblige*.

He was only angry with me on one most memorable occasion and for what seemed to him at the time to be good reason.

There were lots of guns in pioneering South Africa. They came first for killing wild animals for food and hung around long after hunger was no longer a pressing need. They were part of the culture. An echo also of the lamentable needs of the Boer War. We were even taught to shoot at school, and were given regular, compulsory practice sessions at which, happily, nobody was ever shot, as far as I know.

There were three rather fine guns in our house, a .22 Mauser, a 9.5 Magnum Mauser and a Purdey shotgun. One day, for reasons best known to teenage boys, I took down the .22 Mauser from the top of the wardrobe where it lived and, like a well-trained South African boy, checked first to make sure that it was not loaded. It was never loaded in the house and never should have been but, nevertheless, I decided to check.

Stupidly, instead of simply opening the breech and looking, I pointed the gun at the floor and in all confidence, pulled the trigger. Bang! That was a shock. A .22 hole in the wooden floorboards could be quickly fixed but what had happened below? I shot down the stairs like a frightened rabbit to discover that although the hole in the ceiling was small, the plaster around it had come away in an almost perfect circle, a little over 2 inches in diameter and very visible. Both my parents were out and I spent a long time looking for the slug – unsuccessfully. I found it finally at the back of a large oil painting, lodged between the canvas and the wooden frame.

The painting, which hangs in my bedroom to this day, is of a deep forest road in Germany, made before the advent of tarmac. The road is lined by the tallest trees imaginable in full, mid-summer leaf. It has a look reminiscent of a great cathedral. It was painted by the once famous German artist, Otto von Minden. It is imposing and was a proud possession of the entire family.

I extracted the slug and found that it had made a tiny tear, about a quarter of an inch long, in the canvas. Idiotically, I tried to disguise this with green watercolour. There were no oil paints in the house. For the ceiling, as there was no Polyfilla in those days, I ran to the chemist and bought plaster of Paris to conceal the evidence of my wicked doings.

Many moons later my father, my mother and I were all in the living room together and I saw my father suddenly stop – peering intently at the painting. The time had come to confess. I started to explain but had uttered only a few words about the gun when I saw a person I had never seen before – enraged to the limit. He said, 'You shot this picture?'

I could see that this was not the moment for rational discussion and that flight was the only remedy. I shot out of the room, out of the front door, across the road and through a hole in the golf course fence which I was accustomed to using when I felt like a bit of unofficial golf from the eighth tee without having to pay green fees. I stayed there, hidden in the trees, for more than an hour, listening to their calls.

Eventually I crept back, sideways, like a lost sheep and told the full story. My wonderful, kind, generous, intelligent, understanding father understood and accepted with no more ado. He took the painting for repair on the following day without a word of recrimination. No words were needed. My remorse was plain enough to see.

I have no doubt that the sudden restoration of calm bore witness to the influence of my wonderfully motherly mother. I remember once telling a school friend that I much admired his mother who was active in politics and in the tennis club and in several worthy social causes and he fired straight back at me, 'Christopher, you have a real mother. I do not.' Many years went by before I fully understood his message. Taking our parents for granted seems to be helpful to the development of the human being.

Eiulf became a lawyer but nevertheless played test cricket for South Africa for fourteen years, was in the newspapers most weekends and finally captained South Africa against England in December 1930. In the words of one of the commentators, 'He virtually won the test match on his own.' He took 11 wickets for 150 runs and claimed the last England batsmen in the last over of the third day. It was a dramatic race from start to finish and South Africa won by 28 runs in one of the closest fought test matches ever played on South African soil. And the captain had only one eye.

When it was over there was a public demonstration and a call for the South African captain. He came out of the dressing room and in his habitually gentle manner which I wish I could describe more adequately, paid tribute to the England captain, Alf Chapman. He ended with, 'I am glad to have been of service to my side.'

Twenty-eight years later in the private box of one of the leading lights of the MCC in London, Rony Stanyforth, my father introduced me to Jack Hobbs who said, promptly, 'Young man, you should know that your father was the most dangerous off-spin bowler the world has ever seen,' and a fellow sitting about six feet away with his elbow on his knee said, 'I'll second that!' That fellow was the great Wally Hammond who bowled my father out for a duck in the first innings of that famous test match. It is a pity that only cricket aficionados now know how much magic those two names carry between them.

When the South African cricket side toured the United Kingdom in 1924, the professors of Edinburgh University set up a room of tests which they believed could not be done by a person with only one eye. They invited my father to take the tests. In the event he walked quietly through the whole lot without hesitation and without making a single mistake. The professors announced, somewhat ruefully, that they would need to revise their theories.

The Charing Cross Road

*The piano, the Spanish Guitar Centre, Len Williams, John Williams,
the coal cellar, Luc Markies, New Cavendish Street*

•

When I left South Africa for the United Kingdom, I resolved to learn all the Beethoven sonatas during the four years that I was scheduled to be in London. In fact, I could not have done it. I did not have the ability, but I was bold enough to think that I should try.

At School I had started to learn the piano from a sympathetic teacher whom we called Globo Higgins: Globo because he taught geography and had a round and jovial face. He was a likeable and engaging fellow. Unhappily, he left, soon after I arrived and was replaced by a strangely awkward character, fresh from England, who quickly made himself universally unpopular.

Since music was regarded with some reservation in that rigidly sports-orientated atmosphere – and I was already in trouble with some of the inmates for challenging the ridiculous hierarchical rules that were imposed on us – I dared not associate myself with the unpopular new man and stopped having piano lessons. That was just one of my many serious mistakes, although it seemed to be the only workable thing to do at the time.

In London my piano hopes were confronted by two hard facts: I could afford neither the cost of a piano nor the rent on any place big enough to house one. With these problems unresolved I found myself one day in the Charing Cross Road, looking for a bookshop, and came across a glass case advertising The Spanish Guitar Centre. The message inside it claimed that the guitar was a serious musical instrument with a great range of musical possibilities. I noted the address and my pace quickened until I came to the junction of the Charing Cross Road and Cranbourn Street. I shot up the stairs of number 36, to the first floor, and found a lean, questioning-looking fellow who introduced himself as Len Williams and asked what he could do for me. I told him that I was scheduled to be in London for only four years and asked if it was possible to learn the guitar in four years.

His response was explosive. 'My God, most of them come up those stairs and ask whether they can learn the guitar in two weeks. You are in!'. He handed me a guitar, showed me the basic body and hand positions, the fingering of a C major scale and said that he would be back soon to answer any questions that I might have.

He disappeared, but soon afterwards, a young boy appeared and asked me how I was getting on. The boy was Len's son, John Williams, and he had been sent by his father for amusement because there was a South African upstairs who said 'bloody' with entertaining regularity.

Len Williams taught in classes, convinced that it was the best method. I joined one of his classes and did quite well. Len liked me, which was fortunate because he gave those whom he felt were pretentious a very rough time – and Len Williams could be more blunt than anyone else that I have ever met.

To use his own word he was 'uneducated' at a very low-grade school in the East End of London but that did not stop him from teaching himself music, philosophy, chess, politics and much else besides. He was also the sharpest observer of human behaviour that I have ever met. I was captivated and when, one day, he asked me if I would like to go to his home in Bounds Green for the weekend, I accepted with excitement.

Len Williams was a talker and he talked through most of that weekend. There were seven of us in the house including his half-Chinese wife Melaan, his son John, his assistant at the Spanish Guitar Centre, Stella McKenzie, an artist from New Zealand called Bob Wilson and Bob's partner Barbara Green. There is a mocking but friendly drawing of me, made by Bob Wilson, at one of those Sunday lunches. I was often seen as an energetic oaf.

The talk went on until two o'clock in the morning and, as a good South African boy, believing that nothing should phase me, I slept under the carpet in the living room on the Saturday night. I learned that carpets are a great deal less flexible and comfortable than I had supposed. Better arrangements were found on subsequent visits.

Melaan made Sunday lunch for everybody and the discourse – or monologue – continued through it and beyond, until it was time to go home.

Len's critical faculties were staggering: he saw into the heart of things, as few can do, and he saw through falseness and pretence within twenty seconds of any encounter. I began to realize that my supposedly elevated education had been less elevated than it claimed to be. I felt that my education began during those weekend visits to Bound's Green.

My new friends laughed at my ignorance, but it was never malicious and I had too much respect for them to let it worry me anyway. I remember talking to Bob Wilson, who taught at the Spanish Guitar Centre, about my shock at the fire in Len's criticisms and the response came back, quick as a flash, with 'Christopher, haven't you learned that criticism is a rallying point for intelligence?' I had not learned that because I had not learned much of any value about anything.

There were only two things which had brightened the horizon at school; music, which spoke to me in some unexplained way while I knew absolutely nothing at all about it, and poetry which was much aided by an astonishing memory for the plangent phrase. If I heard well-wrought words or words poetically combined with music they seemed to remain with me permanently and I was often able to quote them from memory. I still cherish my school poetry book (*Eight Poets*, Oxford Press) to this day although I know so much of it by heart.

As a jazz guitarist, living in Australia and working at the Melbourne zoo, Len Williams had understood, as I believe very few had understood, what Segovia had done in developing guitar technique. Len Williams became the most gifted teacher of that technique. He taught all who wanted to learn and he taught his son from the age of four. That meant that John Williams was the first person to be taught advanced guitar technique from an essentially early age.

Segovia had been self-taught and was still developing his technique into his late teens. John's technique at twelve became a wonder to all who encountered it, including Segovia himself.

Len and his family moved from Bounds Green to central London, to an apartment at 40 Gordon Square. It included an unused coal cellar – under the pavement. The first reason for it being unused, aside from the prohibition on the use of coal, was that it was shockingly damp. I asked Len if I could live in the coal cellar. He replied, 'For 30 shillings a week, the answer is yes, but you have to deal with the damp.'

I did some research (before the days of the Internet) and discovered the existence of Lillington's Number 2 liquid. This was a product developed for the construction of concrete tanks, built to contain water and, added to cement, it made waterproof concrete. I spent an entire weekend applying two and a half tons of treated cement with a six- inch trowel, making the whole cellar into a tank to exclude water, not to contain it.

When it was over, Len said, 'My God, Nupen, only you and God know what went on in there. I have never seen such tenacity.'

I lived in that waterproofed cellar for about a year and a half until John and I moved, together with an architect called Luc Markies, who was also in my Spanish Guitar Centre class, to a flat at number 42 New Cavendish Street, fortuitously and prophetically close to BBC Broadcasting House.

Len then sold the Spanish Guitar Centre and established the Murrayton Woolly Monkey Sanctuary near Looe in Cornwall. That was where he wrote his unique series of books about primate behaviour, which included some revealing glances at *homo sapiens*. He became the first to raise Woolly Monkeys in captivity and earned international recognition for his achievement.

Len was kind to me and I learned more from him than I had learned from all the rest of my teachers put together. When he wrote his book, *Challenge to Survival*, the fly-leaf carried the following dedication and it struck me like thunder:

> In the evolution of the primate line, an animal emerged that knew it was going to die. It wept, laughed, struggled with the forces of nature, fought

for its children and buried its dead with ceremony. It feared and appeased the Unknown and made it into the Known. It discovered the elements of art, science and history, gave birth to the concept and came face-to-face with itself. This book is dedicated to the survival of that divine and terrifying animal.

For me, those words contain the essence of what made Len Williams the inspiring human being that he was and the great teacher that he was. He knew that they would touch me and so he gave me a copy of the book and added the following, in his own hand:

> To Chris, my spiritual son.
> God bless you
> Len
> Don't forget the Now!

It would be years before I began to understand what that last line meant.

Liberated from the coal cellar I spent many hours in the New Cavendish Street flat watching John playing and enjoying a permanent sense of delight at what he could do – and the magical sounds with which he did them. John also taught me chess. Len was too elevated a chess player to teach beginners.

Being an emigré is often uncomfortable and the kindness of Len and Melaan meant a great deal to me, despite their being decidedly superior about it. In fact, they were very funny about my South African-nesses. I was with John and Melaan in the kitchen one day and suddenly remembered that I was supposed to be somewhere else. I left in a hurry but realized that I had forgotten something. I turned back just in time to hear Melaan say, 'Did you feel that? He does everything with such energy that he creates wind.'

One evening John announced that he had to watch television because his friend, the guitarist Alirio Diaz, was going to appear on a programme called Gala Performance. We watched the broadcast and, at the end, although I had seen almost no television at all up to that time, I said that I felt it was rather poorly done. I felt that it had not held together in its narrative. Without a moment's hesitation, John said, 'If you are ever able to get into television, we will see whether you can do any better.' His statement was fair enough and I have never reminded him of it. I was working in a merchant bank and had never dreamed that I would or could ever work in television.

John had met Alirio at the Accademia Chigiana in Siena where Alirio had been assistant to Segovia and where John had studied in the summers since he was twelve. In the early years his mother had always accompanied him and both of them had regaled me with endless tales of what a magic place it was. They felt that it was the most inspiring summer school of music that had ever existed – thanks to the quality of the teachers and the unimaginable generosity and high-minded aspirations of Count Guido Chigi Saracini and – of course – the magic of Siena itself.

I decided to apply, thinking I would do no better than to become one of the auditors.

That decision was soon to change many things.

8

BBC Radio

PART ONE

Josie Bacon, Harman Grisewood, Oliver Whitley, Public Service Broadcasting, BBC Features, Louis MacNeice, Laurence Gilliam

•

When I decided to follow Lotte Lehmann's advice and join the BBC – if possible – I told my father what I was planning to do. He was doubting, to say the least, despite his knowing that I was unhappy in the merchant bank and he clearly regretted having got me the job there. What father, with a good relationship with his son and who had arranged and paid for what was considered the best education in the land, would welcome the idea of his son taking a low level arty job with very uncertain prospects, six thousand miles away from home?

He asked, 'What on earth will you do there?'

I provided the worst possible answer. 'I don't know, but I want to follow Lotte's advice'.

That did not go down well. Both my parents were concerned about my friendship with Lotte Lehmann, understandably enough, even though they had heard only the very faintest echo of the true story. But I knew that I wanted to do what Lotte had advised me to do – to leave the bank, come what may – and at exactly that moment one of my synchronized lucky breaks floated quietly into place.

My father was a lawyer and had a reputation for being an honest one – rare in Johannesburg at the time. He had a client for whom he had a great deal of affection. He did the work of a rather complicated case for her without charging her anything at all. That, unsurprisingly, further strengthened the happy relationship and prompted him to ask what she thought he should do with his errant son, who seemed to him to be going off the rails in London. His client's name was Josie Bacon.

By astonishing chance my father's question and the close relationship unearthed the welcome news that Josie Bacon was related to the Chief Assistant to the Director-General of the BBC in London: an amiable, elegant, witty and very diplomatic looking fellow called Harman Grisewood. Josie Bacon made the introduction and I am forever indebted to her. My father, to his eternal credit and with my lasting gratitude, followed his grateful client's advice. I received an invitation to go and see Mr Grisewood.

He and his wife took me, in their super-luxurious Bentley, to supper at an imposing country restaurant about an hour outside London. I was struck by the abundance of the Bentley carpets and by a luscious English greenness flying past us in the summer evening sunlight. I felt immensely privileged.

I had not a single sensible thing to say during that supper but the recommendation of the South African relative carried the day and, within a week, I was invited to go and see the Head of Appointments at the BBC, Mr. Oliver Whitley. When I arrived at Mr. Whitley's office at number 5 Portland Place, I once again had nothing sensible to say and, after some fruitless conversation, Mr. Whitley started shuffling, a touch impatiently, through a great pile of BBC job vacancy announcements. At this point I made a strenuous effort to demonstrate seriousness and managed to say what turned out to be exactly the wrong thing:

'Mr. Whitley, I want to apply for a job that I know I can do. I do not want to give the impression that I JUST want to get into the BBC.'

That had the opposite effect from the one intended and the reply was not long in coming:

'Mr. Nupen, I can assure you that you can give no BETTER impression than that you JUST want to get into the BBC.'

Happily, and as I felt my time was running out, he came up with something that seemed to be created expressly for me, less elevated than Mr Grisewood had hoped for but calling for practical skills.

I felt it was right up my street. The job, at that time, was called Studio Manager. It meant everything to do with production in the radio studios of the BBC: setting up microphones, balancing the microphone outputs, making sound effects, opening and shutting doors, making the infinitely varied sounds of footsteps, clinking teaspoons and playing disc recordings of everything from classical music to sound effects and birdsong.

The job description called for some knowledge of audio recording techniques and I had recently bought one of the very first British tape recorders, the Ferrograph. That went down well. The desiderata called also for manual dexterity. I explained that I had a very good sporting track record. It called also for some knowledge of music. I said that I played the piano and the classical guitar and had come to the BBC on the advice of Lotte Lehmann.

I had landed well. Mr. Whitley asked whether I had the ability to think quickly and clearly in emergencies. I said that I hoped my poly-faceted nature which had been commented on since early school days would provide the required ability. I ended by saying that I honestly believed that they would have difficulty in finding anybody better qualified for that particular job. It doubtless sounded dreadfully immodest but was not intended that way. I learned later that it is bad form to draw attention to one's own virtues in England, even when the conversation calls for it.

The job description concluded with the words: 'Applicants should not assume that the job of Studio Manager will lead automatically to promotion to more senior positions in either production or administration.' I wondered at that because it seemed to me to be begging an unnecessary question. There were twelve of us on the induction course. I discovered that six had been promoted from administration jobs in the BBC and five were Oxbridge graduates. I wondered where I fitted in that pattern.

On the course I heard about the great and pioneering doings of the Features Department under the inspired leadership of Laurence Gilliam. It was by far the most wide – ranging and innovative of the BBC radio production departments and it was the only one that I knew anything about, having heard the work of Louis MacNeice,

Dylan Thomas, Douglas Cleverdon, Terence Tiller, Nesta Payne and Geoffrey Bridson on the BBC Third Programme.

Features had its own team of Studio Managers. I applied for membership and was accepted. From the first day I was like a dog with ten tails. I had never been in an atmosphere like that before. Those people were giants for me and, amazingly, they were all welcoming and kind to me. The effect was dramatic.

Helped by the challenges of the war and the wicked doings of Paul Joseph Goebbels, Laurence Gilliam had succeeded in bringing the work of many writers of note in the British Isles into BBC radio. He was a major force in the process that sent the name of the BBC echoing around the world. He, and the circumstances, created an atmosphere in BBC radio that has justifiably been compared to what happened in London in the Elizabethan theatre. Everybody who had anything to say was there and all were competing with each other in the pursuit of excellence, not aggrandisement. Excellence was the goal for all, and the programme was king.

The new medium rapidly attracted the messengers in our midst, of all grades and colours. It was the first time that the people in the land who had something to say could address the whole population, irrespective of circumstance and location. The idea of public service broadcasting quickly became one of the seminal ideas of the 20th century. It changed our perception of the world. It changed the lives of millions of people and it most certainly changed mine – radically. After the disasters of school and the bank I was acutely conscious of how fortunate I was.

PART TWO
Louis MacNeice, BBC Belfast, death at 56, Connemara

The biggest surprise and the happiest, at least in the early days, was the way in which Louis MacNeice befriended me. His was the name that I knew best. I had known and admired it since schooldays and I knew that T.S Eliot had said that he was the best poet writing in the English language at that time. He was a god for me and, at first, I dared not utter a word, especially as I was told that he lived in horror of being accosted and congratulated on this or that line that he had written long ago and long since forgotten.

I was impressed to hear that he frequently started work at 4:30 in the morning to avoid the encroachment of the world and to create time, later in the day, for drinking in The George, a much-frequented pub within ambling reach of Broadcasting House – just around the corner in Great Portland Street.

One day I was given the job of making footsteps for a MacNeice production. I did my very best and lo and behold the great man noticed, complimented me and thanked me. Imagine that for a beginner. I was profoundly touched. I tried even harder and a much loved actress called Betty Hardy said, when I had to shut a door, 'Thank you. There are some who know, and some that don't.' I never succeeded in telling her how much that meant to me.

It is so good to work one's way into a profession from the very bottom. For a change I was at peace with my surroundings. I felt, however, and seriously, that in the merchant bank, I had thrown away the six most important years of my life. I see only now that that generated a very productive sense of urgency and need for concentration.

When Louis MacNeice made his verse translation of Faust he asked for me to do the sound effects. I was everything from the Miller of Hell to a barking black dog. My powers of invention flourished. I began drinking with him and a most lovable (and very good) actor called Denys Hawthorne and the actress Mary Wimbush.

One day Louis asked, 'How well do you play the guitar?'

I answered, 'Not bad, and with a good sound but only if the piece is not difficult – and it is one of the great virtues of the guitar that it can make simple pieces sound very appealing.'

He said that he would write something that called for guitar sounds in his next production. I remember that, with gratitude, to this day. I was at home in the world for the first time since I was thirteen.

Almost immediately after that exchange I was sent on attachment to BBC Belfast. I was delighted to hear, when I got there, that Louis was coming soon to produce a radio play there. He was so valued in Northern Ireland that expectation ran high. There was much talk of his impending visit.

Suddenly the news arrived that Louis had gone potholing to collect sound effects for his new play, had contracted pneumonia and died – at the age of 56. The shock was deep reaching. I felt bereft. I felt that the world had lost one of its most gifted sons. I asked for a week off and drove round the entire coast of the Emerald Isle in his memory. Astonishingly, the sun shone every mile of my way.

When I arrived in Connemara, I saw a man tilling a field and behind him, at quite some distance, an unusually pointed, almost volcanic looking mountain, with something white on top of it. The top looked man-made but was in such an unlikely position that I stopped to try and find out more. I asked the farmer, 'What is that on the top of the mountain?'

He thought for quite a while and then produced the fruits of his reflections. He said, 'On a day like this, it's the contrasts of the colours that counts.' I knew then that I was in the land of Louis MacNeice.

I learned, eventually, that the white cap to the sharp mountain was a man-made chapel which prompted reflection on how the Christian religion strives so hard to come closer to God by probing the heavens in what always seemed to me to be a puny hope – considering the immeasurable height of the heavens. That is not to say that I am unimpressed by the cathedral in Cologne.

I went back to London but neither London nor the BBC were the same without Louis MacNeice and I wondered, long and deep, about what it was that had made him so kind and generous to me.

The Features producers were high level masters of their craft and I felt that that was a prime source of their generosity, that and the awareness that in all the struggles for unrealisable perfection, common to all of them, there is always something beyond us, something to strive for and something to which we all belong. I have carried that conviction with me, from my first year in radio until now, and it sits alongside the awareness that I learned almost everything I know about broadcasting from the people in the Features Department.

I spent the six happiest years of my career in BBC radio. The stresses and strains that came later, in television, and from becoming the first truly independent television producer in the United Kingdom, were nowhere near as happy and were very much lonelier. I came slowly to realize how much it had meant to me to be part of the extraordinarily creative community that had distinguished BBC radio in its great years.

PART THREE
Jim Black, BBC opposition, Siena, Count Guido Chigi Saracini, Martin Elmitt, Giorgio Favoretto

Just as I was beginning to feel truly at home in BBC radio, another totally unexpected event took place that was, once again, destined to change everything.

I had made friends with most of the Features Studio Managers but developed a particular affection for Jim Black, a Liverpudlian who taught me about 'butties' and a back street Liverpudlian life as different as could be imagined from the one that I had enjoyed under the African sun.

One evening, having finished work together, I said good night to Jim and left the Studio Managers' common room. I had gone about ten yards when I heard the door open. I heard Jim's voice calling me and turned around to see him standing in the doorway. What follows remains as bright in my memory as if it had happened yesterday.

He said, 'If you are going to that summer school in Siena and if it is even half as wonderful as you keep telling me it is, why don't you make a radio programme about it?'

I answered, 'I work on other people's programmes. I make sound effects. I have never made a radio programme in my life. I can't do that.'

Jim's reply changed everything. He said, 'I can't. You can.' That astonishing moment started my career as a broadcaster.

Jim persuaded me to propose the idea to Laurence Gilliam and I did so. Laurence asked, in his wonderfully down to earth way, 'Will it make a good programme?'

'Yes.'

'Why?'

'The summer school is held in the medieval Sienese Palace of Count Guido Chigi Saracini, the last member of one of Italy's oldest families, and he is giving away almost the entire family fortune for music – to enable talented young musicians to study, for two months each summer, not with the world's most famous teachers but with the world's most famous performers: Cortot, Thibaud, Enesco, Casals, Rubinstein, Celibidache, Gina Cigna, Segovia, Navarra, Agosti and others. You can imagine the atmosphere that is generated in those scarcely believable circumstances.'

I added that it was essential that I should take with me one of the new Nagra tape recorders, an engineering wonder newly arrived from Switzerland and built like a Swiss watch. I needed this because I would be recording some of the world's top musicians teaching enthusiastic, grateful and unusually gifted music students.

Laurence made enquiries about the Nagra. Permission was refused by the Engineering Department on the grounds that I was not a qualified engineer. Laurence called me to his office, practical as ever, and asked whether I could do the job with one of the interview recorders. I said that with that kind of machine, the job simply could not be done on a level appropriate to the subject. Those machines could not record music on the necessary technical level. Laurence asked if I was sure that I could handle the Nagra properly and safely. I assured him that I could. He sent a memo to the head of engineering: 'If Mr. Nupen destroys the Nagra, I will pay for it out of my Programme Budget.' That settled that.

Next, the head of my department, Brian George, vetoed the idea on the grounds that BBC staff are not permitted to work during their holidays. Gilliam considered this for a moment or two and sent a response saying that he absolutely needed Christopher Nupen to be attached to the Features Department, as a trainee producer, for two weeks because he thought I had potential and his department needed some new blood. That did the trick and Laurence said, 'Well that solved that one, now you have four weeks in which to do the job instead of two.' What a great fellow was Laurence Gilliam, and exceedingly kind to me.

The third, and most dangerous objection came from Howard Newby who was the Head of Third Programme: 'If Mr Nupen, who has never made a radio programme in his life, proposes to go off to

Siena on his own – by the way, does he speak Italian? – to record, as he puts it, "Some of the greatest performing musicians of our time", are we not letting ourselves in for a potentially very expensive failure?'

Laurence replied (this information was given to me privately by Christopher Sykes who was nominally producer of the show),

'Dear Howard, if this programme is a failure I will add it to my list of failures.'

His comment to me, 'Well, that seems to have done it. Off you go.'

I hoped for much but what I found exceeded my highest hopes. With an astonishing rapidity, Siena confirmed all that I had come to believe from John Williams and his mother, Melaan. I arrived at the time of what the Sienese call the Passeggiata, the sacred hour when they take to the streets to greet their friends and enjoy the mediaeval beauties of their home – a custom undreamed of in the South Africa of my birth. The streets around the Piazza del Campo were crammed with leisurely folk who seemed to me to have a peculiar grace.

I dropped my elephantine load with all possible speed and went walking with the Sienese. Siena taught me that culture lives in the stones. In a shop window I saw a huge, heavy, decorated plate with a drawing of the magical Piazza del Campo busting out of the circular inner frame and the words, *Cor magis tibi Sena pandit* emblazoned in the sky above the tower. I felt that Siena was, indeed, opening its great heart to me and I immediately bought the plate – to make my over-heavy luggage for the home journey even more unmanageable. Amazingly, it has survived and I treasure it to this day.

The Accademia Chigiana was a worthy manifestation of that Great Heart. The unparalleled happy atmosphere which it generated came, primarily, from two things: the colossal generosity, both financial and spiritual, of Count Guido Chigi Saracini, and the spirit of Siena itself, its architectural wonders, its own special culture and its enduring civic pride.

The criterion for acceptance at the Accademia was ability – nothing more, nothing less. Each Maestro held auditions, accepted the twenty best or thereabouts and the rest were at liberty to remain in the class as auditors. But Siena offered more than that. It lived up to its motto. The civic centre is so unusual and so beautiful that it drew all of us to its heart like a magnet, students, teachers and the Sienese – day and night.

I remember once hearing the haunting sounds of a cello in the regal Piazza del Campo at two o'clock in the morning. They came from a very young and very gifted English cellist called Martin Elmitt. The recollection of hearing him play, in that way and in those extraordinary circumstances, remains a high point in my memory. There was an unexpected melancholy to his playing, even in some of the brighter pieces and I wondered whether that was what caused a young French violinist, who looked strikingly like Brigitte Bardot, to say, 'Martin Elmitt is the only English musician that I can listen to.'

Martin Elmitt was an unusual fellow and was also interested in guns. He bought an automatic pistol, which is something that one could do in Italy in 1963, and we went target-shooting in the Tuscan countryside. There was an unpredictable side to him and so I went as chaperone because I had grown up in Africa and knew about guns. We didn't kill anything or anybody.

The magic of Siena was augmented inside Chigi's Palazzo where the walls were lined with hundreds of mediaeval and Renaissance paintings. I ran about, recording in as many classes and as many concerts as I could manage. I made recordings with Andrés Segovia, Sergiu Celibidache, Giorgio Favaretto, André Navarra, Gina Cigna, Yvonne Astruc, Salvatore Accardo (as student), Guido Agosti, Nicanor Zabaleta, Bronislav Gimpel, Alirio Diaz and more. I was doing something new and the only reason I could do it at all was that I found the atmosphere so inspiring. And I cherished the wonders of the Nagra. Everything seemed to lead me on.

One of my first encounters was with Giorgio Favaretto, a leading figure in the Santa Cecilia Academy in Rome. He was the Maestro of the singing courses: wonderful musician, generous human being, much loved coach and legendary accompanist. The sounds that I heard in that class and at the final concert, in part because of the setting and the glorious acoustic of the Chigi Palazzo concert hall, flooded me with a sense of what Respighi called the original genius of Italian song. I remember particularly an Armenian baritone, and an Italian Bel Canto tenor who took us all with them to the stars. Oh, what beauty! How could any young man ever have been luckier?

The Armenian was Khacik Pilikian who had one of the richest voices that I have ever heard – a resonant baritone voice of burnished gold which should have had a great career. I still treasure the recordings which I made with him, accompanied by Favaretto in the concert hall of the Palazzo, singing Rachmaninov, Mussorgsky and Monteverdi. But instead of a glorious career he dedicated his life to the Armenian struggle for independence, understandable but a tragedy for music.

To my surprise I seemed to fit in, and I know for certain that my encounter with Lotte Lehmann helped me to create the right atmosphere there. Handling top level musicians is a delicate business but, astonishingly, I seemed to know what to do. I was flying in the air. I had never been so occupied and, certainly, never to such purpose. I seemed to do the right thing at the right time and I had a touching confirmation of it when, after recording for the first time in Favaretto's class he said to his wife and to the students, '*Facciamo una fiesta per questo simpaticissimo inglese.*' (Let's make a celebration for this most sympathetic Englishman.) I had fewer fears after Favaretto's generosity to me. I thought of my father's courage and offered a quiet thank you.

Years later, I realized how important Favaretto's extravagant welcome had been for me and what it had done for my quivering confidence. Lotte Lehmann had been the inspiration, Giorgio Favaretto opened the door and showed me the road. I telephoned the Accademia di Santa Cecilia in Rome and, when I explained my purpose, they kindly gave me his telephone number. I called to thank him. His wife answered and told me that he had just recently died. She had been there, with him in Siena, and clearly remembered his generous welcome to me. She graciously accepted my thanks on his behalf.

I feel at fault for having failed to acknowledge, personally, my immense debt to him. I still see that moment in the mind's eye – in much detail – and I feel its warmth. I can even see the colour of his wife's dress.

Siena became a defining moment for me. It was there that I began to realize that I had the ability to stimulate the elevated artistic persona – with all the glories that so often attend it. My relationship with Lotte Lehmann had been of a different order. It belonged to a magical world.

I saw little or nothing except that engaging face, that winning smile, the sound of that unmistakable voice – even when speaking – and the radiation of glorious femininity. Lehmann was all magic. Siena, by contrast, provided a glimpse into the real world of artistic creativity.

Accademia Chigiana – Siena

Sergiu Celibidache, The Siena tapes, worries, Douglas Cleverdon, Elizabeth Taylor, Hugh Griffith

•

I understood that, as a musician, I would never be a performer on the level of my friends but I soon began to see that radio made it possible to tell the world a great deal about two significant things: first, how gloriously talented were my friends and how extraordinary were the manifestations of those talents. Second, how wondrous music is and how much it can enrich our lives. Those two discoveries became the focus of my life.

On my visit to Siena I was engaged every day from early morning until late at night, almost always ending in the Fonte Gaia (The Gay Fountain), a café in the breathtaking Piazza del Campo where, every evening, some of the teachers would mingle informally with the students.

The first interview that I did was with Sergiu Celibidache, one of Count Chigi's stars, already a legend in the music world despite, or perhaps because of, his refusal to make recordings. I asked him why and his answer was quick and decidedly energetic:

> No! The record is a very objective impossibility. The musical space cannot be reduced to any other dimensions than its own. The record is a bi-dimensional thing and the music space is three-dimensional. On the record, nearly all the qualities get lost, and some others are coming up. There is not a single possibility to transfer or to project on a different field or plane or surface the musical space.

That was big news in 1962. I knew I had recorded something of interest and it made me feel a mite less frightened.

On the night after I had recorded the interview with Celibidache I found him at the Fonte Gaia with about eight of his students. He invited me to join them. He was in expansive form, entertaining them with an account of local builders constructing a house for him on an island within sight of Stromboli. To escape the strong prevailing wind they had placed the main window of the living room on the opposite side of the house with no view of the volcano. He entertained us with an account of his demands for a re-build. When it was done, he remembered, with much drama, seeing Stromboli erupt in the middle of the night and rushing for his camera because it was so spectacular.

For all our deep respect for the teachers, the atmosphere in Siena was gloriously democratic. That allowed me a cheeky question, 'Maestro, how could you, of all people, expect to capture the majesty of Stromboli on a different field, or plane, or surface?'

His eyes widened – a touch frighteningly – and I thought for a moment that I had gone too far but in that atmosphere and surrounded by his students he had nowhere to go and had to live with the joke. That is the sort of thing that could happen in Siena in the great days of the Accademia Chigiana. A similar thing was to happen not long afterwards with the BBC producer, Douglas Cleverdon.

I took my tapes back to London and put them up on a high shelf in the new Cavendish Street flat which I shared with John Williams and Luc Markies.

In London the magic drained rapidly away and began to be replaced by a disturbing and deep-seated anxiety. I woke up repeatedly at something between three and four o'clock in the morning gasping for breath at the prospect of what I had taken on and at my doubts about my ability to do it. I genuinely felt I was in danger of suffocating. It was frightening. Looking back I cannot see why the internal quiverings were quite so profound. The worries increased apace, nevertheless, and I was puzzled by the sense of panic. I suppose that the answer is that creative anxiety burrows deep. I recall standing in front of those tapes on several occasions and thinking that Douglas Cleverdon or Jack Dillon, or Geoffrey Bridson, or any one of the Features Producers could make something rather good out of those tapes – and fearing that I could not. I twice thought that if only the house would burn down I would be able to tell everybody what a wonderful programme had been lost. Fortunately, I dared not burn the house down.

I decided to consult Douglas Cleverdon because we were scheduled to work together for six days on a big production. But on the very day that I planned to approach him something happened that put me off. Perhaps it was the gods again that look after my luck.

Douglas was small but an irrepressible bundle of energy. We were working in studio six which is very tall and has the control room on the floor above the studio, (with a huge window looking directly down into it). Every now and then Douglas would decide not to address his cast over the talkback system, but to go down to the studio floor and address them directly. I was supposed to follow him to take notes. Twice, he went so fast that the studio door closed behind him, in my face, and I was quick on my feet in those days.

Then came a moment at which I was to insert some music of my choosing into a given scene. I offered four different selections. Douglas, in a greater hurry than usual expressed impatient dissatisfaction. Finally he jumped up from the production desk, shot over to the turntables, grabbed the first record he could lay his hands on, lowered the needle, listened impatiently for a few seconds and said, 'That'll do'. He returned to his desk and I noticed that he had played a 45 rpm record on a 33 rpm turntable.

I waited until the moment came to insert the music and did nothing. Douglas turned with his eyes blazing and said, 'Now what's the matter?' I said, 'Douglas, I am trying to decide whether to play it at the correct speed, or the wrong speed as you did – because, at the correct speed it will create an entirely different atmosphere'.

There was a flaming of eyes for a moment not dissimilar from my Celibidache Stromboli exchange but, once again, there were too many witnesses and Douglas was too good-natured a fellow to complain, despite his determination never to allow anything ever to impede his quest for perfection. He appreciated the joke and forgave me. Would that there were more like Douglas Cleverdon in the world. We worked happily together for some years and came closer and closer as time went by but I did not, in the end, ask him to help me with my Siena programme. The moment had gone.

Later, we worked on a remake of Dylan Thomas' *Under Milk Wood* with Richard Burton who arrived, each day, with a case of beer and Elizabeth Taylor. Throughout the recording, which took some days, she sat next to him, much of the time with her hand on his thigh.

When it was over Douglas invited us all to drink wine at his home in Islington. At that time I had a 1934 drop-head two seater Austin 7 which I had bought for £25, perhaps the smallest car that was ever built in the UK and almost certainly the prettiest. It was completely unlike the top-heavy lumbering four seaters of the time. I had the engine entirely reconditioned and it flew along the road most beautifully. I even took John Williams to Paris in it for his debut recital in the Salle Gaveau.

I arrived at Douglas's home in Islington to find the biggest Mulliner Rolls-Royce that I had ever seen parked immediately in front of the house. No prizes for guessing that it had brought Elizabeth Taylor. As it happened there was a tiny space free immediately in front of it, just big enough for my midget Austin 7. I slid into the space and reversed until my spare tyre, which was elegantly perched on the back of the car, was touching, most gently, the imposing silver columns of the Rolls-Royce radiator.

I joined the party and when a suitable moment arrived, asked Elizabeth Taylor whether the Rolls-Royce that we could see through the window was hers. She replied that it was and so I said, 'Well the car in front is mine.' It really was an entertaining picture but she managed only to say 'Oh' with not even a glimmer of a smile. I found that disappointing. A few minutes later she was telling a group of the Welsh actors and actresses including the great Hugh Griffith, just how wonderful they all were. Griffith responded, 'I wouldn't let it worry you my dear, you're a pretty enough little thing.' Such things happened in the atmosphere of BBC radio Features and I was very lucky to be there.

At my last meeting with Douglas he made me laugh, as so often, but the occasion was a seriously sad one. His mind was going and his memory was almost totally gone. That did not stop him from saying,

'It has its advantages you know. Everything comes so fresh to you.'

Douglas Cleverdon gave so much to the world and I am ever grateful for how much he gave to me.

10

Evesham

Elizabeth Grossett, Christopher Sykes, Melvyn Bragg,
Hans Keller, Arnold Schoenberg, BBC politics

•

The Siena programme stayed resolutely unmade on the shelf. The anxiety mounted and then another unimaginable piece of luck came my way.

The BBC sent me to Evesham on a three month training course. BBC Evesham was an ex-army barracks taken over by the BBC as a training centre. There was nothing to do in the evenings except drink in the club, which could be done anywhere, and play silly games which did not interest me at all. There was, on the other hand, all manner of studio equipment and recording machinery freely available. To have that much time, in those circumstances and with all the necessary equipment to make a complete radio programme, was nothing less than a gift from heaven – and, once again, bang on cue.

On the training course I found an unexpected friendship with a bright, direct and gloriously outspoken Scottish woman called Elizabeth Grossett who had, by far, the most interesting personality of all of us. I say unexpected because of the way it started.

On the first day of the course Elizabeth sat immediately behind me and during the coffee break, with no hint of inhibition, asked me to change places with her as she could not bear the idea of having to look at my over long greasy hair for three months.

The course ended at five o'clock and supper was scheduled for seven. I went immediately to the barber shop in Evesham and asked the barber to shave the whole lot off. Having checked that I was serious he started by ploughing a central path from the back to the front which produced a comical effect. Contemplating his handywork he suddenly froze and asked, 'Does your wife know about this?' I told him that I had no wife but wanted to appease a pretty, feisty girl on the training course. I left the salon and bought a beret in a nearby shop to conceal the wicked doings.

When I entered the canteen Elizabeth was already there with an empty place next to her. I sat down and removed the beret. The effect was exactly what I had hoped for. I had judged the character well. We became good friends.

The friendship provided all the conversation that was needed for the early evenings and supper and then, each evening I withdrew to the studio to wrestle with my Siena recordings. I made things. I unmade things; I remade things; I played endlessly with contexts and juxtapositions. I began to warm to the task.

The freedom to experiment, and to learn with no deadline, was crucial. I began to find happiness again. Eventually I sent a draft script to Christopher Sykes who was the nominal producer. I had not consulted him at all before that moment and he had offered no assistance. The script contained, in proper fashion, a beginning and a middle and an end and it was only the beginning and the end that I had to invent. Almost all the rest was a matter of organizing the material to best effect and, fortunately, much of it was glorious material, full of talent, good music and the exuberance of youth in happy circumstances.

I interrupted my peroration with a short adieu from a French cellist called Geneviève. Christopher Sykes made only one comment on the entire script, 'Drop Geneviève' was his message. 'Your conclusion will move faster and be more effective'

I dropped Geneviève, finished editing my tape and carried it with me to London. I had recorded it, constructed it, written it, narrated it and edited it entirely on my own. I called it *High Festival in Siena*. When Christopher Sykes was later asked by Laurence Gilliam how much he had contributed, he wrote, and he showed me his memo: 'I suggested cutting out two lines. That is all.'

When the programme had been accepted into the hallowed BBC

library, Laurence arranged for it to be played on what was called the Ring Main, on the first floor of Broadcasting House, where the Features Department lived. He sent a memo to each of the producers inviting them to listen.

When it was over I was in a state of high anxiety and did not dare to ask any of the producers what they thought of it. There was, however, a General Trainee who sat in the very last office at the end of the long corridor which stretches the whole length of Broadcasting House.

I crept down the gauntlet, earnestly hoping that nobody would emerge from any of the office doors as I passed. I opened the last door, timidly, and saw the General Trainee sitting alone at his desk. I asked him whether he had listened and, if so, what he thought. He said, 'I think you have a big success.' His name: Melvyn Bragg, as yet unknown but destined for great things in arts broadcasting – an auspicious start to my broadcasting career. He has always been kind to me since then. I am grateful for that.

High Festival in Siena ended up on a shortlist of five titles being considered as BBC entry to the Prix Italia – not bad for a first effort. It was not chosen but it had caused some stir.

Melvyn's reaction gave me the courage to go and thank Laurence Gilliam and, as usual, his response was instant and direct. His opening words were also a direct echo of Lotte Lehmann's opening gambit. She had said, 'When you have got over your surprise young man, may I please go to my seat?' Laurence's words were, 'When you have recovered from your surprise, young man, think of another.'

I asked if I could return to Siena in the following summer to make a radio programme about Segovia. Laurence asked the same question that he had asked about Siena: 'Will it make a good programme?'

'Yes, because Segovia's achievement is monumental, he was described by Fritz Kreisler as one of the two greatest performing musicians of the 20th century (the other, according to Kreisler, being Pablo Casals) and because it will be made in Siena which will give it something of the same spirit that contributed so much to the Siena programme.'

Once again, Laurence arranged it and with little opposition this time.

News of the Ring Main playback of *High Festival in Siena* had reached Hans Keller, a leading light of BBC Radio and one of the finest minds that ever joined the BBC staff. He was a Viennese Jew who had suffered appalling treatment at the hands of the Nazis. I could not help wondering how much of the extraordinary focus of that brilliant mind had been sharpened by his experiences but I never dared to ask – although I believe he would have accepted my doing so. His penetrating insights were evident in everything that he broadcast. He made the most instructive, erudite and the most unusual radio music programmes. His work was inspiring. I was a fan.

He had listened to the playback and wrote me a letter of congratulation which included the words, 'Your structure is crystal clear. Impeccable. This is remarkable in a first radio programme.' As a result, he asked me to work with him on a programme about Arnold Schoenberg, another significant step in my career. I worked closely with him over several months and learned from him at every step along the way.

I forged a close friendship with the great Keller and also with his wonderful, irrepressibly bouncy and eternally youthful wife, Milein Cosman, herself one of the most refined of artists.

Hans died, too young, of Motor Neurone Disease, an appalling fate, and the UK lost a truly original creative force. Hans Keller was just one of many Jewish emigrés whom the UK accepted with kindness and who, in turn, enriched immensely the British intellectual, cultural, artistic, medical and scientific communities.

William Glock was the Head of the music department but Hans Keller was the dynamo in my opinion. Sadly not everybody gave Hans the credit that he deserved. I remember being genuinely shocked when Howard Newby, Head of Third Programme, who had almost killed the Siena programme, said to me, and I quote, 'I must ask you to supervise what Keller writes. English is not his first language.' I was not only shocked, I was saddened. Hans Keller was a giant, a truly gifted broadcaster who really had valuable things to say and original ways of saying them. There were some in the BBC who had the broadcasting gift and their work stood head and shoulders above the rest. They are a distinguished breed.

Hans invited me to become a producer in the music department. I declined, on the grounds that I knew too little about music. I said that I would be a joke alongside Hans Keller, Basil Lam, Bob Simpson, Deryck Cooke, Lionel Salter, William Glock and others. Hans replied, 'We have more than enough musicians. What we need more of is real producer mentality.' I understood what he meant but declined nevertheless.

I was shocked again when Laurence Gilliam said to me that the producer mentality was being squeezed out by administrators who were appointing more and more politicians and too few real broadcasters. He went so far as to say that he thought the process was irreversible and that the original BBC idea had become irretrievable. Today, some would say that he was incredibly far sighted. I objected violently at the time, 'Laurence, how can you, of all people, you who have done so much to make the BBC what it is – and made the idea of public service broadcasting famous in the furthest corners of the earth – utter such heresy?'

He replied, 'We shall see.'

11

Diana Baikie
PART ONE

•

My first meeting with Diana Baikie left a deep impression. She was wearing a soft, blue silk blouse, full of seductive promise, which contributed more than a little to her charms. I was transfixed. She was working for Christopher Sykes whom Laurence Gilliam had appointed to oversee the Siena programme. Happily, there were some administrative details to be attended to and so I saw her twice more in the coming days. The effect on me grew apace and, on the third day, I put my arms around her from behind and gave her an all-embracing hug.

But the placing of my hands went too far and she dropped to the floor – like a stone.

Our budding relationship might never have recovered from that impassioned indiscretion but Diana had a generous heart. I apologized profusely and we became friends. More than that, we became friends with the greatest physical attraction that I had experienced in all of my 26 years.

Diana Baikie had every kind of natural appeal known to woman. She was soft-spoken, bright, quick, modest and gloriously pretty with a perfect figure to match – perhaps the prettiest girl in the BBC – with beautiful auburn hair.

The BBC fed the bond by asking me to make a radio documentary about the situation of young musicians in Britain. Using what I had learned in Siena and Evesham, I did all the recordings myself but did the editing with Diana, unofficially, late at night in the BBC studios.

Working so close to the aura of irresistible appeal that radiated from her I fell in love with her, as I was bound to do, and happily, she was warm in response. I remember many walks back to the New Cavendish Street flat with Diana at three and four o'clock in the morning leaving Broadcasting House by the main doors, unquestioned, despite our two cases crammed with the original master tapes.

We were young and full of enthusiasm for the idea of public service broadcasting. It was the happiest time that either of us had so far experienced and particularly so for Diana, who had had an intensely unhappy time at an appalling boarding school. She was too gentle and too sensitive for the rough-and-tumble of that sort of institution at its worst.

In her misery, she once ran away from school, very early one morning and woke her mother by throwing pebbles at her bedroom window to appeal for rescue. Her mother, Cathy, another extremely gentle soul, was so afraid of the consequences and the certain rage of her father that she sent her daughter straight back to school without letting her in. My blood runs cold at the thought of the pain which that caused to each of them.

We rarely spoke of our schooldays – the present was much more engaging. There is no shadow of doubt that the intensity with which we embraced the spirit of the Features Department came in response to the warmth and generosity of the gifted people who gave it such glorious life. We were working with great writers, making fascinating programmes and learning, learning, learning. The exceptional proximity of the New Cavendish Street flat to Broadcasting House increased both the time and the energy that we invested in the BBC.

We were also full of love, both rather innocent and making new, exciting discoveries all the time. But the road to recovery from unhappy childhood can be a long one and Diana felt out of her depth in what she saw as the elevated milieu of my musician friends. She need not have done. She was soon to become much loved by Segovia, his young wife Emilita, Jacqueline du Pré, Vladimir Ashkenazy, Daniel Barenboim and Pinchas Zukerman.

A particularly close relationship would develop between Diana and Jackie, and Daniel fed it by generously taking all three of us with him on concert tours to Sweden, Denmark, Germany and the USA. They were happy days.

12

Andrés Segovia
PART ONE
Siena revisited, Huw Wheldon, BBC Television 'Attachment'

•

After one of the coldest winters on record – with inadequate heating in the camp at Evesham – the summer of 1963 was doubly welcome and I went to Siena for the second time, alone again, to make the Segovia radio programme but with much less equipment and a great deal less to do than on the first visit. The experience was entirely different from the trembling rush of the previous year.

There was a quiet centre to Andrés Segovia that seemed to me to echo the popular idea of the 19th Century Spanish Don. He received me with all the courtesy, grace and generosity that is said to have typified those legendary characters.

I recorded in Segovia's classes every day but we did the interviews in comfortable stages in his spacious mediaeval apartment, provided by Chigi. The terracotta floor and the wooden ceiling added a warmth and acoustic colour to the recording that was particularly appropriate. The right acoustic, in the right place can contribute a great deal to the spirit of a sound broadcast. I knew immediately that I was exceptionally lucky – once again. With less complexity, less rush, less anxiety and with growing experience the work was done surprisingly quickly and I was able to spend a good deal of time in the guitar class.

Andrés Segovia was almost entirely self-taught. He nevertheless revolutionised guitar technique in the same way that Pablo Casals changed 'cello technique. He elevated the hand positions, giving them more power – at the expense of security. In consequence, all guitarists, after Segovia, had to work harder because the old securities of anchoring to the neck of the guitar with the left hand and to the sound table with the right, were gone.

Yet another of Segovia's contributions was in his refined use of the fingernails. He was entertaining on the subject in the Siena classes:

> To play the guitar without nails is to take the guitar in the shadow – always in the shadow. The difficulty, of course, is to be born with a very good quality of nails. To have strong nails, not easy to break, and to have, at the same time, soft nails, for the quality of the tone. And you know very well, my dear, without a beautiful sonority, the charm of the guitar disappears – absolutely.

All of this delivered with poetic flair and with his colourful Spanish accent, so striking that his words remain embedded in the memories of many.

Back in London, the editing went quickly and smoothly, once again all of it done unofficially – late at night – in the studios of Broadcasting House with Diana. The BBC enjoyed a very different existence in those days. We were never once challenged. Today it is impossible to get past the front door without clearing serious security checks.

We were lucky to be in the right place at the right time, without doing any harm to anybody or anything in the process. This went on for quite a long time and the night staff greeted us with broadening smiles on entry and exit. What Diana and I did in the making of that programme came as a true gift from heaven and could not be done in that way today. Slowly, cutting quarter-inch tape with a razor blade, we tried to give a true account of at least some part of our artist's extraordinary story and we had a wonderful time together in the doing of it.

The programme *Andrés Segovia and the Revival of the Guitar* was broadcast on 4 March 1964. At about 9:30 on the following morning, the telephone rang in my office. It was Huw Wheldon, another Welshman and, in my view, the best man that BBC Television ever had. He said that he had listened to the programme, liked it and added 'You should be in television, because that is the future.'

I replied that I knew nothing about television and was very happy in the Features Department of BBC radio. I said also that I had a huge debt to Laurence Gilliam which I wanted to repay.

That produced a typically Wheldonian response: 'I am Controller of Programmes and I would like you to come to my office in Television Centre at 10 o'clock tomorrow morning.'

Another bolt from the blue that would entirely change the course of my life. In the event, the meeting was dramatically short. Huw Wheldon said that he wanted to put me on what was called 'attachment' to the Music Department of BBC Television for two months to see how I got on.

Two of his distinguishing characteristics were the intensity of his gaze and the directness of his utterances. It would clearly have been a cheap mistake to express doubts of any kind and so I think that all I said was 'Thank you', and retreated from Television Centre to Broadcasting House to report to Laurence Gilliam.

Gilliam, also a Welshman and equally direct, said, 'Take it, see what you can do with it – and let me know.'

13

BBC Television

Walter Todds, Peter Heelas, Huw Wheldon,
David Attenborough, David Findlay, Daniel Barenboim,
Vladimir Ashkenazy, *Double Concerto*, the first silent cameras

•

When Huw Wheldon dropped me, unceremoniously, into the Music Department of BBC Television I knew absolutely nothing about television and had no interest in it. I had hardly ever watched it because I was so totally dedicated to the Features Department of BBC Radio which I knew well and admired greatly.

I did not believe that I would find anything on television to equal Louis MacNeice's *Dark Tower*, Douglas Cleverdon's much publicised rescue of Dylan Thomas' *Under Milk Wood*, Terence Tiller's regular poetry programmes, Geoffrey Bridson's *Quest of Gilgamesh* – and so many others.

The situation was not helped by the discovery, when I got there, that the people in television looked down on radio. Humphrey Burton, who was Head of the Television Music Department at the time, warned me that radio was 'Not good training for television'. I looked forward to my return to radio – but he who foretells the future tells lies …!

The Senior Producer of the television Music Department was a most likeable fellow called Walter Todds. He was intelligent, wonderfully well educated, helpful, encouraging and wise. He showed me round the Department and I liked him from the first moment. Soon afterwards he had to go into hospital and asked me – although I had absolutely no experience of television whatsoever – to take over the editing of a programme which he had shot with the opera director Carl Ebert, for a series called *Master Class*. I discovered, to my surprise, that Walter had heard some of my radio programmes and felt that he could trust me. He was a trusting soul and I was lucky, once again.

I accepted and went to the cutting room in what was called the BBC Television Film Studios at Ealing. The BBC had taken over what had been Ealing Film Studios. There I met the film editor, Peter Heelas. We made the programme, or rather I should say that Peter edited it – with very little input from me – because Peter is a truly gifted film editor, and Walter had shot it well.

Peter and I became friends. Watching him opened a world that I had not known existed and when I said so he modestly claimed that he had learned it all by having been apprenticed for a long time to a famous film editor called Harry Hastings. That was all very well but I saw also that he had a natural gift of a high order.

What Peter taught me about film editing changed many things and governs what I do in film making to this day. Despite having had no training and no prior interest in the craft I very soon felt at home in the cutting room. I found that I had a feeling for what Nathan Milstein later termed 'artistic organization.'

The attachment to television had barely begun when Daniel Barenboim, who has the quickest eye for fruitful opportunity that I have ever encountered, reminded me that he and Vladimir Ashkenazy had been trying to organize a concert together with the newly formed English Chamber Orchestra but had been unable to raise the funds needed.

I went to see Huw Wheldon on the following morning, told him about the astonishing musical gifts of my two friends, said that there was a real television story to tell and that I knew how to tell it. It was possible for me to utter that last bold assertion only because I knew so little about what was actually involved in doing such a thing. I was thinking in terms of radio where I had become reasonably surefooted. I knew absolutely nothing at all about television and film production.

I did know, however, that this was going to be something very unusual and of unmistakable quality both from the soloists and the orchestra and with a serious contribution coming from Wolfgang

Mozart. The plan was to play the Mozart Concerto for Two Pianos, K365, which Mozart had written to play with his sister Maria Anna (Nannerl)

The reply came within a few days. Huw Wheldon discussed the proposal with David Attenborough who was Controller of BBC2 at the time and he told me that they had arranged for three days of film effort and £600 to enable me to shoot and edit on film a nine minute introduction to the concert. He had arranged for the concert itself to be recorded on electronic cameras, directed by Brian Large.

I asked for Peter Heelas to edit the film sector and the request was granted. I did not ask for any particular cameraman because I knew none. An experienced cameraman was duly nominated. Then, by what turned out to be another extraordinarily lucky happening, I bumped into Barrie Gavin, a first-class director – probably the best in the music department – in the canteen, and he asked how I was getting on. I told him that we were making progress. He asked who the cameraman would be and I gave him the name. He went off like a firecracker, 'No, no, no, that is not the right man for this job. Try to get the talented young Australian called David Findlay.'

I followed his advice and made the request. Again the proposal was accepted and that too was to change my life. David Findlay was not only exceptionally talented, he had started as a stills photographer and, like Peter, had long years of apprenticeship behind him which had produced an impressive and very sure-footed feel for effective composition. Our shared Southern Hemisphere backgrounds made communication quick and easy.

By amazing good fortune the recording of the concert was to be made on 35mm film by a process known as Telerecording which lasted for only a few years. As the recording was made on film, not on tape, which is the usual format for electronic cameras, it made possible the very unusual thing that we ended up doing – without permission. We edited it as a documentary, combining 16mm and 35mm film.

We shot *Double Concerto* in three days – which is well-nigh impossible to do – and were obliged to edit it in three weeks – which is equally unlikely – because of a Musicians Union regulation governing the broadcast of live concerts. The idea was that broadcasts any later than three weeks from the concert date would replace live concerts and so reduce musicians' earnings.

The real benediction was that we were lucky to be in the right place at the right time and able to do things that had not been done before because the equipment required had not previously existed. The mobility and silence of the first lightweight, silent 16mm film cameras changed the future of television music broadcasting. Thanks to Arriflex in Germany and Eclair in France, we could go to places where cameras had not gone before and were able to come closer to our musicians, both in space and in spirit, than anything that had previously been possible. It seemed somehow both easy and natural. We felt that we were telling a story that was crying out to be told and we used the new possibilities to give life and bounce to the narrative.

14

Double Concerto

Walter Todds, Barrie Gavin, Peter Heelas, David Findlay,
Humphrey Burton, Curtis Davis, WNET

•

When I told Huw Wheldon that there was a story to be told, I knew without any doubt or hesitation that the story was a strong one but I knew with equal certainty that I had no knowledge at all about the physical processes of doing it. It was another demonstration of my capacity to be simultaneously brave and foolish but once again I was lucky in the guidance that I received from Walter Todds and Barrie Gavin. Thanks to them David Findlay, Peter Heelas and I formed a trio, a trio *allegro con brio* that was to endure for more than forty years. Here are some of David's never-forgotten aphorisms expressed along the way:

> Christopher needs to love.
> Christopher would have made a very good man of the cloth.
> Christopher is the unluckiest lucky bastard in the film business.

Together with our super-talented musician friends, we three were able to bring a new spirit into television music programming. David's training as a stills photographer had given him an acute feeling for lighting and composition – above the general level of production expertise in the BBC at that time. He also had a refined musical sensibility and an impressively good ear. Happily, he responded with enthusiasm to my invitation to join us making a film of Mozart's Concerto for Two Pianos K365 with Daniel Barenboim and Vladimir Ashkenazy.

We agreed to meet in front of the White House Hotel, where Daniel Barenboim was staying, just off the Euston Road, at 9 o'clock on the first morning of our allocated three days. David arrived half an hour late which generated much anxiety. Three days should normally be enough for a nine-minute introduction but I was a very worried budding director and felt I needed all the help I could get. In the event, however, his late arrival had an interesting influence on how we began – and continued. As a result of the urgency, everything was done in a kind of shorthand style: a series of grabbed images to help me tell my story:

A shot of the Mozart Double Concerto score open on Daniel's table.

Daniel closing the score.

Daniel putting on his jacket.

Daniel leaving the room with score.

The two of us emerging in a hurry from the White House Hotel, main entrance.

The two of us driving away in the open top Morris Minor which I had recently bought from John Williams.

Daniel playing Brahms for a few seconds in the Steinway piano showroom in the West End of London.

A travelling shot from the Morris Minor of the Steinway façade as we drove away.

Daniel emerging in a hurry from the offices of his agents Ibbs & Tillett.

A shot of the elegant houses in Queen Anne Street passing quickly in front of the camera to say, 'Here we are in London's West End'.

When we arrived at the end of the street David said, 'I see you are after a Tim Hewat style.' I had never heard the name Tim Hewat before but had the good sense not to let on because I realized that David had found something useful to hold onto. And so, without Tim Hewat knowing it, the spirit and the technique of Granada Television's pioneering *World in Action* had been imported into music programming – for the first time – and the idea developed fast. We continued in the same fashion for our allocated three days, ending backstage before, during and after the concert at the Fairfield Halls in Croydon.

1. My father, Eiulf Peter Nupen, in his heyday.

2. Tito Gobbi as Figaro with Italian Opera in Johannesburg, dedicated 'A Christopher in ricordo Tito Gobbi, April 1951'.

3. Beniamino Gigli and his daughter Rina in La Traviata, Johannesburg, 1951.

4. Tito Gobbi as Scarpia in Tosca, Johannesburg, 1951, signed photograph.

5. Lotte Lehmann. The inscription on the photograph reads: 'To C.P. Nupen, my charming neighbor in box 11. Lotte Lehmann, 1955'.

6. Lotte Lehmann. Given to me by Lotte Lehmann after her Masterclasses at Wigmore Hall, London, in 1957. On a wavy stave, she had written the notes but not the words of the Marschallin's sigh of impending separation from her youthful lover, Octavian, in Der Rosenkavalier. The photograph is signed 'For Chris, L.L. 1957'.

7. At the request of Lotte Lehmann, this portrait of me was taken in the Bond Street studios of Lotte Meitner-Graf in 1957.

8. With my mother Claire Meikle Nupen, in Rome in 1955.

9. Andrés Segovia in the Alhambra where we filmed him in 1976 for The Song of the Guitar.

10. Daniel Barenboim and Vladimir Davidovich Ashkenazy rehearsing Mozart's Concerto for Two Pianos K 365 with the newly formed English Chamber Orchestra, for our first film, Double Concerto, in 1966.

As a result of the deadline imposed by the Musician's Union rule obliging the BBC to broadcast live concerts within three weeks of the performance date, Peter and I started editing, already under pressure, on the morning after the concert. Film rushes in those days were developed and processed overnight and delivered on the following morning so we already had the rushes from the first two days.

Again, the friendly gods took a most unexpected hand.

Walter Todds, who was not well, had to go into hospital, and Humphrey Burton, the Head of the Music Department, was in the United States working with Leonard Bernstein, so there was nobody to supervise our adventurous doings and only two people, other than Peter and myself, appeared in the cutting room during the entire three weeks.

We had one five minute visit from Brian Large who had directed the electronic cameras at the concert. He asked, 'Is everything OK?' We said 'Yes' and showed him a few minutes of the last movement of the Mozart Concerto. We made no reference to our story telling antics.

The Film Operations Manager, whom we expected to visit us, did not appear, but twice asked Peter, at chance meetings in the canteen, whether all was going according to plan. Peter replied in the affirmative and we carried on diligently, but quietly. We were unbelievably lucky. It is nevertheless amazing that we got away with it and will be forever a witness to Peter's gifts and his faith in me, in our story and in our superb musicians.

The only other visitor was Barrie Gavin himself, dispatched by the Music Department Administrator, Desmond Osland, who was looking for assurance that I knew what I was doing. Barrie, who has made dozens of fine productions, and really knows production in a way that Desmond did not, watched the opening few minutes and reported reassuringly to the Administrator. I believe that Barrie saved us for a second time because what we were doing was so unusual, and so far from what we had been authorized to do, that I fear Desmond Osland would have taken fright and put a stop to it. We did not tell Barrie that we planned to go far beyond our authorized nine minutes of concert introduction.

During those three hectic weeks, often finishing at three or four o'clock in the morning, everything was built on Peter's quiet skill and my knowledge of the story that needed to be told. We abandoned the nine minute idea on the second or third day of editing and started looking for ways to tell the fuller story. We finished the edit and the cutting copy went to the laboratories just a few days before the scheduled Sunday evening transmission.

The first show print came from the labs on the Friday morning. Peter and I watched it immediately and found quite a number of faults, most of them arising from our unusual attempts to combine 16mm and 35mm film. A panic call to the laboratories elicited a promise that the faults would be corrected on Friday night and Saturday, and the new show print would be delivered on the Sunday morning – the day of the broadcast.

Nail-biting time.

On the Friday, Humphrey Burton returned from America and asked, 'How is the concert going?' I replied, 'We dropped the idea of the introduction plus concert and made a documentary out of the material instead.'

'You have done what? Who authorised that? I need to see this immediately.'

'Sadly, you can't. The labs had trouble with the neg cut and show print because of the combination of 16mm and 35mm negative and the transmission print will only be delivered on Sunday morning.'

Consternation spread like wildfire on the sixth floor of Television Centre and several of the top management officials watched the transmission on the Sunday evening. The impact, at least at BBC Television Centre, was considerably greater than it would have been if that panic and fiery focus had not preceded it. We had been lucky once again.

The film, which we called, rather unambitiously, *Double Concerto*, won the Prague and Monte Carlo prizes and had a decisive and significant influence on the development of music programming – worldwide. *Double Concerto* was much imitated and the best of the imitations came from the USA. A telephone call tumbled out of the blue one day from a fellow called Curtis Davis who was Head of Music at WNET in New York. After introducing himself briefly he asked:

'May we pay you the ultimate compliment?'

'What might that be?'

'To imitate your *Double Concerto* film with one about our American pianist André Watts?'

We both knew that he did not need my permission but he wanted to make a gesture of recognition for what we had done – and the spontaneous expression of generosity has always touched me. We became friends, the PBS project went ahead with our blessing and we were pleased to know that our first film would have echoes so far away and in such a big place as the United States of America.

15

Isaac Stern

Jean Bernard Pommier, Ian Hunter

•

The success of the *Double Concerto* film prompted Ernest Fleischmann, the go-getting South African manager of the London Symphony Orchestra, to suggest that we repeat the idea with Isaac Stern and the London Symphony Orchestra.

He was organizing a concert in the Royal Festival Hall in London with the LSO and Isaac as soloist/conductor.

J S Bach Violin Concerto in A minor
J Haydn Violin Concerto in C
J S Bach Violin and Oboe Concerto in C minor
W A Mozart Violin Concerto No.3 in G, K.216

I advised caution, saying that the excitement surrounding nearly every aspect of the *Double Concerto* project would be missing. In particular, I pointed out that the youthful exuberance that we had in front of our cameras on those three supercharged days would not be equalled and, further, that *Double Concerto* was still very much alive in people's memories and would prompt unfavourable comparison.

I was overruled by Humphrey Burton, Head of BBC Television Music Department, and we embarked on our dangerous quest, despite my misgivings. Things did not go too well and at the end of the Festival Hall concert, David Attenborough said to me, 'Well, Nupen, it seems that you have not backed a winner this time.' I wanted to say that the choice had not been mine but I was very junior and

David Attenborough was at the top of the production tree. He was Controller of BBC2 and so I said not a word, partly, also, because I already had a devilish plan up my sleeve.

The material that we had shot to tell our story was very flat indeed by comparison with what we had had for *Double Concerto* and there was only one way that I could think of to go. We did exactly the opposite of what we had done in *Double Concerto*.

In *Double Concerto* we had turned what had been planned as a nine minute introduction to a 50 minute concert into a 60 minute film including a performance of the Mozart Double Concerto. (A combination which we had been told had never succeeded.) With *Isaac Stern and the LSO*, by contrast, we turned what had been planned as a 40 minute documentary followed by the Mozart Concerto, into a Television concert of the Bach violin and oboe concerto and the G major Mozart Concerto with a very short introduction. The fruits of our edit were broadcast in that form and I felt extremely lucky to have got away with it.

The experience was not a happy one, not for Isaac nor for me and there was no further contact between us for three years. But when, in August of 1969, we made our film, *The Trout* (see Chapter 21) its echoes rang around the world and Isaac sent a message via his agent asking us to show it to him on his next visit to London. We duly did this on the editing machine in our cutting room two days after his arrival.

He came with a friend, a woman who expressed excited enthusiasm, repeatedly, during the screening. At the end, however, Isaac said, 'It seems to me that Itzhak [Perlman] is trying to imitate my personality and Pinchas [Zukerman] is trying to imitate my playing.' His friend exploded, 'Isaac, how can you say that after seeing such a wonderful film?' The atmosphere cooled decidedly and when the time came to leave, Isaac left the room ahead of his friend. I thought that was cheeky and out of keeping with the spirit of her generous enthusiasm. I was capable of being a bit cheeky myself in those days and so I shut the door behind Isaac, leaving the lady with me in the cutting room. 'BANG'! The door flew open and Isaac came storming back. I apologized and tried, unsuccessfully, to explain that my action was meant to lighten the mood, not darken it. My effort failed and certainly did not mend the damage that had been done.

There was no further contact for quite a few years until Isaac started editing his film *From Mao to Mozart* about his pioneering visit to China. He asked me to help with the edit and brought a rough cut to the cutting room. But he also brought the director with him and, out of respect, I said that I would not engage in the edit and that my help would be limited to providing the cutting room and limitless cups of coffee. They stayed for quite a few hours and *The Trout* episode seemed to be forgotten.

The next encounter happened when we bumped into each other backstage after a concert which Daniel Barenboim gave in Paris with the Orchestre de Paris. Isaac told me that he was creating the Jerusalem Music Centre in Israel and would like my advice about technical aspects and video equipment. I shied away, saying that to do this work well needed a long and diligent apprenticeship. I could say nothing useful in snatched conversations backstage after someone else's concert.

Isaac, forceful and ebullient as ever, insisted that I join him for a cup of tea at his hotel, the Georges V, a few days later. I went there and we talked for hours while Isaac made copious notes. At the end he put them in his fiddle case which seemed to me to be rather incongruous – hurriedly written scraps of paper sleeping beside one of the most expensive violins in the world. We parted amicably.

Our next encounter was arranged by Sir Ian Hunter, Isaac's London agent. He had persuaded IBM to sponsor a television concert in Dublin with Isaac and Jean-Bernard Pommier and he asked me to produce and direct it for television. As it turned out, Isaac was not on top form and was dissatisfied with his performance of the Bach Chaconne. He asked the production manager to explain to the public that there had been a technical problem which necessitated the need to shoot it again. The fellow did what was requested of him but he did not at all like taking the blame for Isaac's doings, neither did the camera crew.

We shot the Chaconne again. Isaac was still not satisfied and his wife, Vera, joined the fray, insisting on yet another take and saying that wine would be made available for the whole crew afterwards. That cut no ice with the Irish – who had already started to dismantle the set-up – and one of the more feisty said to me: 'We would rather drink your money in the pub'. I always keep faith with my crews. They are the people who make the films work. And so we went to the pub. I don't know what happened to the wine.

We did not release the Chaconne but we did release a marvellous performance of the César Franck Sonata with Jean Bernard Pommier, and Isaac, bless his artistic soul, wrote in the Observer:

> Christopher Nupen's artistic conscience is extraordinary. He makes the camera an instrument, not just an observer. It is a lesson in how alive the camera can be in response to the inner quality of the music rather than to the static quality of the performers.

Sleep in peace, dear Isaac.

16

Daniel Barenboim

Furtwängler, Rafael Kubelik, Hans Keller, *Double Concerto*,
Mozart for New Year's Eve, Denis Forman, Douglas Terry,
Beethoven, Brahms, Bach

●

Thinking back, my first meeting with Daniel Barenboim had been full of sparks – with an unexpected dash of fire thrown in for good measure. The encounter had taken place in the New Cavendish Street flat which I was sharing at the time with John Williams and Luc Markies.

John had met Daniel in Siena where they were universally admired for their exceptional talents and their youth. They were the youngest students at the Accademia Chigiana and were famous for it. John brought Daniel to the flat one day and we got on well from the first moment, aided, I presume, by John having told him about the successes of my Siena and Segovia radio programmes.

We found much to talk about. There is always much to talk about with Daniel Barenboim. Then, suddenly, we disagreed about something and, to my acute surprise, he flew at me and pinned me to the wall. I do not remember the source of the disagreement but I do remember being totally taken aback and saying, 'You should be careful about doing things like that to a South African rugby player. You might come horribly unstuck.'

The disagreement passed but I learned something from it and the friendship developed fast. Soon afterwards he asked me to make a radio programme with him about Wilhelm Furtwängler. I was still desperately unsure of myself and felt unequal to the task but was borne down yet again by the force of his conviction. I was so impressed by his energetic commitment to the idea that I agreed to try.

I knew nothing about Furtwängler but several powerful elements were patently obvious: Daniel's affection for the subject, his compendious knowledge of it, his gratitude for what Furtwängler had said, publicly, about him – describing his talent as something close to genius – and his burning need to tell the world what he, Daniel Barenboim, had to say about the conductor whom he so much admired. I proposed the idea to the BBC. It was accepted.

We decided to start recording in Munich because Daniel wanted me to meet and interview Rafael Kubelik who was chief conductor there. While waiting for Kubelik, I suggested doing a first interview with Daniel in my hotel room. He agreed and I set up the equipment. Uncertain about quite where to begin, I opened the first question, tentatively, with the words, 'Mr Barenboim......'

That turned out to be a big mistake. Our relationship had already become so close by then that the unexpected formal address was way out of keeping with the spirit of the game. It produced a spontaneous Barenboim explosion. He shot out of his chair, right across to the other side of the room, giving vent to his surprise with decidedly colourful expletives to match. That was another memorable moment – reminiscent of his flying protest in the New Cavendish Street flat and echoing a newspaper report which had described him as the 'Stormy Petrel of the Music World'. Fortunately, I never again provoked a flight of that volatile bird, although I have seen it land on others, in no uncertain fashion. I have never met anyone more articulate in the expression of disapproval when provoked while usually he is the most convivial of companions.

We made the Furtwängler tribute and it caused quite a stir thanks to the power of the Furtwängler recordings, combined with Daniel's glorious gift for choosing and programming music. I discovered also that I had learned more from working with the Features Department producers of BBC radio than I had realized. I was beginning to find my way.

Daniel had caused a great stir when he played his first recital in London, at the age of fifteen. It had included the monumental

Hammerklavier Sonata of Beethoven – something considered way beyond the reach of any 15-year-old no matter how gifted. In the event it was a spectacular success but, curiously, it did not lead to a stream of concerts or recitals, perhaps because it was thought of as a nine day wonder and just too unbelievable a performance for a 15-year-old.

Daniel is a restless fellow, however, and the lack of concerts did not suit him so he booked the Wigmore Hall for two Sunday afternoon recitals which he promoted himself. He was staying with us in the New Cavendish Street flat at the time and was actually in the bath at 14:55, five minutes before the scheduled start time of the recital. Happily, the Wigmore Hall is only three minutes walk from the flat and Diana and I ran with him all the way down Welbeck Street feeding him his jacket, tie, handkerchief and cuff links along the way. We entered the hall through the stage door and Daniel bypassed his dressing room and went straight onto the stage sounding the first chords before Diana and I had reached our seats.

That was a genuine Barenboim moment. Others were to follow.

The friendship continued to grow. I went to all his concerts in and around London, sometimes turning pages for him. One day he decided that I needed more appropriate clothes to appear on the stage with him. He sent me to a tailor called Mr Richards who had the smallest rooms in all of Savile Row, the same Savile Row which had provided the tails that were *de rigueur* for my entry to the State Opera in Vienna at the grand re-opening in 1955. After three visits I came away with an elegant blue suit, at Daniel's expense and, with it, travelled to several countries with him.

Following the Furtwängler transmission on the BBC Third Programme I introduced Daniel to Hans Keller which was to have fruitful consequences for both of us. Hans offered Daniel a considerable number of radio broadcasts which made him known in many parts of the United Kingdom and he asked me if I would make a radio feature about Schoenberg with him. I could not have thought of anything better than to collaborate with the great Hans Keller although I knew virtually nothing about Schoenberg. One thing I did know, however, was that even five minutes in Hans Keller's company was both enlivening and instructive.

After the success of *Double Concerto* which had gone down well with the BBC management, I proposed a studio programme called *Mozart for New Year's Eve* with Daniel Barenboim, Vladimir Ashkenazy, Fou T'song, and the English Chamber Orchestra, once again all Daniel's idea. The ECO had made great progress in the world thanks to their exceptional qualities, their radio broadcasts with Daniel and the *Double Concerto* film which was seen in eighteen countries. The players were all looking for more television exposure and I was pleased to provide it.

Mozart for New Year's Eve, shot in the BBC Television studios, included the Haffner Symphony, the Rondo in A major for piano and orchestra with Vladimir Ashkenazy, the Rondo in D major for piano and orchestra with Fou Ts'ong and the Mozart concerto for three pianos with all three of them and Daniel directing from the keyboard. I was becoming more secure and we were all very pleased with the result. It had a happy spirit to it.

Soon after the New Year's Eve broadcast the BBC erased the tape in order to re-use it for a gardening programme. In my view something of real quality and historical value was lost by that strange decision.

To my horror the BBC did the same thing to each of the next five programmes that we made for them:

> Max Bruch's Kol Nidrei with Jacqueline du Pré as soloist and Daniel Barenboim conducting the Israel Philharmonic Orchestra
>
> Schubert's Great C major symphony —with the IPO and Daniel conducting
>
> Both of the Brahms 'cello sonatas with Daniel and Jackie
>
> The Brahms Clarinet Trio with the two of them plus Gervase de Peyer

The television broadcasts were greeted with impressive enthusiasm and there was talk of our having solved the traditionally insoluble problems of putting chamber music on television. But the tapes were nevertheless all erased soon after the first broadcasts.

That was too much for me. I decided to try to do things differently in the future and looked for ways of setting up the next project entirely independently despite the general belief that it would be impossible for us to do so. Even my dear Huw Wheldon said, 'You cannot succeed,

Christopher. There is no infrastructure to support you.'

As far as the UK was concerned, he was right, of course. At that time the BBC management was not at all keen on taking programmes from outside sources and paid dramatically little when it did, and so we put our faith in Granada Television, Channel Four Television London Weekend, German television, and the international appeal of music. I would not have had the courage to do that had it not been for the sure-footed commitment that radiated from Daniel and his confidence in me. We made a good team.

Our bid for independence was helped by three lucky events that were truly crucial to our survival. The first was the closeness of the relationship with Daniel and his staggering abilities; the second, the loan of the money with which to make *The Trout*; the third was the courage, the intelligence, the managerial skill, the far-sightedness and the status of Denis Forman at Granada Television – allied to the universal esteem in which he was held by everyone who came into contact with him. We shot *The Trout* in one week, in London, in August of 1969 and *Mirabile dictum*, it was to become the most frequently broadcast classical music film of its era.

In 1969, with the 200th anniversary of Beethoven's birth looming I offered Denis a 13-part series with the working title *Barenboim on Beethoven*. The idea was simple: Daniel would choose the music that charted Beethoven's progress, I would direct and we would write the script together. Denis asked just a few questions, we talked for about twenty minutes and he said, 'Come back tomorrow and I will let you know what we think of this.'

I returned, as requested, on the following day and he said, 'We want you to make a pilot programme. I have asked Douglas Terry to be the Granada producer.' This was decision making at a speed unimaginable for such a project today.

I had met Douglas Terry through John Williams, which was a help, and we got on well. We shot the pilot in the newly converted Round House in Chalk Farm, built originally as a workshop for the repair of railway locomotives. It was an ideal location because of its all-round gallery which enabled us to place a battery of 10KW lights exactly where we wanted them. When we had a rough cut of the pilot, Peter

Heelas and I showed it to Denis Forman and Douglas Terry in the basement theatre of Granada Television, at 36 Golden Square.

Every detail of that defining event stays in my mind. Both Denis and Douglas suggested improvements which we accepted immediately. Denis said, 'Come back tomorrow and I will let you know our decision.' We went back on the morrow and Denis said, 'Make the series.'

Unbelievable as that sounds, that is what happened. That was Denis Forman.

Another brightly remembered highlight of those dramatic days was Daniel's first complete cycle of the Beethoven sonatas in the Queen Elizabeth Hall. I learned more about music at those recitals than at any other time in my existence. At the end of the final recital I felt bereft. It is impossible to describe what I experienced but I can say that it happened in the heart, not the head. I was reminded of it many years later when I sent Daniel, in Berlin, the first copy of our film *Remembering Jacqueline du Pré*. He telephoned to thank me and said, 'Cristobalin, you have a gift for structure which the others do not have.' That was a great moment for me and it prompted an instant response: 'If I have any gift for structure then it comes from Ludwig van Beethoven, as I learned to understand him from the hands of my young friend the Swaffo.' Swaffo was Jackie's private and affectionate name for him and I use it here to involve her in that high moment.

After those heady days Daniel and I made some series for French and German television and shot the *Goldberg Variations* for our mutual friend Michael Fuehr in Munich – a bold project that worked surprisingly well and pleased Daniel greatly. It set the seal on a happy working relationship that has so far produced more than twenty television productions and one for radio.

Since then, over a thousand kilometers have come between us, and pioneering ideas – of the order which we developed in those early years – grow from closeness, physical, spiritual, intellectual and emotional. Nevertheless, I thank the gods and John Williams for bringing us together and enabling us to capture the spirit of a glorious time long gone and which, through the films, still resonates in the world today.

17

Andrés Segovia

PART TWO

BBC Television Centre and *Segovia at Los Olivos,*
the intervention of Sol Hurok, *The Ghost, The Song of the Guitar*

•

Following on the success of *Double Concerto*, my next attempt at a contribution to BBC Television was an invitation to Segovia, on a visit to London, to make an item for a television magazine programme called *Music International*. It did not go well. To use his own words, he "disliked profoundly" the atmosphere and the dead acoustics of television studios and so we were toiling uphill from the start.

Segovia described the guitar as 'An orchestra but with smaller sound size' and since it incorporates so many different kinds of wood, 'a synthesis of the forest, with as many voices.' He said that those many voices needed to resonate with timber – and timber was notably absent from our television studio. He was not at ease and I was too young to do anything useful about it.

When the interview was over, I asked, 'Maestro, would you like to see what we have done?' He replied, 'Very well, my dear' and we went down into the basement of BBC Television Centre where the videotape recording machines were located.

In those days they stood about three and a half feet high and made aggressive, hissing and clanking noises. Confronted with about fifteen of these machines, making a huge racket, Segovia suddenly stopped dead in his tracks, right in the middle of the entrance doorway, took me by the arm and with disarming honesty, said, 'Ay, Christopher my dear, I am not a modern artist. I cannot play for the machine'.

I saw it all in a flash – a great moment in my memory – and I asked him, right then and there, still blocking the doorway, whether we could come to his new home on the Costa del Sol, in the summer of the following year, with one of the new, lightweight, almost silent 16mm film cameras, to try and do better. It took him about two weeks to respond. He accepted. I wonder how many international superstars would have agreed to do that with an untrained, aspiring young film maker in whom the only discernible virtue was love for his subject?

The summer of 1967 duly arrived and we set off from London for the Costa del Sol in three cars. There were no motorways in those times. It took us three days but nobody minded because it was an exotic project and every member of the crew was looking forward to it. We took with us an Arriflex BL camera with the serial number 00008. That is to say, the eighth camera off the new production line and it is as good a proof as any of what I mean when I say how lucky we were to be in the right place at the right time. Our adventure would not have been thinkable without that new kind of quiet camera.

What we produced was a simple film, an early film – we were just beginning – but, in his own surroundings, our star was the real Segovia again, the same Segovia, who could step out in London's Royal Festival Hall with his very small but many voiced guitar and hold a full house of nearly three thousand people in thrall.

Contrary to what most would expect, he usually started his recitals with quiet pieces to make the audience attune its ears. For many the quiet beginning was a shock but, slowly, the Grand Master drew the public into his world of magical sounds. His quietness may also have been an echo of nervousness. I once went backstage immediately before a recital in the Royal Festival Hall and found him in a state of acute anxiety. He was breathing heavily and looked mightily stressed. I was alarmed and asked if all was well. He answered, 'You know, my dear, to begin the concert is always a torture, and I would like to cancel.' Just as I was wondering whether he had in mind to cancel this particular recital, with more than a thousand people already in the hall, he added, 'And then, you know, at the end, I would like to begin again.'

His newly built home, *Los Olivos*, had been carefully situated on the top of a steep hill overlooking the Mediterranean, almost due south of his much-loved Granada and the Alhambra. Segovia heard our cars fighting their way up the hill and when we got there he was outside and waiting for us – sprightly, full of smiles and generously welcoming. He was 75.

We shot everything for that film with only one camera. That is the best way to do things, if circumstances allow. That is how most cinema films used to be shot but, sadly, it is seldom possible when shooting musical performance for television. It takes too much time and there are some specific technical difficulties associated with shooting music. At *Los Olivos*, however, it meant that we could have as many camera angles as we could dream up because we reset the lights for each new position and Segovia was willing to repeat every take as often as we wanted.

In that sense it is good to be both producer and director, as I was, provided that the most important truth is respected: namely that the film is king – not the director, not the producer, not the commissioning editor, not the lighting cameraman, and not even the star. Once that principle is established, everything falls into place and many of the tensions that arise in film making disappear. I learnt this truth from Federico Fellini who told me: 'If you know your craft, the film will tell *you* what to do.' The film is a better mentor than any individual.

Our Spanish adventure was not helped by the fiercest heat wave that southern Spain had experienced in a century. We were all impressed, nevertheless, by the quiet grace with which the great man received us as private guests in his new home – a reminder that he had been born into a very different culture and a long time ago.

His young wife, Emilita, was equally kind to us and one day decided to make lunch for the entire crew, spiced with lashings of cold sangria. We drank it like lemonade, with the result that our work in the afternoon fell apart and the atmosphere became highly charged. Everybody had problems, including the Maestro himself, and everybody eventually became grumpy – again including the Maestro himself. We retreated to siesta in a very unhappy state but the next day all was forgotten and we carried on with one of the happiest film making trips that I have ever experienced.

One evening, Segovia introduced me to a man whom he described as the official architect of the Alhambra. He took a shine to Diana and offered us the keys to the Alhambra. He said that we should go there one night and experience its magic with the city noises quieted and the cascading water accompanying our every step. He said, 'You will have your whole honeymoon in one night.' Segovia had made a similar remark in our Siena programme: 'The water, coming from the Sierra Nevada, comes in great abundance, cradling the thoughts of every person sensitive to poetry.'

The architect kept his word – a fine Spanish gesture. We accepted the keys to the Alhambra for one night and it remains forever in a happy corner of my memory. It also planted a seed that would bear fruit some years later.

At the time when *Los Olivos* was broadcast there were regular weekly meetings of the programme department heads in BBC Television to discuss and assess the output of the preceding week. I think they were called Programme Review Meetings. Humphrey Burton, as Head of the Music Department of BBC Television was usually present. On this occasion I bumped into him in the corridor as he emerged from the meeting and he said, 'Huw liked your Segovia film. He said that the trouble which went into its making showed around the edges. Nobody understood what he meant but that is what he said.'

Huw Wheldon knew what he meant and so did I. Once again I was indebted to him for his all-important understanding of what we were trying to do and his encouragement to us to continue doing it. Everything in a film must belong to everything else in the film, even at the edges.

Segovia at Los Olivos fared well in the world but, as the years went by, I began to feel that one film with Andrés Segovia was not enough. I wanted also to do something which might help the viewer to understand how a young Andalusian boy could suddenly see so far beyond the horizons of his time and transform a folk instrument into something worthy of Fritz Kreisler's memorable tribute. I wanted to do something more poetic than the first film with more music and less talk and with the talk focused on the spirit of his quest rather than on the facts and events of his life and career.

I arranged with Segovia that during his next visit to London he would keep one day free for filming. One day is not a lot but he did not have more time and I did not know how much longer he would go on playing, nor indeed how much time he had left on this earth. I felt it important to film whatever we could and I believed that we could produce something worthwhile in a single day if we stuck to shooting performance only. We had learned from *Los Olivos* that he was so wonderfully secure, so willing to do instant retakes to remove small scale imperfections, and his tempi were so rock solid, despite his famous rubati, that the edits always worked.

I booked St John's, Smith Square, London, (a church that had recently been converted into a concert hall) for the 11th and 12th of May 1970. One day for set up and lighting and one day for shooting. I booked the hall, a film crew, the sound crew, three cameras, the lights and the lighting electricians. All expensive commodities.

With only a few days to go Segovia's American agent, Sol Hurok, heard of our project, doubtless from Segovia himself, and reacted vigorously. He told Segovia that Sol Hurok could do a lot better for him in the United States than the young, unknown, Nupen could do for him in London. Further, that if he did a film with me it would undermine the possibilities for the USA.

Segovia was a very serious and very correct fellow. This put him in a difficult position. He asked me to go and see him in the Westbury Hotel and I found him clearly perturbed. I said, immediately, that I would not contemplate getting into a tangle with the mighty Sol Hurok and that it was anathema to me even to think of causing embarrassment to my Maestro. I offered to cancel.

That was something highly dangerous for me to do. It was not a matter of courage this time. I felt that I really had no alternative. It was *force majeure*. But what to do?

Not long before, I had heard Daniel Barenboim, Jacqueline du Pré and Pinchas Zukerman play Beethoven's *Ghost Trio*, Opus 70 Number 1 in the Town Hall in Oxford. It remains one of the most memorable concerts that I have ever heard and so, as soon as I left the Westbury, I called Daniel in Brighton where the trio was performing at the Festival, and asked whether they were free on Tuesday, the 12th of May. I thank all the gods in all the heavens that they were and so, instead of filming the Grand Master we filmed three of the most abundantly gifted young musicians in the world at that time, playing Beethoven's *Ghost Trio*.

The cancelled Segovia project remained dormant for seven years but then, one afternoon, I went to have tea with him in the Westbury and decided to try once again. I reminded him of the happy spirit of our work in Siena and our fruitful days at *Los Olivos*. I reminded him also of my night in the Alhambra with Diana. Both Segovia and his wife Emilita had great affection for Diana and so, in a significant way, she helped to unlock the door. I suggested that we shoot the second film in the Alhambra and discovered that I had played the trump card. Segovia had long claimed that the beauties of Granada had so penetrated his imagination in his youth that the Alhambra had become the Leitmotif of his life. I knew what he meant and that he really meant it.

Then for no reason that I can recall he suddenly said, 'Christopher, my dear, to have one beard well-controll-ed is very well, but this esplosion (sic) of hair will never do.'

I picked up the opportunity as fast as I dared. 'Maestro, if we make the new film in the Alhambra I will remove the beard entirely when you arrive in the Alhambra for the first day of shooting'. I do not know what impression that made but it certainly did no harm and I confirmed it in a follow-up letter. Shortly afterwards a telegram arrived:

> I am moved realy (sic) by your letter and happy with the results of your enthusiastic work Stop I give you green light but be careful not to get in economic troubles by excess of optimism Stop our affectionate greetings for Diana you and your collaborators Stop Segovia.

Hurok's project never flew and, after he died, Segovia discovered that the fee which the grand impressario had offered him was exactly half of what Hurok had negotiated with the television company!

Happily, our project flowered and in the summer of 1976, we made Andrés Segovia: *The Song of the Guitar*.

When our 83-year old star appeared in the Patio de Los Leones, at midnight on the first day, I kept my word and – in sight of all – removed the beard. Sadly, with very little hair on the top of my head, the result was visually unappealing – with so much skin showing I looked much too much like a hard-boiled egg. Many months later, when the film was finished and with Segovia's approval, I grew a smaller beard well-controll-ed.

In the first film, *Segovia at Los Olivos*, he talks about his life, his career and his music and, most of the time, he talks on camera. By contrast, ninety-eight per cent of what he says in *The Song of the Guitar* is out of vision. The first film is documentary, the second is made as a poetic reflection, in late maturity, on the spirit in which a passionate youth had set out on his remarkable quest. The films are entirely different from one another.

Segovia sums it all up, in *The Song of the Guitar*, with the words:

> My life has been an ascending line, slowly, but ascending line.
> It came, everything came,
> But I was not to be distracted, not to answer another call.
> In that consists the miracle of my will,
> In persisting in the road I had taken.
> The rest was in the mysterious stars of my firmament.

Andrés Segovia was a poet in almost everything that he did.

When the Alhambra shoot was over he invited the whole crew to supper in a very elegant restaurant. There were 17 of us. Suddenly one of the Spanish lighting electricians stood up and said, 'El Baston', just those two words, nothing more. He was referring to the silver topped cane that Segovia often carried. All of us who spoke Spanish knew instantly what he meant. Segovia handed the stick to Emilita who was sitting on his left and from there it went from hand to hand around the table until it came back to the Maestro himself – a symbolic gesture of unity.

For me, knowing how much the spirit of a shoot contributes to the finished film, that was a truly great moment.

Segovia ends the second film with the words:

> If I had chosen another instrument – the violin or the piano – I would have considered my life absolutely spoiled. I am telling the truth. I believe, objectively, that the guitar is the most beautiful instrument that man has created.

There speaks the passion and conviction which, allied to a heaven-sent gift and a lifetime of dedicated hard labour, enabled him to give so much to so many people.

18

Jacqueline du Pré

A Gift Beyond Words, Hugh Maguire, the Brahms Double Concerto,
The Ghost, the interview, DVD of the Year, Janet Baker

•

Jacqueline du Pré loved surprise and surprise followed her like her shadow, seemingly permanently attached to an effervescent spirit and an irrepressibly spontaneous nature. It was just one of her many great gifts. She added a dimension of surprising depth to almost everything that she touched and people responded to it even when they did not fully understand it. Her unusual doings caught my imagination many times. The first of them left an indelible impression.

One evening in 1961, I came home to the New Cavendish Street flat which I shared with John Williams and Luc Markies and found it empty but with the radio playing. This was already unusual. My attention was caught and held by sounds that were arresting, to say the least. It was instantly clear to me that this was something special.

I dropped my bags in the corridor, crept into the living room and listened in the half light. All the internal lights were switched off but a street lamp peeped in through a window which had such ancient glass in it that the imperfections in its structure threw strange patterns on the wall. The effect was magical and the visual impression seemed to relate to the music.

I listened, transfixed, until the last note died away. An unusually subdued BBC voice followed. I felt that it was trying not to tread too heavily on the magic which had just preceded it. I learned that I had been listening to Jacqueline du Pré. I had not heard the name before.

The broadcast was a live relay of a solo Bach recital from Fenton House in North London. Jackie was sixteen years old.

Some weeks later the doorbell rang. John was practising and had not told me that he was expecting a visitor. I opened the front door and was confronted by a Junoesque figure with one arm extended, resting on her cello case. The other was on her hip. I was struck by the image and the imposing stature but also felt instant sympathy. I was so bewitched by what I saw that I stared at her for much too long, without inviting her in. There was an awkward pause during which she showed quite clearly that she was painfully shy. Eventually, she asked, 'Is this where John Williams lives?' and rather timidly explained that she had come to rehearse with him.

I stepped back and she strode past me into the flat, surprisingly suddenly, with her cello case held high. I was amazed by the speed of the transformation and the striking contrast between the manifest shyness and the expansiveness of her generous movements. Jackie was tall and when she was intent on something, her being and her energy were elemental. The shy girl on the doorstep had been instantly transformed and she strode past me like an Amazon. The impact of that first impression and its apparent contradictions have remained with me ever since.

Jackie had come to rehearse with John for her first commercial audio recording. After about an hour of working with John, during which I eavesdropped intently, they took a break. We made tea in the kitchen and talked. I found Jackie irresistibly appealing. It was the start of a friendship that was to last for 26 years and to bring into my life an extraordinary richness – including the opportunity to keep something of a great artist's inexplicable magic alive on film.

I went to her concerts and her rehearsals whenever I could. When I went backstage she was always smiling and welcoming. But a real friendship only began to grow once she and Daniel Barenboim were in a relationship. A friendly closeness also developed between Jackie and Diana. Those were happy days.

Jackie's curious combination of shyness and ferocious determination struck me repeatedly throughout her life but one instance, in particular, remains bright in my memory. I was present at a rehearsal in the Albert Hall in which the ensemble fell apart at a certain moment. Jackie had taken her time for one of her 'sumptuous glissandi', as she called them, and this did not please the conductor. He stopped the orchestra and a discussion ensued. Jackie was advised that her largesse was inappropriate at that particular point and she rather quietly agreed to restrain herself. A few days later I reminded her of the incident and asked what had happened at the concert.

'I did it anyway', she said.

'And how was it?' I asked.

'Gorgeous!' came the reply.

Jackie obeyed what she felt inside her and because what she felt came from so deep, it spoke from the heart to the heart, often with surprise a major ingredient. She could play a phrase in such a way that one felt it should not be otherwise and yet, at the same time, she could make us catch our breath at an unexpected shift in the phrasing, the tone colour or the dynamic.

What she did was always full of wonder. 'When I put the bow on the string' she says in our first film with her, 'it was always a source of wonder that it made such a beautiful sound.' There was nothing that Jacqueline du Pré was happier doing than going out on the stage and sharing that sense of wonder.

In one of our early films her mother remembers her participating in a competition when she was very young. She went skipping down the corridor with her cello in the air, tossing around her always generous shower of smiles as she went. She was greeted by one of the officials who said, 'It's easy to see you have just had your turn,' to which Jackie replied, 'Oh NO! I am just GOING to play'. There is no story more true to her.

The opening image of our first film with her, *Jacqueline*, was of Jackie singing a French folk song and accompanying herself, pizzicato, on her 'cello in a train on the way to Gatwick airport. It has become one of the best remembered images of a musician enjoying the gift of music. Jackie was one of the first to see that film remembers the artistic persona in a way that not one of the other media is quite able to equal. That in turn enabled her to co-operate in the film making process in ways that were new and with not a single moment of difficulty.

Film crews are usually kind to first time directors because they know just how deep is the water and I remember that after we shot the Elgar Concerto members of the crew came looking for me repeatedly, to rehearse and re-live the enthusiasm which Jackie had generated in them. They frequently used the word 'inspiring.' The production could not have been better served.

I was later to see many examples of the way in which her magic worked on all around her. In *Jacqueline du Pré: A Gift Beyond Words*, the violinist Hugh Maguire gives a vivid account of how Jackie elevated him to the highest level that he ever reached when they played the Brahms Double Concerto together in the Royal Festival Hall with the Philharmonia Orchestra. That concert was the most moving that I had heard up to that time. When it was over I rushed backstage to thank them but was able to say only three words: 'Thank you, Smiley'. Jackie responded with, 'Kitty, why are you always crying?' I answered 'Smiley, because of the way you play'. Not another word. I turned and left in a mist. I spent four hours wandering the streets of London that night, finding my way through a haze of tears. I had not known that music could affect the human being in quite that way and to that degree – I was shaking. It was unlike anything I had experienced before.

When we shot the Elgar Concerto it was the first time I had ever directed cameras 'live'. Cutting 'live' is a complicated business that normally requires a great deal of training and experience and I had none at all. I had, however, deliberately chosen the best drama crew because the drama people know their craft better than the rest of us. We also had a very talented, musically sensitive and sympathetic vision mixer called Ron Isted. Those elements made all the difference. Nevertheless, looking at the result today, I can only explain its quality as evidence of the inspiration which Jackie generated in the people who came close to her.

When we shot the Barenboim, Zukerman, du Pré Trio playing Beethoven's *Ghost Trio* in St John's Smith Square concert hall we shot the whole piece three times with three cameras in three different positions. The idea was to give the impression of a nine camera shoot – provided it could all be cut together convincingly. In the event that proved extremely difficult to do because the electronic time-code techniques had not yet been applied to 16mm film and keeping track of it all generated nightmares for many weeks.

In the end we were forced to do what we had done with *Segovia at Los Olivo*s, to make multiple cuts in both the sound and the picture to keep them in synchronization. Fortunately, the tempi of our astonishing musicians were so rock solid that what we did is very rarely noticeable – and never disturbing. That is only possible with musicians who have unshakable internal metronomes.

Some months later, I showed the first show-print to the three musicians in a theatre in London. I started by apologising for the fact that the results of our labours came nowhere near the level of what they had achieved at their concert in Oxford.

Twenty eight minutes later, as the last credit rolled, Jackie, uncharacteristically, was the first to speak and she was both quick and blunt.

'You are wrong,' she said.

I asked, 'What's the matter? Don't you like it?

Jackie replied, 'What you said about it not being as good on the film as it was in the concert in Oxford'.

I asked what had made her say that and her answer remains with me to this day. It is one of my most important lessons. She said, 'It's better on the film because you can see what's going on and it adds another dimension to the music'.

Twelve years later, when she was already seriously handicapped by her illness, I was having supper with her in her flat in London when the telephone rang. It was Daniel calling in the interval of a concert he was giving in Paris, and Jackie's telephone was on loudspeaker because she could no longer hold the instrument in her hands. As a result I heard both sides of the conversation.

Daniel asked, 'What are you doing this evening?'

'Having supper with Kitty'.

'Well tell Kitty that I showed *The Ghost* to Jean-Pierre Ponnelle [the French opera and film director] last night and he said that it is the most successful translation of musical performance onto the screen that he has ever seen.'

Then came the great moment. It took Jackie less than three seconds to say, 'You see! I told you so.'

Nobody on earth would have expected Jackie, who often did not know what day of the week it was or what things cost or even when her next concert might be or what she would be playing, and who had almost no interest at all in the trivia of daily life, to remember that exchange twelve years later. But she did remember it because, with the things that really matter, the things of the heart and the soul, she saw deeper than the rest of us and she had seen something in our filming of *The Ghost* that nobody else had seen with such clarity.

Her easy-going ways meant that she was often undervalued and not given due credit for her exceptional insights. For many people, their image of her was of the budding young musician, not of the mature performing artist which she had already become.

If ever there was an artist who did not deserve the rubbish with which some have sought to invest her memory, it was Jacqueline du Pré. In all of the 26 years that I knew her I never saw anybody come into her presence who did not go out brighter than they were when they came in. She lifted the spirit. I watched closely during all those years and I can say without any hesitation that she was one of the kindest, one of the purest and one of the most honest of human beings. Several of her closest friends bear witness to that in our film *Remembering Jacqueline du Pré*.

When Jackie fell ill with Multiple Sclerosis she asked me to try and persuade the BBC to show the first film again. It took a long time for the answer to come back from the BBC and when it did it was a resounding 'No' for two prime reasons. The first was that the Musicians Union rights had expired and were not renewable. The second was the fear that it might lead to confusion, that the public might be tempted to think either that she had returned to the concert platform or that she had died.

That did not please Jackie and so I proposed the idea of re-making the film, which we had shot in black-and-white, and adding an introduction in colour, to remove any possibility of the feared confusion, by showing what she had done since the onset of her illness and what she was doing currently.

Fortunately, the Head of the BBC Television Music Department was an intelligent and far-sighted fellow called Richard Somerset-Ward. He understood all the issues immediately but it took him quite some time to fight his way through the BBC red tape. Finally, the BBC agreed, provided I could obtain the permission of the Musicians Union, of Jackie and Daniel, and of all the contributors, and provided that I would be entirely responsible for whatever production and clearance costs would be involved. Fortunately, the Musicians Union was kindly disposed towards Jackie and to me and agreed – at a price, of course.

We finally began the re-make in 1980 and the six months that we spent doing it were the only time in the entire 14 years of her illness during which its progress seemed to be arrested. Jackie did not have any remissions, as many sufferers from multiple sclerosis do. In her case it was a slow fourteen year descent into the dark but during those six months and only those six months, there seemed to be no deterioration or, at very least, it was masked by her enthusiasm for the enterprise. That may have been a coincidence and it may not. I think not and, in support of my belief, here are some of her memorable words.

'Kitty, Kitty, you cannot imagine what it feels like to me to know that I am playing for people again in our film'. She said 'our film'. She did not say her film, or my film, or the film. She understood, at the deepest level, that it was a collaborative enterprise, that neither of us could have done it without the other and that this was something that needed to be acknowledged – another demonstration of her finesse.

When we were working on the remake we shot an interview with her in her home of the time, Margot Fonteyn's house in Rutland Gate. We shot it on the 13th of December 1980, seven years after she stopped playing and seven years before she died. But, in the end, it did not fit in the remake of the film. Her honesty would have been too raw for many and her circumstances too sad.

Twenty five years later the world was a different place. Many things had changed and among the changes was the arrival of DVD. Our first DVD with Jackie had been so well received that we decided to release a second.

When we began editing the interview we started, out of habit, to cut it television style. That is to say, to try and extract the essential elements in the most condensed framework possible. We cut the first seven minutes, which took us a day, and I suddenly asked myself why we should be working so hard to reduce it when it was destined for DVD, which is so different from television. Television is always in a hurry. DVD is never in a hurry.

We undid everything we had done and started all over again. This time we allowed it to take its own course and its own time. We left in all the hesitations, the retakes and the fluffs. We even left in the clapper boards in the hope that the viewer would feel part of a real event in the presence of Jacqueline du Pré, just as we ourselves had done on that memorable morning in December 1980. The result is much slower but much more appropriate for DVD.

When it was done we decided to enter it for the Midem Classical Awards competition in Cannes, thinking that it had no chance whatever of winning anything, especially as our first DVD with her had won DVD of The Year Award three years earlier, but I thought that it was worth exposing it to people in the music and television worlds anyway. In the event, something which I had felt was too sad and too raw for release in 1980 had become a deeply revealing testament by 2007. *Jacqueline du Pré – A Celebration of her Unique and Enduring Gift* won DVD of the Year in January 2008. I am in no doubt that it was, once again, Jackie who won that award.

She battled on bravely for another seven years, with the disease taking an ever greater hold on her and yet she managed to be cheerful for at least a part of almost every day – right to the end. I can honestly say that for those of us who were close enough and courageous enough to be uninhibited by the appalling manifestations of her illness, her essential character remained unchanged. I made her laugh two days before she died and we both enjoyed it.

On the 19th of October 1987, we knew that she was failing and everybody who could possibly be there came running. There were about twenty of us in the apartment and three of us in Jackie's bedroom, her teacher William Pleeth on one side of the bed holding her left hand, Daniel standing in the corner looking haggard as I had never seen him before, and I was on the other side of the bed holding her right hand.

Somebody put on Jackie's recording of the Schumann concerto

and Daniel snapped immediately. 'Take that off'. In the silence that followed Jacqueline du Pré breathed her last breath.

As soon as the news reached *The Daily Telegraph*, the Arts Editor called and asked me to write something for the paper. I started immediately and words have never come to me so quickly or so easily. I wrote it in a single session, conscious, all the way, that Jackie's extraordinary capacity to elevate people was sharpening my concentration and urging me on. The article appeared in *The Daily Telegraph* on 21 October 1987.

At the memorial service for Jackie in London, Janet Baker sang Schubert's great song *Die Junge Nonne* (The Young Nun) accompanied by Daniel Barenboim and if ever there was proof that Jackie's spirit survived her departure it was there. Janet's interpretation echoed Jackie's cello and her repetition of the words *das Grab* (the grave) at the end of each of the first two verses was the most heart-breaking expression of grief that I have ever received from music.

We talk blithely of human beings being born equal. There was nothing equal about Jacqueline du Pré, neither in her prodigious suffering nor in her ability to deal with that impossible burden, nor in her glorious gifts which meant so much to so many people and touched them in ways that are given to so few.

She is remembered as few are remembered.

19

Diana Baikie

PART TWO

Regina Resnik, Placido Domingo, Huguette Tourangeau, the Hamburg State Opera, *Carmen*, the summer that never came

---

After many happy years in the New Cavendish Street flat, John Williams married Lindy Kendal and bought a house at 33 Brunswick Gardens close to Kensington Church Street. John and Lindy, plus, in time their daughter Kate, occupied the ground and upper floors and Diana and I rented the basement.

Later, when we started to talk about having children, we bought a house near the magical Primrose Hill. At the time, it was an area which was suffering from inner city decay. Prices were consequently just about affordable – with a massive mortgage. Diana called the house, at 29 Quickswood, 'Railway Cuttings.'

Our happiness was unclouded until we were invited to make a film about Regina Resnik producing *Carmen* for the Hamburg State Opera. The invitation came from a wealthy American friend of Regina's called Ed Swann. Some productions are unlucky and this was most certainly one of them. Several things went wrong from the first day, starting with restrictions on when and where we could film, imposed on us by the Hamburg State Opera, where Regina was directing for the first time.

Bizet's *Carmen* has left a long trail of catastrophes in its wake and in trying to make our film I was to find out why. The music is so inspired, so emotionally charged, so full of passion and so full of tragedy that it has at times penetrated the hearts and minds of the people engaged in producing it, to a degree that has often caused them to make the strangest of mistakes.

We were not given sufficient time nor the appropriate access to make the sort of film which we had been asked to make and I saw catastrophe looming. I advised Ed Swann to abandon ship and to cut his losses which, at that stage, were relatively small in relation to what I feared they would become if we carried on. I offered to take no fee. During much of the following day Ed pleaded with me to continue, repeatedly putting further pressure on me by saying how much confidence he had in me and how much he appreciated the quality of our existing films. Film making is a nerve wracking game at the best of times and the right word of encouragement at the right moment can have a powerful effect. We carried on.

Then, suddenly, two knights in shining armour arrived on the scene and I began to see something promising unfolding in front of our cameras. Our two saviours were Placido Domingo (Don José) and Huguette Tourangeau (Carmen). I was totally captivated by them and by some warm, velvety quality in their voices that stole my heart away. The magic flew high on the waves of Bizet's inspired music and I was transported by our unexpected guests.

The feeling soon changed however. I felt I was falling, falling, falling and I realised that, with absolutely no conscious intention, I was falling in love with Huguette. I was to learn also just how unexpectedly, how uncontrollably and how fast these things can happen – especially in hothouse circumstances. Brahms' words to Clara Schumann kept echoing in my mind: 'What have you done to me? Can you not release me from this magic?' The atmosphere was magical in the most convincing sense of that term, warm, tender, giving, generous and pure. As we were both married, there was a limit to what we could do about it, but we exchanged affections and met in dark corners, hidden by scenery. I went back to filming with new hope.

At the end of the shoot Huguette and I parted painfully. I promised that if any film at all emerged from our struggles, I would make it for her – and that is what I did.

It took two years with three additional shoots in France to turn it from a film about a production of *Carmen* into a film about Bizet and the tragedy of what happened to his masterpiece, all potentiated by the power of his music, the very nature of the story and the glorious gifts of our heroine and our hero.

The music of *Carmen* is heady stuff and it is not for nothing that productions of the opera have a widely acknowledged history of going wrong. I am in no doubt that the catastrophe of the first production is what killed Georges Bizet. He died of heart failure, exactly three months after the disastrous first night, having swum in the Seine at Bougival – in despair and against strict medical advice.

Unhappily, before starting to try and edit the film, the fates had a disturbing surprise in store for me. The Decca Record Company sent Huguette to London for recording sessions with Richard Bonynge and Joan Sutherland. In Hamburg the cast had all worked and lived closely together in a particularly happy spirit. Now, transported to London for the recording sessions, it was inevitable that Huguette and I would meet socially. We made strenuous efforts to maintain the secrecy which we had achieved in Hamburg but the circumstances were very different and there were no dark corners to hide in.

Diana, who was famously intuitive, sensed that something was awry. She taxed me with it and I had no choice but to reveal what Huguette and I had kept so entirely and diligently secret in Hamburg. The real world suddenly came at me like Birnam Wood. What had been so happy, enlivening, and well controlled, suddenly became deeply threatening.

Neither Diana nor I had been in anything like that situation before and we were both lost. We separated for a time but soon came back together, trying to rebuild what we had had before. Unsurprisingly, it took time. Then, one day, Diana stopped me on the stairs of our Quickswood house and said, 'Being in love with somebody is the gratification of a selfish need. Really loving somebody is something entirely different and I know now that I really love you.' Her warmth and her generosity flooded me as nothing had ever done before. Everything dissolved in mist. I gave thanks to Diana and to all the heavens.

Our relationship moved onto a new level and, in time, Diana, who had a great wit, even made us laugh at what had happened. She was very funny and a great mimic. One day, with about five or six people present in the living room, she had us all in stitches with a direct reference to the Hamburg story, 'Haven't you noticed Christopher when a pretty woman walks into the room?' and she followed her question with an imitation of a pigeon strutting its stuff in courtship display with wings dragging on the carpet and appropriate curru-curru-cuccu sounds. It was a demonstration of a great humorous talent and I wish that we had filmed her at it.

Her grace and gentle nature enabled us to restore what we had lost and carry it onto a deeper level of understanding but then on one terrifying day, Diana was diagnosed with cancer.

She suffered the trauma of a mastectomy and, having little faith in the capacity of Western medicine to cure breast cancer at that time, we turned to Michio Kushi and his macrobiotics for help. Kushi said to her, 'You have no illness now and you are very beautiful. You will remain beautiful and will have no more cancer if you follow my advice. You will even stay unusually young and people will come to you for guidance and solace.'

For five years we followed his advice and his macrobiotic diet – scrupulously. There was no sign of the cancer reappearing and, coincidentally, a string of troublesome but not mortal ailments that had affected my own health for some years, disappeared entirely. We seemed to have made the most important health discovery of our lives. Diana said, 'I haven't got cancer. I used to have cancer.' But her mother, Cathy, who was living with us and who came from solid Scottish stock, felt that the macrobiotic diet was dangerously lacking in fortifying ingredients and started to cook a normal Western diet.

One day, without preamble Diana said, 'The summer is coming and I am not ready for it.' I felt that she was telling me something ominous and it sent a shiver through me. The cancer suddenly reappeared in several places and nobody will ever know what part her diet played in that.

After a short illness in the Charing Cross Hospital, in Hammersmith, during which she earned the admiration and affection of most of the staff, and several of the patients in her ward, she suddenly started fading. The news flew around London and on 29 May 1979, her thirty-ninth birthday, her visitors included an impressive number of the world's leading musicians. Diana asked, 'Why so many? I am not dying am I?' Nobody answered that question and two days later, she slipped away forever. Following her body to the mortuary, I was profoundly shocked by the deliberate and repeated disrespect of the porters. I had no idea that such things were possible.

And so, Cathy lost her Diana, I lost my Diana and Jackie lost her Diana. She had been a different kind of angel for each of us. It was an overwhelming catastrophe for us all but for Jacqueline du Pré, in some ways, particularly so, because Jackie already had so little left of what had been such a wonderfully rich but mercilessly short life – and Diana had meant so much to her.

Andrés Segovia, who saw extremely deep and who loved both Jackie and Diana dearly, could only say, 'I do not understand – and never will – the cruelty of nature.'

20

Vladimir Ashkenazy

Scriabin, Iceland, David Attenborough, Daniel Barenboim,
the birth of Allegro Films, *The Vital Juices are Russian*, Alan Dykes

•

In the making of my first radio programme, *High Festival in Siena*, I did every first and last thing myself. That was partly through force of circumstance, partly through nervousness – I could say fright – and partly a matter of temperament. The only other person who had any influence at all was Christopher Sykes whose contribution was limited to his suggestion that I drop two lines at the end – a brief adieu from a French cellist called Genevieve.

My role with the Furtwängler programme, by contrast, was limited to structure and artistic organization. Ninety per cent of the content came from Daniel Barenboim and when it was broadcast, Daniel invited Vladimir Ashkenazy to listen to the transmission on the BBC Third Programme. On the following morning Ashkenazy telephoned me and asked me to make a radio programme about Scriabin with him.

I said that I knew nothing at all about Scriabin and was much too new to the game even to try. I told him that all the content in the Furtwängler broadcast had come entirely from Daniel and that my contribution was limited to the organization of it. I did not know enough about Scriabin in particular or about making radio programmes in general and, despite the generosity of the request, I felt that I had no choice but to turn the offer down.

Undeterred, his immediate response was 'Well, we can easily fix the first of those problems.'

He invited me to his house in Hendon on the north side of London on four consecutive evenings and he sight-read through the entire piano works of Alexander Scriabin, in chronological order, from first to last and apparently without mistakes. I was staggered by his speed and accuracy and was later to discover that he is one of the most capable sight readers in the profession. His wife, Dódý, a pianist herself, describes his sight-reading as 'scary'.

Together, we made a radio study of Scriabin and called it *Prometheus: Bringer of Fire*. It was the beginning of the most extensive working relationship that I have had in my entire career. It has endured, so far, for more than 50 years. We have made 24 television productions together and forged the warmest of friendships, without a single moment of tension or personal difficulty. I owe him many grateful thanks. Spasibo bolshoye, Vladimir Davidovich.

The success of the *Double Concerto* film with the BBC Television Management encouraged me, at Daniel Barenboim's prompting, to propose a follow up film about Ashkenazy alone and I expected the BBC to jump at it. It was at the time when Ashkenazy was planning to move his home from London to Reykjavik in Iceland and I knew that the move would give the film a valuable extra focus.

Unhappily, I ran into trouble from the start.

David Attenborough, as Controller of BBC2, had to make the final decision and he warned me that it would be very difficult, perhaps impossible, to make a convincing film with Ashkenazy because he was so shy. He made the point that what I was proposing to do was very different from what we had done with *Double Concerto* which started life as a straight performance film, shot in three days.

I said that I had put in a lot of effort, during the making of the *Double Concerto* film, to foster a good relationship between Ashkenazy and our cameraman, David Findlay, and it was essential that we should all be there together in Iceland when the family arrived there on the scheduled day – 8 June 1968. I asked also that Peter Heelas should edit the film because of the way in which we had worked so successfully together on *Double Concerto* and the Carl Ebert programme. I had already learned from *Double Concerto* that respecting the importance of the working relationships is vital in the making of a film.

My requests to the BBC management, which seemed so obviously sensible to me, met with a stony reception. I was told that I could have neither David Findlay, nor Peter Heelas and we could not go on 8 June. I protested vigorously which elicited the response, 'You cannot expect us to run the BBC around you.'

I answered, 'No! I do not expect that, but do you not organize your facilities in the way best calculated to serve the productions? Remember that I have had very little experience and this team has, nevertheless already given you a major success.'

That was seen as bragging and promptly made matters worse. In turn, that made me grumpy because although I didn't know much, I did know what a difference it would make if both David and Peter worked with me on the film. Unfortunately, grumpy is a dangerous condition. The atmosphere became tense and the more I tried to convince my interlocutor that I was speaking on behalf of the film, not of my ego, the less progress I made.

Finally, in a moment of desperation and ill-concealed bluff, I said, 'If you go on like this, I will end up resigning or something.' I expected that to be understood as forgivable youthful exasperation in trying to underline a passionate conviction. Instead, it prompted the reply, 'Mr Nupen, if you resign, you will be back on your knees in two years.'

That did it – well and truly. I very seldom get cross because I learned a long time ago, that it usually makes matters worse but I lost control, packed up my papers and said, 'In that case, I am resigning now.' I left the room, closing the door, very gently, behind me.

Ten yards down the corridor an idea came to me. I turned around, went back, and opened the door. I was greeted with the words, 'You do not need to apologize now, let's calm down at the weekend and meet again on Monday.'

I answered, 'Mr Wadsworth, I have not come to apologize, I have come to say that I plan to spend the whole of this weekend trying to persuade David and Peter also to resign so that we can make this film.' I closed the door, quietly again. Memory suggests that he said, 'Oh go away,' but that may well be just wishful thinking.

I did what I said I would do. David Findlay resigned on the Monday and Peter Heelas resigned about six weeks later. Michael Rosenberg then joined us and we all four went to Iceland on 6 June 1968.

By dint of ill-advised, grumpy behaviour we had embarked on our first entirely independent production: *Vladimir Ashkenazy: The Vital Juices are Russian*. Diana hung on at the BBC a bit longer to generate some income but worked for the film in the evenings and at weekends. With her permission we edited the film in the kitchen at 33 Brunswick Gardens and we registered our bold venture as Allegro Films.

I have said that my work with Vladimir Davidovich Ashkenazy produced not a moment of difficulty in all the years. That is not quite true. There was one fleeting but memorable moment of tension.

When we were making the Schubert film (*The Greatest Love and the Greatest Sorrow*) and were shooting the music in the Siemens Villa in Berlin, Ashkenazy was practising while David Findlay was battling with some tricky lighting problems. Suddenly, Vova stopped playing, got up, and came towards me. He had some distance to go and his walk was quite visibly lacking its usual bounce —it was even a bit awkward. I knew immediately that something was wrong. As he approached he said, 'Christopher, why is it taking so long?'

I answered, 'Vov, because it is so difficult.' On that very instant he said, 'Oh, OK, turned on his heel and went back to the piano, not to practise Schubert, he had already done all of that, but Shostakovich for which he won a Grammy Award shortly afterwards. This interlude says all that needs to be said about his open, honest, practical and generous nature in response to the ever-present difficulties of production.

The *Vital Juices* brought an unexpected blessing in its train. It added a new and unlikely part-time member to the team, the dubbing mixer, Alan Dykes. I knew Alan and I knew his work. It was different from the other BBC dubbing mixers in the same sort of way that David Findlay was different from the other cameramen. He had a questioning attitude, a strong identification with the programme content, and a directness and determination to push things through to the right conclusion, no matter what obstacles might stand in the way. He also had an exuberance and original way of looking at the things which concerned us and an uninhibited readiness to express his convictions.

But there was a problem about using him for the Ashkenazy film. We had left the BBC under something of a cloud and Alan was on the permanent staff of the BBC. I went, cap in hand, to Mr Wadsworth and asked whether we could produce the sound track of the *Vital Juices* film with Alan in his BBC dubbing theatre. Remembering our previous stressful encounter, I did not have much hope but it turned out that the BBC had forgiven us or, at least, wanted to show the finished film. And so we did the sound mix with Alan and paid the BBC a facility fee. The BBC showed the finished product and even paid us a small acquisition fee. We had survived.

Alan had been the right person for our kind of film and he proved it again and again with many others over many years. The BBC remained understanding. Alan also contributed his own special humour, a gift that pulled us through many a tricky moment in his dubbing theatre where there is always an acute sense of pressure. When mixing the sound, one is obliged to try and perfect – in just one day or two – work that has taken months to build, and passionate convictions about how to do it sometimes collide. Alan's directness and humour defused quite a few of them. 'Christopher, you do not have your friendly voice on today. Go home and come back when you know the whole script by heart.' He was right and he saved us. He always made a big difference because he cared so much and he looked for a matching commitment from others. He once said in an interview that of all the people who came into his dubbing theatre the two who cared most were Tony Palmer and Christopher Nupen.

We have very much to thank Alan for, for so many lively soundtracks, for so many laughs along the way, and most particularly for helping to bridge the BBC gap that followed on our resignations. The *Vital Juices* was broadcast twice by the BBC and then in eighteen countries around the world.

21

The Trout

John Denison, Daniel Barenboim, South Bank Summer Music,
a different orientation, Corti Rosenberg, a 'vintage' moment in music

•

Daniel Barenboim's star was already on high when John Denison, as General Manager of the South Bank Centre in London, came up with his bold idea for the first season of South Bank Summer Music. His first announcement was the appointment of the 26-year-old Daniel Barenboim as Artistic Director. That was in August 1968.

Daniel's astonishing repertoire was already legendary. He also had an unusually wide circle of friends whom he knew he could call on to join him with enthusiasm. I remember only one complaint: Itzhak Perlman, backstage, with a bad cold, dripping with sweat and with no shirt on, saying 'I'm suffering from Barenboim scheduling!'

The pace was dramatic, riding on Daniel's exceptional gifts for programming. The public quickly picked up the spirit and came running in large numbers. John Denison programmed a second season for 1969 and Daniel came up with a surprise that was to scamper around the world in double quick time, and continues to delight many thousands of people to this day.

He invited Itzhak Perlman, Pinchas Zukerman, Jacqueline du Pré and Zubin Mehta to join him in a Saturday afternoon performance of Schubert's *Trout* Quintet. Zubin had not played the bass professionally in many years but he agreed to do it nevertheless and there is no more telling testimony to the spirit of the occasion.

I knew, at the very moment when Daniel first told me of his idea, that this was something that should be filmed. More than that, I knew that it had to be filmed in close up – as distinct from the way in which concerts were generally shot at that time.

I asked John Denison whether he would give us permission to put five cameras on the stage with the artists. Such a thing had not been done before. A tradition had grown up of shooting concerts from the audience point of view. The reasons are obvious and fair enough. That is how we usually see and hear concerts but I wanted to tell this story from the **inside,** because of the nature of the event, the quality of the artists and my close relationship with them.

I expected either an outright rejection or a long, weary battle but the same far-sightedness that had prompted the idea of South Bank Summer Music in the first place took boss Denison straight to the crucial question. He asked whether I could disguise the cameras in some way and suggested importing stand-alone vegetation. That gave me the idea of building tongue-and-groove hides for the cameras, removing just one plank from the front face of each at the appropriate lens height.

John Denison gave us the permission that so many others would have refused and hundreds of thousands of people have since owed him thanks for his decision.

After filming rehearsals and other story-telling material during the preceding week, we shot the complete performance of *The Trout*, live – and with not a note retaken – with five film cameras on the stage or near it. The look and the feel were immediately and strikingly different from what usually appeared on television. We had done the right thing.

We try always to allow our films to choose their own paths and this one grew rapidly into something which flew directly in the face of two specific BBC warnings. First, we wanted to call it *The Trout* which the BBC advised against in no uncertain terms. They said that it would sound to the public like a fishing film. Second, they insisted, again, that documentary material and musical performance could not be successfully combined. We were in limbo and did not have the necessary money to dig ourselves out, but suddenly, and precisely on cue, another wholly unlikely but exceedingly happy benediction floated quietly into place.

We had left the BBC in order to have more time and more freedom to make the sort of films that we had been developing. Our lawyer, Martin Bayer, knew that we needed money and he presented me with an offer from an American client of his named Harold Shaw, a partner of the mighty Sol Hurok. The proposal was to set up a film making business together, to make independently produced music productions for television.

Hopes ran high but Mr. Shaw, who later became a good friend, wanted 85% of the equity in return for providing all the money. I felt that the price was too high and said so – most politely. Martin then approached a wealthy South African called Corti Rosenberg who offered to lend me the money to make *The Trout* if I would teach his son, Michael, the film business.

Michael learned quickly and eventually became one of the world's most successful Wild Life film producers. In homage to Corti Rosenberg, there is a shot of him pacing around in front of the Queen Elizabeth Hall just before the start of the *Trout* concert.

The Trout gathered momentum and, happily, fortune and the five Arriflex BL cameras functioned perfectly. Nobody expected it at the time but, over the years, *The Trout* has established itself as a unique document in a category of its own and in a form that was said, at the time, to be unworkable.

One can never know how a film will turn out – and one should not. Films need to grow under their own steam. We have had films tell us – on six different occasions – to abandon the original project entirely and produce something completely different from what we had originally set out to do, bending the same material to a different purpose.

Double Concerto, for example, started as a concert with a short introduction and became a documentary film of a kind which had not been made before. A Brahms recital with Pinchas Zukerman and Marc Neikrug became a film about Brahms and Clara Schumann. A film about Regina Resnik became a film about Bizet and his opera *Carmen*. A recital by Nathan Milstein and Georges Pludermacher became a portrait film of Nathan Milstein. A planned recital by Andrés Segovia became a performance film of Beethoven's *Ghost*

Trio by Daniel Barenboim, Pinchas Zukerman and Jacqueline du Pré. *The Trout* started as a performance film and ended up in a category of its own. Unexpected success always rings louder and, many years later, Jackie herself had this to say:

> Nine years ago we were five friends linked by our youth and the pleasure we had in making music together. Any excuse was good enough for fun and music-making.
>
> When we played *The Trout* it would have evaporated, as all concerts do, but Christopher Nupen saw a film in it and suddenly there was a statement of our happiness, forever.
>
> You know, when you're not actually giving concerts you can forget the immediacy of the feeling even though you still live every note totally; but when I see *The Trout* it gives me back something of that feeling which will always be so precious to me.

It is often difficult to know exactly which ingredients in a film contribute most to that strange alchemy that sometimes results in enduring success but I have long known that the most powerful radiations which continue to flow from *The Trout* come from the unspoken relationships between us, both in front of the cameras and behind them and between the cameras and the protagonists. We were lucky to be in the right place at the right time, to capture a spirit which so perfectly matched Schubert's youthful masterpiece.

We kept our title *The Trout*, despite the BBC's fishing worry and it still swims happily today in many parts of the world, preserving a moment in music which Itzhak Perlman calls vintage and which he fears has forever gone.

Pinchas Zukerman

Here to make music

A new exuberance, a new trio, *The Ghost* in Oxford,
the English Chamber Orchestra, The Hercules Hall protest

•

Daniel Barenboim and Jacqueline du Pré returned to London one day from a trip to New York, bubbling with excitement at a new discovery. They had heard Pinchas Zukerman for the first time and Jackie said, 'Just you wait till you hear him. It is really something different.'

Pinchas came to visit them in London not long afterwards and I had never before seen such ebullience in a musician. What made it especially intriguing was that it clearly reflected both a huge generosity of spirit and a surprising vulnerability. A friendship grew out of those first moments, a friendship that has endured to this day and has manifested itself unmistakably in the work that we have done together.

The three of them immediately began to play trios, initially just for the fun of it but it was not long before the agency, Ibbs and Tillett, found professional engagements for them. There was a warmth and a centre to their sound which was instantly recognizable, most memorable, and the public responded to it.

I remember many concerts of theirs, one a late afternoon weekend concert at a girls' school north of London at which several professional musicians were present. Wine was offered in the evening sunlight after the concert and every person that I spoke to was full of wonder, if not disbelief, at what we had just heard. Uppermost in my memories was their concert in the Town Hall in Oxford, which led to our film

The Ghost – a key moment in our work together and one for which I will be forever grateful.

Daniel Barenboim soon became intent on introducing Pinchas to Quintin Ballardie and the English Chamber Orchestra with whom he had developed such a close relationship and done so much productive work. A similar relationship developed quickly with Pinchas. They were soon playing Baroque music together with Pinchas leading from the violin. That led to Mozart concerti and, not long afterwards, the ECO invited him to conduct Mozart symphonies.

Pinchas had no established conducting technique at the time but with those true chamber music players, and full of the excitement of mutual discovery, he did not need it. The communication functioned so well that he had only to be there in front of them, responding to the music and, above all, looking at them with musical intent, for them to produce performances that were unmistakably 'Zukermanesque' and had a vitality which appealed as much to the players themselves as to their audiences.

What developed was heartening to see, especially with the string players. They wondered endlessly at what he could do and the warmth of the sounds that he produced. They hung on his every word, his every gesture and his every look and mostly it was the looks that gave the shape to the music making. They even acquired a 'Zukerman sound'.

Clearly, we had to make a film about him, and his relationship with the ECO players had to be a major part of it. The leader of the orchestra, Kenneth Sillito, had this to say about Pinchas Zukerman: 'I never cease to be amazed at the range of achievement of this artist. Everything seems to be in style. He is such a tremendous musician. I think he could probably succeed at anything he wanted to do. He's a born chamber music player, concerto player, conductor – anything you like. To me, he has the greatest talent the world has seen for the past 25 years – on the fiddle.'

This led to a momentous decision, to give a Mozart concert in the Hercules Hall in Munich on the 21st May 1973, at which they would play the Rondo in C, K373, the Fourth Violin concerto, K218, the Bach Concerto for violin and oboe, BWV 1060, with Neil Black as oboist, and the Mozart A major symphony, K201 with Pinchas conducting.

We all knew that this had its dangers but that was one of the main reasons why I decided to take a five camera crew all the way from London to Munich to film it. Films of this kind thrive on being in the right highly charged place at the right time. In the event it proved even more dangerous than we had feared but for entirely unexpected reasons.

Immediately before Pinchas was due to go on stage to play the Rondo, three separate small groups of people in the audience began chanting, '*Licht aus, Licht aus, Licht aus*' (lights out, lights out, lights out).

I appealed to the promoter of the concert to address the public and say that it had been announced on the posters, in the programmes and on the tickets that the concert would be filmed, that the crew would make no noise but that the stage would be more brightly lit than usual. The promoter refused and asked me to send Pinchas onto the stage, urgently.

I replied, 'Pinchas is 24 years old and is about to play one of the most important concerts of his career so far. I will not ask him to go onto the stage and do battle with the public and in a country which is not even his own.'

I had no choice but to go onto the stage myself – noticeably ill-dressed for the occasion.

'May I speak?'

'*Nein, nein. Licht aus, Licht aus.*'

I was in deep trouble and I knew it but at exactly that moment some words in elevated German which Manfred Gräter had taught me for an International Music Centre Congress in Munich a few years earlier suddenly tumbled from the heavens and I was able to trot them out verbatim:

> *Entschuldigen Sie bitte, meine Damen und Herren, wenn ich mein Referat nicht in deutscher Sprache halten kann. Bedauerlicherweise habe ich niemals deutsch studiert, aber glücklicherweise scheinen die meisten von Ihnen englisch zu verstehen.*

Excuse me please, ladies and gentlemen, that I am unable to address you in German. Unfortunately, I have never studied German but happily it seems that most of you are able to understand English.

The surprise and, I suppose, the national respect for High German, produced instant silence.

I managed, somehow, to stumble on in German, to explain that I had brought a five camera film crew all the way from London as a direct result of Pinchas Zukerman's past successes in Munich, where he had even made front-page news. I said that the crew would make no noise but the stage would be more brightly lit than usual. I said also that we could not continue without their approval but that if they would allow us to continue we would make something that I expected to give pleasure to many people in many parts of the world for many years to come. Some light applause followed and I retreated awkwardly, fearing that my knees would give way before I reached the exit from the stage.

Pinchas then went on to the stage and plunged quickly into the C major Rondo. He had not gone far when all the lights went out. Night descended and everything ground to a halt. Unsurprisingly, the public assumed that it was our additional lighting which had caused the problem. Some emergency lighting came on but was not enough to enable us to expose a single foot of film.

What to do? In the hope that the problem could be quickly fixed I went on the stage again and said that the emergency lighting was not enough to play the Mozart pieces but they could play the scheduled Bach piece because they knew it by heart – and that is what they did.

We soon discovered that we were not responsible for the problem. The whole of that quarter of Munich was dark and it was causing major concern with the police because Brezhnev was staying in the Vierjahreszeiten Hotel, just around the corner. The police feared that there might be some connection.

During the Bach Concerto the power supply was restored and I arranged with Pinchas that he would play both the Rondo and the Concerto before the interval. To our astonishment, when he returned to the stage, the protests began anew. I say 'to our astonishment' because the German public is usually a respectful one and the problem had already been publicly resolved.

This time Pinchas was on the spot and had no way out. He turned, slowly and reflectively, to the public, put his fingers to his lips and said, 'Whoever doesn't want to stay, should leave right now. We're here to make music.' This prompted further cries of '*Licht aus, Licht aus*'. Pinchas responded with 'Tell me, how many times have you been in a concert that has been filmed?' 'Never before!' came the reply. 'Well, I have played in concerts that have been filmed, including Germany, and I have never had this kind of problem.' This produced the instant retort, 'Will you give ze money back?' Pinchas had his wallet in his breast pocket. It had no money in it but he took it out, waved it confidently and said, 'Yes, I will give you, personally, the money back.' This produced a further response, 'It's not a question of money. It's a question of taste.' Pinchas, now angry, replied with, 'Well, my friend, if it's a matter of taste, I must say that you have very bad taste.' That produced a deciding round of applause. The concert went ahead, we filmed it and we were saved from bankruptcy by a worryingly narrow margin.

The silver lining to this story is that my crew continued filming during the whole exchange and the material which they shot gave a gloriously unexpected and very effective sequence and change of direction to our film. It also gave us our very appropriate title: *Pinchas Zukerman: Here to Make Music.*

That is one of the occasions on which I learned that it can be exceedingly unwise to presume that we know what is going to happen next in the making of a film – another echo of the Arabic proverb: 'He who foretells the future tells lies. Even when he gets it right.'

On the following day, a leading Munich newspaper, in entertainingly hostile mood, reported the events (translation follows):

Zukerman, wie im Filmstudio...Eiligst trat ein Mitglied des englischen Kamerateams vor. In perfektem Deutsch obwohl er behauptete, kein Wort Deutsch gelernt zu haben, schmeichelte er den Anwesenden mit dem Hinweis, man hätte bei diesen Filmaufnahmen gerade München vor London den Vorzug gegeben.

Das Lokalpatriotische Zuckerstückchen wurde mit Dank angenommen.

Zukerman as in a film studio.

A member of the English camera team presented himself, in the greatest haste, and in perfect German, although he claimed never to have studied a word of it, flattered those present with the announcement that he had chosen Munich, even before London, to make this film. This sugarplum was received by the local patriots with thanks.

What the local patriots gave us in return has generated smiles in many parts of the world since then. We had survived the most dangerous moment of our existence and by a slender thread. If we had not been able to film that concert it is very likely that Allegro Films would not have lasted. But, what doesn't kill you makes you stronger, or so they say.

The drama and the danger pushed the camaraderie that already existed between all of us onto a higher level than before. It was also a glorious proof of my relationship with Pinchas which has been distinguished by the qualities of warmth and generosity – on both sides – right from the start. That trust and affection saved us on that evening and continues to this day.

23

Itzhak Perlman

I know I played every note!

Confusion, polio, Toby Perlman, duos with Pinchas Zukerman, generous recognition, the Perlman Music Program

We could not make a film about Pinchas Zukerman without making one about Itzhak Perlman – for a number of good reasons, quite aside from their extraordinary musical talents. From a film maker's point of view, high on the list, was the astonishing amount of public confusion about who was who, and we thought that with the power of film and television, we could do something about that.

The origins of the confusion are not far to seek: both are violinists, both were born in Israel, both studied at the Juilliard School, both won the Leventritt Award and both lived at 173 Riverside Drive, New York. The extent of the confusion was, nevertheless, genuinely surprising because they are so unmistakably different both in appearance and bearing, starting with the fact that one of them has to walk with the aid of crutches and the other does not – a difference, one would think, hardly likely to go unnoticed. The high point of that curious confusion came when one of them was being harangued by a passionate fan, telling him how much better he was than the other, only to discover that he was talking to the wrong one – an event which caused much merriment at 173 Riverside Drive.

Itzhak Perlman contracted polio at the age of four and a half and it has left several life-long legacies but, as I say in the film, it takes more than that to stop talent of this calibre. In the event Itzhak has forged one of the top musical careers of our time. The grace with which he comes to terms with the difficulties is one of the threads of our film, not baldly stated but quietly observed in the way that film can do so tellingly.

In conversation Itzhak is impressively open about his disability – easy-going and accepting – with no scrap of embarrassment or rancour, although the world does make it difficult at times. When that happens the weight quite often falls on his wife, Toby, but she too rises to it with impressively good humour. In the film she recalls air hostesses asking, 'Does he take sugar' and other similar moments. Toby and Itzhak have learned how to teach embarrassment to smile.

These are the very virtues that Itzhak gratefully acknowledges and praises in his parents. He attributes much of the happy relationship which he has established with his public to the open, honest and practical way in which his parents dealt with the problems of his disability – and what they taught him by their attitude.

At one point, quite early in the film, I ask, 'How often do you fall down?' He answers: 'Well, I don't mind falling down. What I don't like is *almost* falling down. That's the worst, because that gets your adrenaline going like mad and I say "Dammit! You should have fallen down. I almost fell down. Fall down already. Either do something or don't do it!" '

He was quick to acknowledge the effects of the film and the impact on his career: He called me from China, on his first visit there and said, 'My public is not the same in any country where that film has not been shown.' The warmth and generosity of spirit touched all of us.

I Know I Played Every Note rocketed around the world on prime-time television slots bringing Itzhak into the lives of millions of people. And so, naturally, we shot a few extensions to our story: the Brahms violin concerto with the Philharmonia Orchestra conducted by Lawrence Foster, the E major and D minor Bach Partitas, shot live at a BBC lunch-time concert in St John's, Smith Square, London and two Duo films with Pinchas Zukerman shot at a concert which we arranged, expressly for filming, in the Royal College of Music in London. The audience was composed almost entirely of musicians – all of them in transports of delight, reflecting that particular sense of fun which can inhabit both performers and audiences on rare and unforgettable occasions.

No words about Itzhak are complete without singing the praises of Toby. When she was a student, also studying the violin, she fell in love with Itzhak Perlman and, apart from a short *entr'acte* when he dallied briefly with another student – and which Toby describes lightheartedly in the film – they have been together ever since.

Aside from the not inconsiderable labours of managing one of the biggest careers in music today they have produced five children who have, in turn, produced twelve grandchildren for Toby and Itzhak. They remain a close-knit family and circulate ever-growing family photographs at the end of each year – smiling testaments to a continuing happiness.

We were lucky to be there in the developing years when so much was new and so much was happening. We did things which had not been possible before, for many reasons, one of which was television's readiness to take more chances than it does today. It gave more time to classical music than it does now. It was a special time in music itself. As Itzhak says of *The Trout* in our film *Jacqueline du Pré: A Gift Beyond Words*, 'I think *The Trout* film is a wonderful little piece of history. It captured a real musical time that I don't know exists anymore.'

In the spirit of those glorious times we began a new project: to make a film about the Perlman Music Program, their summer music camp on Shelter Island, about 100 miles from New York. We started but sadly we could not find the funding to complete it.

Itzhak and Toby and The Perlman Music Program continue to inspire talented young musicians and generate a sense of purpose and gratitude in them which has a real influence in the world of music. I can still hear John Denison's voice backstage after the performance of Schubert's *Trout Quintet* at the Queen Elizabeth Hall:

'Bravo, Ishtak (sic) well done!'

24

Origins

*The bored child, King Edward VII School, Michaelhouse,
petty restrictions, the Padre and his wife,
the devout Rector, the science test*

Daniel Barenboim once said to me, 'When we were making the films the process seemed tiresome but looking back at what we produced, we see something entirely different.' His remark prompted me to look back at how it had all started.

Kindergarten was fun. The teachers liked me and were kind to me. They left me with two enduring memories. The first was of lying flat on the floor, learning, under instruction, how to write my name for the first time – and the amazing discovery that it contained eleven letters. A happy moment, well remembered.

The second is more complicated. The Kindergarten inmates were all assembled one morning and given a lecture on the grave dangers lurking in some brilliant red berries which grew temptingly in the back garden and which somebody had apparently been picking. The berries were said to be extremely poisonous and we were instructed not to pick them, not even to touch them, and to report anybody seen doing so.

At the first break following this intriguing announcement I saw, to my amusement, a row of about ten bottoms belonging to members of the class, all elevated on desks and peering through a high-level window at the back of the classroom – intent on detecting illegal activity.

It was obvious to me that nothing was ever going to happen in front of that array of enquiring bottoms. More than that it seemed to me that since what they were doing was so unlikely to achieve anything at all, I should draw attention to the silliness of it. I went directly to the Garden of Eden, armed with a page from my exercise book to ensure that I did not actually touch the forbidden fruit, ostentatiously picked a berry and returned with my prize to the classroom.

I was reported to the authorities, with bubbling excitement. On being asked by the head teacher to explain my wicked doings I told her exactly how and why it had all happened. Kindness prevailed. I was understood and pardoned with some half suppressed smiles thrown in for good measure. I was lucky. There must have been some warnings and advice attached but I can remember nothing of them and it was only later, when I saw terrible things being done to sensitive young people who trod innocently on the tail of authority, that I realized just how lucky I had been.

It was also the start, although I did not know it at the time, of the discovery of just how important truly gifted teachers can be in the development of our lives and just how few and far between are those wonderful beings. In all my years at school I encountered only four of real quality. Those four still glow, radiant and beckoning, in my memory: my kindergarten teacher whose name has long been lost in the dust of a hyper-active life; then came Kitty Oldroyd, who had also taught my father and who was an angel in every aspect of the classroom, followed by Piet Barnard and Fanie Gouws both of whom taught me Afrikaans and were kind to me when kindness was much needed. Fanie also introduced me to the mysteries of opera and Lieder and to the magic of Lotte Lehmann but I feel that I owe most to Kitty Oldroyd who was kindness, feminine warmth and wisdom personified and who tried, so valiantly, so diligently, so patiently but unsuccessfully, to teach me how to work.

The cause of the problem was that by the age of eleven I was already a 'Bored Child' but a bored child in a South Africa where that concept was apparently not yet known and most certainly not respected. As a result I dropped, in a dramatically short space of time, from top of the class to somewhere very near the bottom of it and

Kitty Oldroyd wrote her great lines in my final report, 'He has the capacity to be a fine student and a fine man but he must learn the meaning of WORK.' I had no work ethic. I did everything for fun.

The happiness that I had enjoyed in my Kindergarten days was rapidly eroded when I entered King Edward VII School in Johannesburg., a process exacerbated by a surprising event. One morning every pupil in the school sat the same Cattell Intelligence Test – a thousand boys, aged between seven and seventeen. When the papers were checked mine scored the third highest from the top, a fact divulged to my mother in the hope that it would help her to get me started on learning how to work. When I graduated to the high school not long afterwards, that result went with me and I was labelled lazy – not a good reputation to have in a fiercely competitive environment.

My situation in the King Edward VII High School was further complicated by the fact that my father's name appeared on the imposing oak panels of the Great Hall as both Head Boy and Victor Ludorum. He was known also for having played cricket for the Transvaal while still at school and for having had only one eye from the age of seven. All of this was thought a bit too much by some of my peers. It generated a hostility that was new to me.

Sadly, I fed the flames because my father was such a lovely fellow, so unusual, so caring, so loving, so enlivening, so encouraging, so engaging and so unmistakably heroic that I felt obliged to explain all this to my jealous classmates. The effect, unsurprisingly, was negative – an early manifestation of a trusting naïveté that would land me in trouble repeatedly in the next few years.

During all of my King Edward VII time I had one great friend. His name was Allen Brooks. He was as instantly likeable as anybody I have ever met and he was a spectacularly gifted sportsman.

My father had once been given a practice cricket bat. The blade was about half the width of a normal bat, obviously designed to develop accuracy but a very dangerous companion at the crease. The weight was the same as a normal bat and to compensate for the reduced width it was twice as thick. That meant that if one managed to hit the ball in the sweet spot of the bat, it travelled a great deal faster and a great deal further than the equivalent stroke would have achieved with the standard willow blade.

I gave up using it in the nets because I dared not risk too many glanced strokes which would appear incompetent and might be taken as showing off. Unsuccessful showing off was mercilessly mocked in that competitive climate.

Allen Brooks was different. He was a real hero. He not only took the bat into the nets but he also used it in official matches. We very soon became best friends in the way that only the young can know. I gave him the bat. That friendship was the happiest event of my single year at King Edward VII High School.

Unfortunately, my father, with the very best of intentions, had put my name down, very early on in my existence, for what he and many others thought was the best school in South Africa, a boarding school called Michaelhouse planted in the Natal countryside where, between the ages of 13 and 17, I was seriously ill at ease in a rigidly controlled society that did not suit me at all. With a strongly democratic Norwegian father and grandfather behind me, I rebelled against what I saw as petty and frankly unintelligent restrictions where infringement merited what the organization itself called flogging, a brutal practice.

I never suffered from that physical maltreatment, I was too careful to avoid it but the sort of restrictions that were imposed can inflict subtler wounds. I knew it, I saw it and it prompted me to become active in developing opposition to it amongst my peers and their parents. There was not only the barbaric practice of excessive canings but many other restrictive regulations which were all designed to reinforce hierarchical domination and to generate a sense of inferiority in the juniors.

Among them there were two that amused me greatly: a prohibition on shutting the lavatory door, regardless of what one might be doing there, and a prohibition on wearing swimming costumes in the swimming pool. Nakedness was *de rigueur* and I remember seeing one of my schoolmates with extensive, severe red and blue bruise marks not only on his bottom but right round his ribs and up to his chest. The sight was shocking and it looked as though the administrator of the punishment had done it deliberately – an unusually heavily built prefect, well-known for his sporting achievements. He could not have made a misjudgement of that kind by mistake.

Most of the petty restrictions would have been laughable, if they had not conveyed hurt. At breakfast, for example, the seating was arranged according to seniority with the most junior at the tail end. It was the duty of the youngest to serve the porridge and to ensure the removal of all the frequently occurring lumps. In the event that a single lump arrived with the seniors an order was passed down, 'Fork the kak.' Kak was the pejorative term for juniors, used on all possible occasions. The boy sitting next to the unfortunate fellow who had served the porridge was obliged to stick a fork in the bottom of the unfortunate server and in the event that he was deemed to make too light of it, he received, in turn, the same treatment. I watched all of this with amazement and disgust.

In the spirit of my pioneering ancestors I fuelled a campaign of complaint during the first two years but was smart enough not to confront the management directly. Schooling normally ran for four years with the pupils divided sharply into Juniors for the first two years and Seniors thereafter. During the first years I was known and cautiously appreciated by many of the others for my critical views but then a strange and totally unexpected lesson fell on me.

At the end of the second year we all went home happily for the Christmas holidays, rejoicing in the fact that we were escaping from the idiocies imposed on juniors. When we came back in January I was shocked by the rapidity with which my peers began insisting on their new privileges and being unkind to the juniors in exactly the same way that had so incensed us during our first two years.

For the rest of my time there I stuck to my guns and continued to advocate the need for more equality and more intelligence but slowly and steadily my maverick views estranged me from most of the school with the welcome exceptions of Ralph Morkel and Dick Ridgway who became much appreciated friends in a hostile world.

One of my clearest memories of school years was a surprisingly revealing moment with Ralph. He was taller than most of us and stronger, both attributes which he put to good effect on the rugby field. One day, in a crowded corridor, he pushed me out of his way.

My Norwegian blood boiled up and I gave him a short, sharp and decidedly pointed jab in the ribs. His face fell a mile. I had not seen a transformation that was anything quite like that before, neither in its speed nor in its message. I was amazed.

His pushy gesture had not been nasty. He was not a nasty fellow, he was a very likeable fellow, but he was a very pushy rugby player and he was not accustomed to letting anybody stand in his way. His attitude towards me changed radically in that moment. As a direct consequence of it he became my best friend at Michaelhouse and we maintained a warm contact until he died recently.

Among his virtues he liked to listen to Johann Strauss's Blue Danube Waltz. He was also a good boxer and said to me, in another revealing moment, that he would like to go into the ring to the accompanying strains of the Blue Danube. He said that he could not imagine losing with that music behind him. I was instrumental in helping to develop his existing appreciation of some of the other virtues of music.

Aside from Ralph Morkel and Dick Ridgway my best companionship and greatest solace at Michaelhouse came from William Wordsworth, Samuel Taylor Coleridge, George Gordon Byron, Percy Bysshe Shelley, John Keats, and Alfred Lord Tennyson, all in a book called *Eight Poets* which I cherish to this day.

One of the biggest Michaelhouse surprises for me was the behaviour of the resident priest who, while charged with taking care of our spiritual well-being, seemed to me to be consciously hostile. I remember a school concert in which he appeared on the stage and – being significantly lacking in artistic talent – resorted to two cheap tricks for the entertainment of his audience, tricks which I have not forgotten.

One of the students was a painfully shy fellow whose family name was De'Ath. Quite early on, his peers named him Dubsy Death, dubs being the school slang word for the lavatories. As a result, this gentle, sensitive fellow, who needed all the help he could possibly get, had to spend four years of his young life known to his peers as Lavatory Death. Everything about him called for sympathy and encouragement but he received none from the priest who, at a school concert, publicly made vicious fun of his Dubsy Death nickname, in front of 400 of his peers. I was shocked. Then, just as I was reeling from the awfulness of what I had just heard, the priest turned his fire on me with the words, 'And we have a special prize for Christopher Nupen for giving the best imitation of Keith Miller that we have seen this season except that he never took any wickets.' In fact I was the opening bowler for the second eleven and twice took a wicket with the first ball of a match. The priest, of course, knew all of that. It was my first direct encounter with verbal sadism.

Amazingly, our Padre had a very sympathetic and very pretty wife. We often wondered how she had come to accept him because she seemed to be his opposite. She was a kind, helpful and gentle soul; perhaps another unhappy childhood striving to remedy past hurt. On one unfortunate day, three senior boys, at least one of them a prefect, were talking about the considerable virtues of this most desirable woman. They were close to a thick, tall hedge unaware that the Padre himself was eavesdropping on the other side of the bushes. The man of religion took a heavy complaint to the Rector insisting on the severest punishment possible.

The commonly accepted standard for canings was between one and the famous 'Six of the best'. The grapevine had it that the Rector, who declared himself a man of God on all suitable occasions, hit each one of those boys ten times – with the others within earshot. Unimaginable!

Those boys were at the age when young human males need education about the glorious mysteries of sex, not caning. They insisted that they were not being vulgar or disparaging. On the contrary, they were full of admiration but sex speaks loud and temptingly at that age and they talked as boys talk, particularly in an all-male community – with almost no female contact at all.

A somewhat similar tale concerns a fellow pupil called John Montgomery. He was a gifted scholar, particularly in history. I, by contrast, was probably the worst student of history that the school had ever seen. This was at least partly because of the nature and the manner of my history teacher, a fellow called Hugh Carey who was also my Housemaster. In Mr Carey's presence my ability to absorb lessons so quickly in English, Afrikaans, Geography, Geometry and Trigonometry deserted me entirely.

The last of the matriculation exams that year was history, just a few days before the end of term, and I knew that I was in serious trouble. I then learned from John Montgomery that he was planning to hide himself away in the clock tower on the night before the final history exam because he wanted to secure a Distinction. I asked if I could join him. During that night I studied six and a half of John Montgomery's essays and I was astonished at my luck when I discovered that I could use four of them in the final history exam on the following day. I received a very mediocre mark but I passed and I most certainly would not have done so had it not been for John Montgomery.

But the story does not end there. On the last day of term many parents came to collect their sons, my father among them. His fame as a sporting hero meant that his arrival caused some stir. He was greeted repeatedly with 'Hello Buster' by other parents wherever we went. I was with him from the moment he arrived but, towards lunchtime, I was given a whispered message that Hugh Carey wanted to see me in his rooms. I asked why and received the news that he had somehow got wind of our late-night studies, had called John Montgomery to his rooms and flogged him for his wicked doings. That was on the last day of John's school life, within three hours of his leaving forever. I wondered what kind of a mind could do that in those circumstances. I ignored Mr. Carey's invitation to see him in his rooms. I never saw him again.

Some weeks later a registered letter arrived at my home in Johannesburg. By another of my life-saving coincidences, I happened to be in the garden, met the postman and signed for the package. It included a letter addressed to my father which I kept in a safe place until my next visit to the lavatory where it served its only possible useful purpose. I now wish that I had kept that letter as evidence of Mr Carey's doings.

I distanced myself both physically and mentally from that unhappy place for sixty years. But then, suddenly, from an Old Boys newsletter, I heard that the school has improved itself beyond all recognition and is now a true paragon of all the appropriate virtues: considerably expanded academic curricula and a vast range of sporting and leisure activities. I rejoice with those who are there now and am truly sorry that I missed it all. I lament for those who were there in my time in a much bleaker landscape. It was not a place for artistic sensibility or critical intelligence.

The saddest day of my four years at Michaelhouse came like a thunderbolt. In the middle of a science test I was summoned to the Rector's study. With the most perfunctory of warnings that he had bad news for me, he announced that Allen Brooks had shot himself and was dead.

Something happened inside me which was beyond my control, beyond my ability to understand. The Rector's sentence had scarcely ended when I felt tears streaming from my eyes, well before my mind had grasped the import of what I was hearing. I shot out of the chair, out of the room and into the quadrangle. I saw shooting tears hitting the ground ahead of me as I went. I could not understand those tears either. It was the strangest sensation that I have ever had.

Behaviour of this kind was not what was expected of pupils in that rigorously controlled society but the Rector had to do something and so he followed me into the quadrangle where I had stopped short, transfixed by a startling brightness that etched every line and corner of the quad into my befuddled brain. The shock of this event was totally new to me. The Rector asked if I would like to spend some time in the garden. I was unable to answer. I shook my head and ran away from him, straight back to the science test. He did not follow.

Then an extraordinary thing happened. Although there was very little time left to complete the test, or perhaps because of it, my mind worked with a clarity that it had not known before. I seemed to have instant recall of everything that I had ever been told in science classes from day one. I wrote furiously with tears still splattering from eyes that could not understand them and blurring the page. I scored 100% in that test. I had not done anything remotely like that before and have never done anything like it since.

To this day I do not understand it, except to say that my body or heart or soul had understood something that my head could not yet grasp, even though I knew that I had lost the closest friend I had ever had. I heard Tennyson's great cry:

Deep as first love, and wild with all regret;
O Death in Life, the days that are no more.

25

Michael Nupen

The accident, the triple first, Head of Politics,
Rick Turner, the banning order, the murder, Manfred Gräter,
Respighi, *A Dream of Italy*, the legacy

•

My first encounter with my brother – before he had a name – was when my mother took me in her black Chevrolet coupé to the nursing home where she had given birth just a few days earlier. I remember two nurses putting my new brother in a cradle on the back seat. My mother introduced the new arrival and said that it was important to welcome him into the family. She was good at such things.

The age difference was four years and four days. Not a good gap, especially when the older one reaches teenage. Thirteen-year-old boys do not have much in common with nine-year-olds. To make the differences more pronounced I was the active one, Michael was more contemplative, as time was to prove so abundantly and so fruitfully.

Apart from the age difference, our childhood was normal enough until my parents decided to send me to Michaelhouse, an institution decidedly ill-equipped – in those days at least – to receive and nurture intelligent, questioning and sensitive small boys. I advised my parents not to send my brother to that school under any circumstances and, happily, they listened to me and believed me.

But sadly, a great misfortune was soon to befall Michael. When he found his first girlfriend he asked our mother for permission to drive the girl just once around the block in the Chevrolet. As both Michael and I had driven extensively on our uncle's farm in the Transvaal, and the block to be circled was in a quiet suburb, my mother agreed, insisting that it should be just once, carefully and slowly. Half way around the block, another vehicle, driven at high speed, crashed into them and then cannoned into a brick wall. The driver died.

For many years Michael visited the dead man's mother regularly, doing everything he could to help and console her. They became good friends – a tribute to both of them.

Unsurprisingly, Michael's academic studies collapsed under the weight of the anxiety which these events generated and Michael plummeted to the bottom of his class. His teachers warned my parents that he would not pass the matriculation examination which he was due to take in two years' time.

The accident and its impact on Michael's studies were exceedingly bad news for my father who, to make matters more complicated, was very much in the limelight as a national sporting hero and an honest lawyer to whom many turned for guidance.

My father, bless his courage, his intelligence and his practical good sense, took Michael to a brilliantly gifted teacher, Isaac Kriel, who ran a tutorial college in Johannesburg called Damelin. In a little over a year Michael passed the matriculation exam with flying colours. A few years later, in 1959, he scored a Triple First at the University of the Witwatersrand in Johannesburg, in Moral Philosophy, Political Theory and Government, and History of Music. I remember a prominently placed newspaper article headed, 'Cricketer's son scores Academic Hat-Trick.'

In 1961-2, still at the University of the Witwatersrand, Michael completed an Honours degree in Political Theory and Government followed by an MA in 1966. He then went to the University of Heidelberg in Germany, where he followed courses on the Frankfurt School. Subsequently, he returned to South Africa to teach and to write his thesis on Heidegger.

In the words of his fellow-philosopher, Professor Andrew Nash,

> He soon became a celebrated and controversial figure, known as a brilliant lecturer and public speaker. Nupen articulated large and potentially life-changing themes, then and throughout his life, with great erudition and panache. In the opinion of his colleagues, he was the most gifted social philosopher in South Africa for as long as we could remember.*

In 1969 Michael was made Head of the newly-established Department of Politics at the University of Natal in Durban where he is said to have given powerful accounts of Nietzsche as an important forbear for Heidegger. He also headed a selection committee which appointed the renowned academic and anti-Apartheid activist, Rick Turner, to the Department – an event which was to have far reaching consequences.

Michael and Rick Turner became the closest of friends and colleagues, and formed a powerful and influential partnership. According to Professor Andrew Nash, their work together was to have a significant influence on the developing political conscience of South Africa.

> Together, Nupen and Turner played a major role in what became known as 'The Durban Moment' in South African politics with Turner focused on engagement and activism and Nupen on philosophical questions. Many of their students were active in the independent union movement that emerged from the Durban strikes of 1973.**

Together they provided a critique of capitalist society and culture which was new and unexpected to white students of that generation. They brought European thought to Africa and brought white students and black workers together in a way that had previously been unimaginable.

Rick Turner's wife, Foszia is of mixed race and so official marriage to Rick would have been illegal and criminally punishable under the Apartheid regime. As a result they made an Islamic marriage which was not officially recognized. The government nevertheless placed Rick under house arrest for his political activities and for what they considered his subversive influence on the students.

The banning order lasted for five crippling years until, early in the morning on the 8th of January 1978, shortly before it was due to expire, a man, who has never been identified, came to the window of Rick's daughters' bedroom and when Rick went there to investigate suspicious sounds, the intruder shot him dead in front of his two young daughters, Jann and Kim aged 12 and 9.

---

* In Memoriam: Michael Nupen, by Prof. Andrew Nash, Dept. of Political Studies, University of Cape Town, SA.

**Ibid. page 1

Michael was with me in London when the news came through. We were in the kitchen at 29 Quickswood. His distress was appalling. I will not forget it. It seemed to me that it re-activated the scars of his earlier disaster and I saw his spirit sink. He and Rick had complemented each other perfectly in a moment of inestimable significance for their country and the high point of Michael's professional existence had lost an essential element. He was never quite the same again.

A little over a year later an equal tragedy fell on me. On 27th May 1979 Diana died of cancer, two days after her thirty-ninth birthday. I had no idea that despair could penetrate so deep. I was lost in a black hole in which I barely stirred for a whole year. Twelve months after her death Diana's handbag was still where she had left it next to the bed.

In a gesture of huge generosity Michael came to live with me in London, to keep me company and to help run Allegro Films. My Professor of Philosophy brother, with touching good grace, did much of the day-to-day management. He also did most of the cooking. The memory of those gestures remains with me.

In an undisguised attempt to get me going again, Manfred Gräter, Head of Music at WDR Television in Cologne, asked us to make a film about Respighi. With Respighi no longer alive and without my exuberant musician friends in front of our cameras, I doubted our ability to make it work. I remember saying to Michael, 'We can't just go and shoot Italy and photographs of Respighi'.

I was slow to respond to Manfred but with Michael's energetic encouragement, we worked our way into it. Michael did the research, both historical and musicological, and, speaking good Italian, struck up a warm friendship with the composer's wife, the indomitable and long-living Elsa Respighi. Sustained by that friendship and Michael's research, we made *Ottorino Respighi: A Dream of Italy*. It proved difficult and, notwithstanding my earlier conviction that we could not 'just go and film Italy', we went there three times to photograph its glories.

When the Respighi film was completed, we decided to take it to Johannesburg to show it to SABC Television and to our mother. The SABC arranged a screening for us, for our friends and for SABC staff to assess it for possible broadcast. As the lights came up at the end of the screening Michael and I, on opposite sides of the room, both got up simultaneously, turned, and went to our mother. Her closest friend, Yetta Stone, said that it was the most touching thing she had ever seen. Of course the unhappy background events were known to Yetta in all their detail.

Respighi had shown us a new path and given us some new confidence. We owed Manfred Gräter a deep debt of gratitude. It enabled us to follow with films about Brahms, Schönberg, Wittgenstein (entirely Michael's idea), Schubert and the complex relationship between the Jews and German music in *We Want the Light* – a film which was extremely difficult to make, needed a great deal of invention and, to our surprise, ended up winning a number of international prizes.

Film making of this kind is always a voyage of discovery – with an uncertain outcome – and frequently calls for a great deal of courage. Michael's courage both physical and mental was a great help and, on one occasion, actually saved his life.

He often sought solace in the sea and went swimming regularly when he was in Durban and Cape Town. One day, in a place on the Cape coast where he had swum safely before, he was suddenly swept out to a considerable distance by a fast running offshore current.

After battling, unsuccessfully, for more than three hours he saw a fishing boat approaching and then suddenly veering away. He called out for help and was told by the fishermen to keep as far as possible away from them because they had sharks following them. At the same time they pointed to an area where the current was flowing in the opposite direction. Michael followed their advice but it took him a further hour to reach land – a fitting testimony to his physical and mental courage and strength.

Ten years after Rick Turner's death Michael was able to write two tributes to Rick's legacy: one was a contribution to a philosophical conference held at the University of the Western Cape in January 1988, and the other a Turner Memorial lecture given at the University of Natal in Durban in April of that same year, 'A virtuoso piece' in the opinion of Andrew Nash.

The exceptional powers of his mind, allied to a truly astonishing memory, plus a real gift for research and his ability to speak flawless academic German, fluent Spanish and passable Italian meant that every film that he worked on achieved a distinguished and unusual result. These are the titles of those films:

Ottorino Respighi: A Dream of Italy

Elegies for the Deaths of Three Spanish Poets – Antonio Machado, Miguel Hernandez and Federico García Lorca

The Language of the New Music – Arnold Schoenberg and Ludwig Wittgenstein

Tchaikovsky's Women

Franz Peter Schubert: The Greatest Love and the Greatest Sorrow

We Want the Light

Michael spent most of his days immersed in music and in the graphic arts, where he had, again in the words of Andrew Nash, 'Compendious knowledge and formidable powers of criticism and interpretation.' He also dedicated himself for years to intensive study of the most advanced contemporary European philosophical thought – ending with Lacan.

Deeply depressed and alone, he had said for quite a while that when he felt that he had understood Lacan he would leave this world in much the same way as Arthur Koestler and his wife had done and that is exactly what happened.

When the time came he took a carefully prepared overdose which he had carried around with him for years. A close friend, sensing what was coming, found him forever still, but smiling. Michael had asked that his ashes be given to the sea off Cape Point .

The world is a poorer place when a spirit so individual, so engaging, so astonishingly erudite – and which had worked so hard to put its knowledge of the world and of human thought to beneficial use – is suddenly no more. To give an idea of the inner world of my super-gifted brother, here are some words which he sent me, unannounced, on a Sunday evening some years ago:

Der Segen von Johann Sebastian Bach.
(The Benediction of Johann Sebastian Bach).

Christoff, dear Brother,

I am going to bed tranquil and serene. I want you to know this because I know you love me and worry about me in my present frustrated state.

The cause of this happy, balanced, being is none other than Johann Sebastian Bach. I am convinced that, if you want

(1) to experience the awesome power of music as a pure phenomenon;

(2) to have an experience which exercises and by so doing delights the mind and puts it at rest ;

(3) to experience the rhythm of the life force;

(4) to traverse every emotion known to man and transcend all that is negative and limiting, opening a perspective on what is liberatory sub specie aeternitatis;

(5) to experience gratitude and wonder at an instancing of complete order and coherence;

(6) in short to extend and integrate the mind and the emotions (and they are one, not two) totally,

why then, you only have to approach (and I use the word advisedly because nobody can seize hold of it), the music of the supreme musical genius (and, I sometimes think, because he is so German, the greatest German who ever lived), and perhaps the purest, most noble spirit who ever lived, Bach- (or, as Beethoven said he should have been called, Meer.)

For a couple of years now I have been studying with the aid of innumerable recordings and the Dover edition scores, the sonatas and partitas for violin and for keyboard instruments. The supreme alchemist transforms European dance forms (but let nobody say that they are simple or humble in themselves; they tap into limitless strength) and transforms them into cognitive/emotional structures - at once so audaciously artificial and so unbearably direct in import - that go to the centre of life itself. *Du muss Dein Leben aendern* Rilke said. I honestly believe that, if anyone were truly able cognitively/emotionally to experience Bach's music completely, he would be in what the Christians call a state of grace, that is to say that his life would, at a stroke, be utterly transformed.

Modern neurological research has shown the primacy of emotion over cognition in human thinking. It could have learned it two centuries ago from Bach. More importantly it could have learned that emotion needs an infinitely complex cognitive elaboration in order to live. Surrender to the impulse without trying to follow through its articulation and you arrive at a music of effect without a cause (a phrase of either Schoenberg's or Adorno's)

Enough my dearest Christoff. You will understand these ravings because, as Vova [Ashkenazy] acutely said, you have a pure spirit.

With my love,

M

26

Hayat (Nieves de Madariaga)

Franco, Van Gogh, Tchaikovsky, the professor,
the telephone lines

•

The Minister of Education in the Spanish Republic was the much respected and much loved writer and philosopher Salvador de Madariaga. Unhappily the bloody arrival of El Caudillo, Generalisimo Franco, forced him to flee for his life most urgently. Had he stayed in Spain, he would certainly have fallen victim to Franco. By contrast he was welcomed at Oxford where he remained for the rest of his days.

Don Salvador had two singularly bright daughters who grew up in Oxford, Nieves and her sister Isabel. Both became noted writers, each speaking several languages at a professional level. I knew nothing about the daughters but I knew a fair amount about Don Salvador because of my interest in the Spanish Civil War. Segovia encouraged me to make a film about Don Salvador but, sadly, I could not raise the money.

Then, in London, in 1987, I was invited to supper by Diana Burlton who had been my first girlfriend in London. She wanted me to meet several people including Salvador's daughter, Nieves. During the supper, I was asked by one of the guests, a German professor, to describe my current project. She had heard that I was planning to make a film about Tchaikovsky – a subject which she had studied.

I presented my ideas, in quite some detail, and noticed that Nieves de Madariaga was looking at me with increasing intensity from the other side of the table. She had deeply enquiring eyes and an equally enquiring eagle nose. The intensity of her gaze disturbed me and I felt that I had gone over the top – again – a long-ingrained habit. I brought my discourse to a rapid close.

The professor announced that I was on a completely wrong track, that I should do some serious study of Pyotr Ilyich Tchaikovsky and revise my plans accordingly. The combination of this attack and the seeming ferocity of the gaze from the other side of the table, shut me up completely but as we retired to the drawing room an entertaining surprise stopped me in my tracks. The German woman had gone first with some of the other guests. I was the last to leave, immediately behind Nieves de Madariaga, who suddenly stopped, turned, and whispered to me, 'Ignore everything that woman is telling you, stick to your convictions and stick to your guns.'

One of my most valuable, most interesting and most stimulating friendships was born in that moment. Nieves, who had held a leading position in the Food and Agricultural Organisation in Rome, lived in Italy, near Cortona. The friendship grew so fast by mail and telephone that I drove, several times from London to Cortona to visit her. On my first visit I had been there only a day and a half when she suggested that we record our conversations as a first step towards making a book about my experiences and the artists I have worked with. I went immediately into Cortona and bought a tape recorder. The recordings which we made during the next two days became the first stirrings of this book.

Nieves did not much like her given name, with its reminders of the snow and the cold, and so she adopted, instead, the Sufi name Hayat, which means life. It was the right name for her – she was vital in everything that she did, but above all in the speed and resilience of her mind.

I learned much from her. I called her whenever I had a problem – language problems in particular. She published work in English, Spanish, Italian and French. She was also a very helpful critic of my films in their early stages. I remember sending her a rough cut of the Schubert film and receiving, in return such a paean of praise that I could not believe it was justified. I called her and said, 'I fear that you are judging it at the level of its best intentions rather than its actual achievements.' She replied, with startling speed, 'Christopher, have you not yet learned that a thing's best intentions are its essence?'

She called me at 7:30 in the morning on almost every day of the last ten years of her life. She died, listening to me playing the guitar for her in the summer of 2003. I had often been surprised to find that I played better for her than for anyone else, including Segovia. I should not have been surprised: friendship and music are happy companions and it was Hayat who taught me that nearness is not experienced in space but at the centre of the heart.

I miss Hayat – and always will. Here is her own account of that first meeting, written some time later:

First Encounter

At dinner, in the house of a warmly welcoming mutual friend I was holding an interesting conversation on one side of the table when I was drawn to the face opposite me, your laughing blue eyes and widespread beard. You were listening to your neighbour, an art historian, as I later heard, who insisted that if you were going to make a film about Tchaikovsky, you must make every effort to visit, in Russia, the places where Tchaikovsky had wandered. You explained that there were difficulties, particularly financial, and you might not be able to go, but your interlocutor insisted that your forthcoming film could not afford to do without those shots.

"Yes it could", I telegraphed to the still unknown but overflowing face, while still following my own conversation on my side of the table. The art historian continued to insist. I continued to flash my disagreement with her across the space between us. I was recalling a Dutch documentary film on Van Gogh in which every picture he painted was matched with a photograph of the exact spot, rippling water, reflected trees and all. And each photo, as it appeared, killed the painting. Then I remembered another 'Life of Van Gogh', a French one, 10 minutes of it, made exclusively of his paintings. Switching from picture to picture, gloriously light and tragically dark, we were lifted each time, as on a new wave, to new heights – or depths – of spirit.

'Don't listen,' I flashed across the intervening space. 'What she is telling you is wrong.' At that point you came around the table, crouched by my side and asked. 'Why are you looking at me so critically?' The as yet unknown you had picked up my conviction that it was not necessary for us to see the same leaves as Tchaikovsky had walked past, the piece of sward that he trod. As we left the dining room I encouraged you, quietly, to stand firm.

I could not know then what your film was really about – all your films are full of unexpected, imaginative touches – the way a carriage wheel went on turning in the air, the switches, like those in the Van Gogh film, from one portrait to another as we hear a few lines from a heart-rending letter, the swirl of dancing skirts, or three instruments on three chairs. None of which could be found in the places where your protagonist had walked.

This unspoken dialogue was the beginning of a mysterious friendship, made almost entirely of an absence of those trodden places, that literal grass, since we hardly ever meet, and which we owe to the blessed telephone lines that carry our sighs and chuckles and prolong the thoughts that come together as fast as they first crossed the space between us at that dinner table.

11. Diana Anne Wishart Baikie Nupen with our dog Huffi on our wedding day. Diana died of breast cancer on 27 May 1979, two days after her 39th birthday.

12. Our wedding day.

13. A characteristic Jackie moment while making Jacqueline du Pré and the Elgar Cello Concerto.

14. Rehearsing The Trout in Abbey Road Studios in 1966.

15. With Pinchas Zukerman and David Findlay in the courtyard of Munich's Hercules Hall, setting up to shoot an interview for Pinchas Zukerman: Here to make Music.

16. With Manfred Gräter, head of music at German television channel WDR. He coaxed us into making a film on Respighi which brought far-reaching changes to the nature and the future of Allegro Films.

17. My brother Michael, who came to rescue me and Allegro Films after the death of Diana and who helped us make the Respighi film.

18. With Elsa Respighi, wife of the composer, after showing her our film Ottorino Respighi: A Dream of Italy.

19. Being presented with the BAFTA gold mask by Richard Attenborough in 1979, for Elegies for the Deaths of Three Spanish Poets.

20. With the 101 year old Alice Sommer Herz, Theresienstadt survivor, pianist and star of our film Everything is a present – the Wonder and the Grace of Alice Sommer Herz.

21. Being presented by Michael Grade with the Jewish Cultural Award 2003/2004 for our film We Want the Light which looks at the fruitful but complex question of the Jews and German music.

22. Making Franz Peter Schubert – the Greatest Love and the Greatest Sorrow, 1994.

23. Caroline, having supper with me in Alsace. I took the photograph.

24. With Matthew Percival, Caroline's son, at his graduation in 1994.

25. Sporting my father's tails, with Caroline at the Ball to celebrate the 200th anniversary of Lord's Cricket Ground in 2014, photographed by Matthew.

26. The author by his long-term cameraman and great friend, David Findlay.

Huw Wheldon

A happy coincidence, Chicago,
Robert Anderson, Joan Harris, the 81st floor

•

About twenty years after we made the *Double Concerto* film, Huw Wheldon was invited to address the assembled dignitaries of the PBS Network on the 81st floor of the Standard Oil building in Chicago and to explain the BBC's successes with arts programming.

It was a fitting Wheldon setting. The 81st floor was an impressive enough address on its own but, to add spice to the occasion, a great wind was howling off the lake so that the very building itself seemed to sway in the gale, an experience somewhat unnerving to visitors but no surprise to the inhabitants of the windy city. We were assured that the building was designed to bend in the breeze.

It was my first visit to Chicago and the fact that Huw and I were both there on the same evening was pure chance; another seemingly impossible gift from the gods. I was there because the Chicago PBS station, WTTW, was planning to show four of our films with the group title of the *Here to Make Music* Series, under the sponsorship of the Atlantic Richfield oil company.

I had shown *The Trout* at the Aspen Institute when we were filming there for the Itzhak Perlman film and the student audience went wild – so much so that they asked me to show it again on the following day for those who had missed it and for those who missed some of the jokes because of the uproarious laughter. News of the excitement reached Mr Robert Anderson, the adventurous Chairman of Atlantic

Richfield who happened to be in Aspen and when we screened the film again on the following day, he came to see what all the fuss was about. Another very influential person, Mrs Joan Harris, came too. Together they arranged with WTTW, the Chicago station of the PBS Network, to put four of our films on the national Network under the sponsorship of Atlantic Richfield.

Pinchas Zukerman: Here to Make Music

Itzhak Perlman: Virtuoso Violinist. I know I played every note!

The Trout

Pinchas Zukerman and Itzhak Perlman, filmed during their memorable duo recital at the Royal College of Music in London.

Atlantic Richfield was later to say that the *Here to Make Music* Series produced the best feedback to any sponsorship in which the company had ever engaged, in any medium. That was the beginning of our discovery that the citizens of the United States are the most enthusiastic in the world about our work although they have seen so little of it. They are also the most articulate about their enthusiasms and yet it remains difficult to find sponsorship for classical music programming in the USA. We have succeeded only five times.

Huw Wheldon had been invited to talk to them because of the success of his Monitor arts series on the BBC. In his address, he likened television to book publishing and pointed to the vitality of the book scene in America – so evident in all the packed bookshops. But he pointed to a fundamental difference between the ways in which book publishing and television in America were addressing the same questions. He asked whether anyone present could imagine an American publisher commissioning Saul Bellow to write a novel and then sending a committee down to read the first chapter and tell him how to write the rest of the book. There was much laughter.

By contrast, stony silence greeted him when he said that in television, 'The only thing to do, not the *best* thing to do, but the *only* thing to do, is to find talented people and then let them have their heads. You will either have success or you will have failure or perhaps something in between, but if you interfere you are certain to land yourself with mediocrity'. He begged his audience to remember that the programme is king – all very welcome echoes of what Fellini had taught me.

Huw was never at a loss for the telling phrase when he needed one and, among many memorable moments that evening, he delivered himself of the following: 'I reckon that forty top quality ideas are born in the BBC every week but I can think of no week in the past 15 years that saw the broadcast of more than three top quality programmes – and that was a damned good week!'

At the tail end of his speech, out of pure generosity, and only because I happened by chance to be there, he referred to Laurence Gilliam giving the unknown Nupen his head in Siena and how he, Huw Wheldon, had heard the broadcast and invited the same Nupen to move to BBC Television. He went on to say that he did not wish to give the impression that life in the BBC was a bed of roses, quite the contrary. He said that the going was extremely tough and he assured all present that 'At least 40% of all the supposedly creative people in the BBC are there for no other purpose than to keep their bottoms warm on the radiators. It is not an easy life in the BBC,' he said, 'but Nupen and I, we are the ones who made it.'

He had no need to say that but it was a touching proof of the generous expansiveness of Huw Wheldon. Television will be forever indebted to him and so will I.

Nathan Mironovich Milstein

Master of Invention

Honesty, Ian Hunter, Chester Square, Isaac Stern,
the painful first finger, the Paganini ploy

•

Of how many people can it be said, legitimately, that honesty is their most distinguishing characteristic? I have so far met only two, Jacqueline du Pré and Nathan Mironovich Milstein, and it was very interesting to see how their honesty worked in the world.

Most of our deviations from strict honesty come from good intentions and the wish not to cause hurt but with Nathan Milstein the honesty was so authentic, so palpable and the source of it was so clean that he was able to say the most critical things imaginable without giving offence. I saw that happen several times. Jacqueline du Pré could do something similar on occasion.

I was introduced to Nathan by his agent, Sir Ian Hunter, who had asked me to produce and direct a television recital with Nathan and Georges Pludermacher in the Berwaldhallen in Stockholm. I said that I never shoot anything before getting to know the artists and making sure that they have the patience and the selflessness needed to accept the complicated disciplines and imperatives of filming.

Ian Hunter took me to Nathan's Chester Square home in London for our first meeting. I was captivated by a degree of quiet sure-footedness that was unusual. I accepted the invitation to produce and direct the recital. Not long afterwards, Nathan and I had a preparatory meeting at his home to talk about the dozens of things that needed to be agreed. The telephone rang. It was Isaac Stern who asked whether he could come over. Nathan declined saying that he was in the middle of working with Christopher.

'What are you doing with Christopher?'

'Planning a recital for television.'

'Did you see the film of Rostropovich on the television last night?'

'Yes.'

'What did you think?'

'Very bad.'

'Why?'

'Very poor artyistic arganization.'

That was all the reassurance I needed. I knew from that brief exchange that Nathan Milstein saw into the heart of things and I believed he would understand whatever we asked of him. We went ahead and shot the Berwaldhallen recital on the 17th of July 1986.

Nathan's performance was a revelation. I was amazed by his accuracy, his articulation, the storytelling quality of his interpretations and that great ingredient which we all recognize but cannot define, the expression of the artistic persona. I understood why the leading American critic, Harold C. Schonberg, had described Nathan as, 'Perhaps the most nearly perfect violinist of his time.' I felt privileged and grateful to Ian Hunter for the introduction.

Nathan was playing, I believe, as no other violinist had ever played at 82, but that was not all. He played with a seriously painful first finger on his left hand and was forced to adapt his fingerings during the concert to spare the finger – a remarkable feat made possible only because he had been doing exactly that, in mid-performance, all through his career, to the repeated astonishment of orchestral musicians.

I felt an urgent need to make an Allegro style portrait film with him and I made the proposal. Nathan refused the offer, adding, 'I don't make publicity. My mother taught me that and I never did it. I would not know HOW to do it.' I tried to persuade him that there were a thousand miles of difference between a publicity film and the intimate portrait film genre which I and my colleagues had pioneered with *Double Concerto* and the first Jacqueline du Pré films – to no avail.

I often had tea with him and his wife, Thérèse, on Sunday afternoons and so I continued to press my case for three long years. Finally, on one happy Sunday, inspiration floated out of the blue. I arrived at Nathan's home in London's elegant Chester Square and said,

'Nathan, I have some astonishing good news for you.'

'What's that?'

'You know that Paganini played in Frankfurt.'

'Yes.'

'Well, what you do not know, is that a very early German film maker was there and he filmed part of the first rehearsal.'

Nathan had saucer-eyes for a second and a half and then said, 'Why you tell me such nonsense?'

'Nathan, if there were film of Paganini anywhere in this world, you would be the first in the queue to see it because you are more enquiring than the others.'

He gave me his famous Nathan Mironovich quizzical look and, after a telling pause said,

'Okay, you win.'

'Nathanski, mi querido', I replied, 'this is not a competition. This is something that we have to achieve together, side by side, with dedication and enthusiasm.'

So that is what we did and, in the process, I discovered that he had been a reluctant violinist since the age of seven when his mother bought him a violin to keep him out of repeated trouble with his schoolmates. He recalls it in our film:

> My mother insisted I play violin. She didn't come with a revolver. She didn't force that way. She simply insisted, and if a mother insisted at that time, she would win. I wouldn't win. She wanted me to play violin and I succumbed to it. I don't mind actually. It didn't do any harm to me.

Instead, it led to one of the longest and most admired musical careers of the twentieth century. Nathan had done virtually no television at all in his many years on stage because he wanted to remain ever true to his mother's injunction about not promoting himself. Our film adventure was nevertheless a pleasure all along the way, full of memorable moments.

When the lighting for the recital was done – a process that took us two days – we made a small mark on the floor and I asked Nathan to stay as close to it as he could, as long as it did nothing to upset his concentration. My words were entirely unnecessary. Nathan was an accomplished painter both with water colours and oils. He knew about images and light.

Before one of the most difficult pieces we saw him take extra-long time and trouble with tuning and then – glorious moment – look down at the floor, step up exactly to his mark and instantly launch into a dazzling display of brilliant virtuosity, from the very first note. In the process he carried us with him to the heavens on the wings of his muse which spoke so directly to the heart.

What a dear, wonderful fellow was Nathan Mironovich Milstein.

29

Manfred Gräter, Sten Andersson, Gidon Kremer, José Montes Baquer, Hasso

At a music Congress in Munich in 1968 I saw a tall, elegant fellow wearing a black and white striped shirt coming, somewhat diffidently, towards me. He said, 'My name is Manfred Gräter. I am head of music at the German television channel WDR in Cologne. I hear from the BBC delegate that you have made a very good film about Vladimir Ashkenazy and I would like to be able to show it on German television.'

That was the first sign that we might be able to survive as independent producers in a world which had no appropriate infrastructure. In the event Manfred and WDR became our best supporters for more than 40 years both financially and artistically.

There were none in television music to match Manfred and that was widely acknowledged. He had a rare combination of skills. He knew music both academically and as a keyboard player, he understood the demands of television production in a way that few heads of department did because of his exceptionally high intelligence and because he stayed so close to, and so interested in, every aspect of production. He also understood the needs of directors better than any of the others.

As a consequence of the reputation which had now preceded us, I was asked to tell the Munich delegates what we had done in the making of the Ashkenazy film and how we had done it. That was worrying news because I did not speak a word of German at the time and during the entire week every one of the delegates had spoken

German. I turned to the sympathetic Manfred Gräter and asked if he could help me with a few appropriate words in the language of the land. In an impressively short time he produced the following:

> *Entschuldigen Sie bitte, meine Damen und Herren, wenn ich mein Referat nicht in deutscher Sprache halten kann. Bedauerlicherweise habe ich niemals deutsch studiert, aber glücklicherweise scheinen die meisten von Ihnen englisch zu verstehen. Es gibt im übrigen eine sehr gekürzte deutsche Übersetzung meines Referats, aber ich muss hinzufügen, dass es keine präzise, sondern in Eile verfasste Übersetzung eines ebenfalls in Eile geschriebenen Originals ist. Ein einigermassen sinnvoller Eindruck kann sich nur ergeben, wenn sie diese deutsche Kurzfassung im Zusammenhang mit dem vollständigen englischen Text lesen.*

> Forgive me, ladies and gentlemen that I am unable to address you in German. Unfortunately, I have never studied your language but happily it seems to me that most of you understand English. I should say also that there is a shortened German translation available but I must add that that it is not a full translation but rather a hurriedly written précis. It can only give a true impression if it is read in conjunction with the complete English text.

Uproarious applause followed. Those self-same words saved me on another occasion, also in Munich, in a much more serious situation – filming Pinchas Zukerman in 1973 (see chapter 22).

Shortly after our meeting in Munich, wanting to do everything possible to develop the relationship, I visited Manfred in Cologne. Four things impressed me: the unbelievable size and majesty of the Cathedral, the striking smallness of Manfred's nearby office, the happy spirit which inhabited that office and Manfred's helpers, one of whom, Lore Ebeler, had pinned up on the wall behind her, written in German, of course: 'And out of the chaos a voice spoke to me: "Smile and be happy, things could be worse" and so I smiled and was happy and things duly **GOT** worse.' And alongside that: 'Only small spirits maintain order. Geniuses overlook the chaos.' I knew I had landed in the right place.

Manfred Gräter's rescue plan of coaxing us into making the Respighi film brought fundamental and far-reaching changes to the nature and the future of Allegro Films. It also brought two new members into the team – albeit on a part-time basis – Alan Dykes, already mentioned in chapter 20, and the Swedish man of many gifts, Sten Andersson. Swedish writer, producer, radio and television broadcaster, fiddle player, poet, playwright, violin maker and the very embodiment of the voice of sanity, Sten is one of those rare people who lift the heart and brighten the world. He became our contact man with Swedish Television and the Swedish Film Institute, and he contributed hugely to the productions that we made in association with those impressive organizations.

Among his many virtues Sten had the rare gift of bringing instant cool when production fire threatens. I remember him working with a senior English producer who was having difficulty with the Swedish Radio Symphony Orchestra and complaining that orchestral musicians behaved like children. On that instant, and ever so quietly, Sten said, 'If you treat them like children they may well behave like that but if you treat them instead as what they are, skilled, dedicated, questioning musicians striving always for effective artistic expression, then you will find them among your most valuable partners in work of this kind.' The stage was a lot quieter after that. Another memorable Sten moment produced these words:

> Time goes by. But working with classical music is like living in a beautiful and dramatic landscape which still will be there when we are gone. I once wanted to write a poem about the Gates of Paradise but I found that it is already there in the last part of Mahler's *Das Lied von der Erde*.

When Manfred asked us to make a film of Mark Neikrug's theatrical piece *Through Roses*, I looked at it carefully and said that I feared it would cost too much to produce something convincing from this unusual base. Manfred answered immediately, '*Mein Gott! Everything you DO is so interesting*!' It is impossible to describe fully how much difference an expression of confidence like that can make when it comes from a trusted source. We made the production and it won a prize. We could not have done that without Sten Andersson.

Not long afterwards Manfred asked us to make a film about Gidon Kremer who was a close friend of his. Gidon and I both had immense respect and affection for Manfred and wanted very much to do it but the opportunity never arose and then catastrophe intervened. Manfred died of cancer – too young – much too young. I gave the funeral address, written in English and translated into High German by a colleague in WDR. We buried Manfred in Cologne but his friends all knew that he wanted to be buried in Capri – the one place on the face of the earth where he really felt at home. We were finally able to do that and the close friends gathered in Capri for the re-burial. Gidon made the music and I delivered the words.

Manfred's love of Capri was very much in response to the island's breathtaking natural beauty. He was hypersensitive to beauty. The island's smallness also played a part, so that, in time, through hundreds of walks, and studying all the histories of the island he got to know every corner of it and felt more and more at home. The moment he set foot there he became more Italian than the locals and called himself 'Dottore Amato'. He loved Italian cooking and soon knew the individual virtues of every restaurant of note on the island. He also knew the wine lists.

At the supper which followed the funeral Manfred's hope that Gidon and I would make a film together duly surfaced, as it was bound to do, but both of us were cautious: Gidon because he is so demanding of himself, and I at the prospect of doing months of work and spending more than a hundred thousand pounds on something that his perfectionism might not approve. None of the artists with whom I had worked previously had ever asked for a right of approval, nor did Gidon, but I feared that his worries might just bring the exception and I saw too many warning lights flashing.

We both retreated and once again, nothing happened, but some years later Gidon telephoned out of the blue. He said that he was approaching his 50th birthday and asked whether this might provide the key and the necessary stimulus for a film together. My reservations sprang vividly to mind, and this time I had the courage to say, 'Forget about it Gidon. You are far too demanding and your perfectionism will never be satisfied. You cannot even listen to your own audio recordings. You will never be content with such a complex and intimate a thing as a Christopher style portrait film'

We had already made a performance film of Vivaldi's *Four Seasons* for the Munich company Unitel. That is a much less dangerous format because the main focus is on the music rather than the performer and so, half joking, I said, 'Why don't we make a film about Vivaldi, we would have a quieter life.' Gidon, sounding none too enthusiastic, said he would think about it.

A few weeks later we had a rather lukewarm telephone conversation about Vivaldi and then discovered, by pure chance, that we were both reading books – two different books – about Niccolo Paganini, another extraordinary coincidence, seemingly heaven-sent. We were both touched by the tragic story, by Paganini's Herculean commitment in the face of mounting health problems and the developing hostility of the world. I said, 'Forget about Vivaldi, let's do Paganini. The story is stronger.'

One of my dangerous failings is that I have a habit of committing myself to projects out of enthusiasm, without pausing to calculate what they will cost in terms of time, or money or difficulty or energy. I realized that I had done it once again. I had absolutely no idea about how to make a Paganini film. All our early films had been based on intimate relationships with living musicians: performers who were full of a now legendary exuberance and who could be persuaded to do almost anything in front of the camera. A new spirit was alive in the world and we were making the most of it.

In stark contrast, I had no relationship of any kind with Niccolo Paganini or his history. I had, of course, heard the violin concerti played by several people and I knew that there were countless legends to draw on, but legends are mostly misleading and I was wary. More significantly, Paganini was not available to appear in front of our cameras and so there was the huge question about what to use for images.

I have always tried to limit the use of photographs in our films because they are so two-dimensional. In addition, film moves too fast. A great photograph needs time to convey its message. Film does not like to wait that long but I feared that that was the road we were going to have to take. I started to wonder how on earth I had got myself into this pickle.

My research took me to the Paganini Institute in Genoa and the lovely fellow who ran it, Edward Neill. It proved to be a revelation. I discovered dozens of drawings, paintings, portraits and caricatures. Niccolo's charisma sprang off the paper. Looking at those images I discovered that Paganini was so remarkable, so unusual and so individual that he sparked the most lively, even inspired, responses from many different artists. I saw with startling clarity that something of the legend had been preserved in their imaginations, and that each had put something of themselves into their work, so there was tremendous visual variety – and film loves variety. It also loves the unexpected, just as it loves drama and virtuosity. All of these qualities, and many more besides, were offered in extravagant measure by the images I found in the Institute.

What's more, the story was animated by hot and widespread controversy – film also loves controversy - and Paganini provided more than his fair share. I decided that we should try to tell this story through those paintings and drawings and, of course, through the music. This was all new to us, but films, like music, are made in the making and so I put my faith in the physical processes of trying to do the job in the cutting room. In a very real sense this was a bigger factor with Paganini than it had ever been before.

First, we shot the Paganini music that seemed best suited to telling our story, with Gidon and the Radio Orchestra of Lugano, conducted by Lawrence Foster. Then I brought dozens of wonderful images to Peter Heelas in the cutting room and we started looking for Niccolo Paganini.

We have always allowed our films to determine their own lengths and the lengths have all been different. This one came out at 73 minutes. Melvyn Bragg, who liked the film and had agreed to show it on the South Bank Show, requested the required 73 minutes from his Management. Unhappily, his bosses would give him no more than 50. We had to cut the film down. We did so, but the deletions stole its heart away.

John Williams, who plays an important part in the film, watched the transmission and I bumped into him two days later in Regents Park Road. He said, 'That was a bit of a downer, wasn't it.' I accepted that we had failed for the first time.

Ten years later, BBC FOUR included the full-length version in a series of our composer films. Less than a minute after the broadcast ended the phone rang. It was John Williams. This time he said, 'Eight of us have been watching the film together. We were riveted from start to finish. It's wonderful!' We felt better and released the film on DVD for the first time.

The making of the Paganini film had served its original purpose. Gidon and I felt that we had found a way of working together. We decided the time had come to try and make the portrait film after all. We began shooting and, of course, soon ran into the problem that had held us back all along: what Gidon now called his 'Virus of perfectionism.' The number of retakes spiralled exponentially and so, without telling Gidon we constructed a sequence in the cutting room to demonstrate that impressive process at work.

The sequence begins with a series of failed attempts by Gidon to play the thirteenth Caprice, in a pool of light, in long-shot, on a single camera. The virus duly manifests itself with multiple restarts while Gidon, with mounting anger, wanders in and out of shot. We strung several failed takes together and overlaid some appropriate words of his from an earlier interview:

> I am not the one to say OK it was a nice performance, we enjoyed it, let's have fun. I am suffering from it and it drives me crazy to such an extent that I actually can't listen to myself in recordings because something ... most of the time ... something disturbs me and these are things that relate to perfectionism. So I am in conflict. On the one hand I am infected by the virus of perfectionism and I am striving for it, on the other hand I just resent it as an idea. So I am in conflict.

With that he plays the entire Caprice, straight through, at a level which his perfectionism allows him to accept. He then makes a broad sweep with his bow and walks quietly out of the shot. The pool of light remains, empty but full of resonances, underlining, yet again, one of the differences between the effects of the aural and the visual.

Gidon knew nothing of that sequence until he saw the finished film and we waited for his reaction with quite some apprehension. It is a tribute to his character and his honesty that he enjoyed it and said so.

Manfred's assistant during almost all the years that I knew him was an extremely gifted Catalan called José Montes Baquer. He played the cello, the piano, the guitar and had a gorgeous flair for the visual. Among other things he made – in collaboration with Salvador Dalí – one of the most imaginative visual television productions in the history of the medium. They called it *Impressions de la haute Mongolie* and visually it was in effect a kind of trompe-l'oeil from start to finish. It won many prizes and made José famous.

Josélito, as I called him (a diminutive form of his name used by the Spanish to convey affection) was a man of kindness, of integrity, of refinement and high intelligence, all of which were employed to the full in his quest for a life that had meaning. And José lived a life worth living although sadly it was cut short – just as he was entering a new phase in his development and just as he was adapting to, and enjoying, new circumstances.

In his professional life he was one of the very few television directors who was truly distinguished both as an artist and as an administrator. As administrator, he had the good fortune to grow up in the best school – the television music department of Westdeutscher Rundfunk, under the inspired leadership of Manfred.

When Manfred died José inherited that department and, astonishingly, expanded it just when the lean years for music programming were beginning to engulf the television world. The age of the ghetto channel, the 'special' channel, the small channels, the under-financed channels, was ushered in – silently, without shame and without ceremony.

The big hope was Arte, the most enlightened of the ghetto channel ideas and covering both France and Germany but access, for an independent producer, was often difficult, even with the support of WDR. José managed those tensions adroitly and won the respect of almost everybody in the process.

As an artist he produced a body of work that is distinguished from start to finish, something which is extremely difficult to do as a full-time employee of a television station. In José's case the secret lay in his high intelligence, his critical eye, an extensive knowledge of the arts, a fine sense of humour and an elevated sense of purpose.

His work was instantly recognisable by its originality, its inventiveness, both visual and thematic; its wit and its dry look at the usual, making it, instantly, unusual in the process. Nothing quite like his *Impressions de la Haute Mongolie* had ever been made, and unsurprisingly, Salvador Dalí became both a mentor and a friend.

On the personal level José and I drew huge pleasure from each other's films and, as a direct consequence of shared ideals and convictions, we called each other 'hermano' (brother). I am proud and grateful for the forty years I knew him, just as I am grateful, in a different way, for the professional support which he gave us.

In the nine years of his retirement Josélito occupied himself with adding to his impressive collection of fine art; playing the piano, mostly in search of Joseph Haydn and Johann Sebastian Bach; his friendship with the artist Rebecca Horn and devoting himself to enjoying life with his lively companion Hasso, the most intelligent and communicative dog that I have ever encountered – qualities developed in part I am sure – by José's tutelage. Hasso was an endless source of surprise, delight and infectious joie de vivre. He also demanded considerable physical energy from his friend – which is no bad thing.

Lamentably, Hasso died young, of a mosquito bite, leaving José saddened and very much the poorer. We buried Hasso with ceremony and with love. José delivered the farewell address and he ended it with heartfelt thanks for what Hasso had taught him about responsibility. The scene was deeply touching and reminded me of a very typical Josélito remark, when Hasso was still a bounding puppy, 'He is waiting to become my friend. At the moment he is still convinced that I am his slave'. There you have a small window on the soul of José Montes Baquer.

Suddenly and unexplainably José fell ill. After several failed investigations he guessed that it might be serious and asked the doctors to tell him everything, to hold nothing back. A week went by without producing a diagnosis or any clarification except that his liver was infected but his condition – and his appearance – deteriorated drastically.

Having recently been given a CD entitled 'Great moments in the History of Cello Playing', I asked Josélito whether he would like to hear some of them. He said yes and I brought three on the following day:

> Casals playing a Haydn Minuet, arranged Piatti.
> Maurice Maréchal playing Caix d'Hervelois' Plainte .
> Ennio Bolognini playing his own Serenata del Gaucho.

All three are highly unusual and totally captivating. The effect was dramatic. That music brought Josélito to life in a way that I would not have thought possible. He became animated. He responded instantly to every musical twist and turn. Even the colour of his skin changed from an unhealthy shade of grey to a more natural colour many tones lighter. The transformation was, quite literally, unbelievable.

As I left the hospital, full of wonder at the power of music, one of the doctors stopped me in the entrance hall and said, 'I must tell you that your friend is very seriously ill.' I realised that the kind, concerned people who had seen many deaths had decided, contrary to José's specific instructions, to spare him the pain of living the last few days of his life in the knowledge that he was dying. I was floored. I could not even ask the obvious questions. I left with a nod of acknowledgement but without saying a word. Two days later mi querido Josélito was dead.

I gave the funeral address in Castilian Spanish and played the Caix d'Hervelois Plainte recording to bring us closer to the spirit of José Montes which still lives on in all of us who loved him. I believe that that moment and the nature of the event, and the love and the words and the music, all together stirred many of the souls present in a way that they had never experienced before. José's two brothers had the same conviction.

30

Gigi
Alice Sommer

Sage, Saint, Maven

•

The world likes to remember its heroes in their own lifetimes but there have been precious few so deeply loved and for so long – and by so many – as Alice Sommer who died in London in 2014 at the age of 110. She died in exceptionally good physical shape, living alone in a small flat near Belsize Village in London and mentally as good as few achieve at any time in their lives.

She had been called Gigi (hard G's) by all who knew her since she was six years old. She could not remember how or where the name originated but she knew that she liked it and that it suited her. In time that name came to be loved by almost every person who ever came into contact with her. Among her many virtues she was wise and kind.

Her story is astonishing, inspiring, overwhelming and is told in full in her book, *Ein Garten Eden inmitten der Hölle (A Garden of Eden in Hell)* compiled by Melissa Müller and Reinhold Piechocki from hundreds of conversations with her. That book has so far been published in six languages. I commend it to all who read these lines. The book gives her name as Alice Herz-Sommer but she asked me to call her Alice Sommer in the two films we made with her because she wanted to give more prominence to her husband's name.

The title of her book refers to the two years that Gigi spent as a prisoner of the Nazis in the Theresienstadt concentration camp. She survived because of her music – playing more than a hundred concerts there. She was just one of several top class musicians imprisoned there and she described the effects of the concerts as being akin to a profound religious experience. She survived also because of her unwavering determination to take care of her six-year-old son, no matter what it cost her personally.

She was extremely reluctant to say anything at all about the horrors which she witnessed in the camp but described, graphically, the nightmare of being unable to give her child enough to eat or to explain the absence of his father who had been sent to Dachau. These concerns accentuated her conviction that the greatest gift which nature has granted to human beings is the phenomenon which she called 'the love of the mother to the child. This is the basis of everything.'

I met her through her son, the cellist Raphael Sommer, who was a neighbour of mine in London. At the time she was an astonishingly sprightly 75-year-old who walked a long way almost every day to a swimming pool where she spent more time in the water than anyone else present because she believed in the therapeutic powers of exercise in water. I was impressed by her physical bearing, her engaging personality and the depth of her perceptions, long before I knew anything of the gigantic story that lay behind her.

I began to visit her and drew something from her at each meeting. She had a quiet grace that was immensely attractive and I found her more enlivening, more interesting, more entertaining on each occasion. I went also because I thought, mistakenly, that she must be lonely living in a small flat, alone, at seventy five. I was wrong. I discovered soon that Gigi was never lonely. She had an endless stream of knowledgeable visitors, she had her piano which she played for two hours every day, starting at exactly 10 a.m. She listened to BBC Radio 3 and when she heard that there was talk of shutting Radio 3 down, she came up with the instant response, 'Don't they realize that it is one of the best things this country has?' She watched television from time to time and had a tireless interest in music in all its guises. She knew so much and had such insights that almost every one of my visits brought something new and engaging to light:

> I sit here and I think, uninterrupted, *(ununterbrochen)*, about the wonder in the world. Everything is a wonder. Our eyes are a miracle, and our ears.

> Nature is a miracle. Everything is a present. How can people live without music? I am thankful for everything and thankful for my mother who helps me even now.

She welcomed everybody and when I came through the door she always said 'Da ist er' (there he is), with unmistakable warmth. She understood the power of the warm welcome and the power of love as few can do. Our relationship blossomed with every visit.

When I told her that Manfred Gräter, at WDR Television in Cologne, had asked us to make a film about Respighi, Gigi asked whether there was something that her son Raphael could contribute, and there was. He gave a marvellous, soaring performance of the *Adagio con Variazione* for cello and orchestra which gives much to the finished film and which Gigi watched many times after Raffi died. It brought a measure of solace to her for the loss of a relationship that had quite literally saved the lives of both of them in appalling and life-threatening circumstances.

Gigi had given him life and sacrificed almost everything to keep him alive and feeling loved in the concentration camp. They were there for two years with almost nothing to eat but in later life Raffi remembered Theresienstadt as a happy place where he made music with his mother nearly every day and sang in the first performance of the children's opera, *Brundibar*, more support for her conviction that in the life of the human being there is nothing more important than the 'love of the mother to the child.'.

That Raffi should have died while Gigi was still alive was unimaginable but that is what happened. After more than sixty years of close relationship Gigi, maven to the end, said, 'He is with me still and I rejoice that he did not have to suffer the agony of declining powers in his music-making through old age.' Raffi was 61 when he died. Gigi was 98 at the time. She was to live twelve more years without him.

When we shot the first interview with her for our film *We Want the Light*, I had known and admired her for more than 35 years but I had never seen her so engaged. Her intelligence, allied to what she had l earned from her shocking experiences, meant that she understood, better than anyone else, the potential importance of the project. It soon became obvious to me that she would be the star of our film and I know that in the final analysis, it was due to Gigi that the film won its many prizes.

I extended the shoot in the hope that we would both collect our best material for the film we were making and perhaps, additionally, enough to make something else, focused on Gigi alone – somewhere further down the line. The opportunity did not present itself for some years but when Gigi was approaching her 106th birthday I suddenly realised how much time had gone by and felt real urgency. I picked up the telephone immediately and said, 'Gigi, we must do something for your birthday'. She replied, 'I don't celebrate my birthday. I celebrated my mother's birthday.' It took a few days to persuade her and then, with her blessing, we made the film, *Everything is a Present*.

Such is the magic that radiated from Gigi Sommer that the film was nominated in 2010 for the ICMA DVD of the Year Award and the Social Award at Rose d'Or. In the same year it won the World Documentary Bronze Medal at the New York Film and Television Festival and the Czech Television Prize at Golden Prague. It also picked up the Accolade Award in 2012. Those prizes were won by Gigi.

She had a spirit that was not only beautiful itself but which sought beauty, sought to create beauty and drew beauty to itself in a way that few, very few, have ever been able to do. Right to the end she remained one of the three deepest seeing people I have known, the other two being Jacqueline du Pré and Isaiah Berlin. What I mean by that is what William Wordsworth described as seeing into the life of things:

> While with an eye made quiet by the power
> Of harmony, and the deep power of joy,
> We see into the life of things.

31

Len Selby

Doctor to the Stars

A long time ago I asked a Weymouth Street osteopath whether he thought there were any really gifted doctors in Harley Street. Cheeky, perhaps, but it turned out to be the right question. He sent me to Len Selby at number 52 Harley Street and I never looked back.

I asked the question because, since my school days, I had been troubled by a long series of unexplained symptoms which had entirely defeated all doctors. One of the most memorable responses came from a very important Harley Street doctor who said, after a short consultation 'I have patients with trivial symptoms and mortal complaints and others with troublesome symptoms and trivial complaints. Luckily, I put you in the second category.' End of consultation – no diagnosis, no prescription but a disgracefully large invoice followed soon afterwards. Len Selby, by contrast, was of a different order, both as doctor and as human being.

In a profession where the demands are often too much for ordinary mortals, Len Selby never once deviated in either his dedication or in his honesty. His patients knew this and at times it was hugely reassuring for them. I was so touched by his dedication that I remained close to him for the next 50 years.

His greatest natural gift was his uncanny talent for diagnosis. He once told me that he generally knew, at the moment when his patients walked through the door, whether there was anything wrong and, surprisingly often, he knew what it was. When he said that to me it had a curious and totally inappropriate effect. I never again walked through that consulting room door without throwing my arms in the air and shouting, 'Hello Len!' with all possible youthful vigour. He knew, immediately, what I was up to and we both smiled about it – every time. Len Selby was good for smiles.

At first sight, his credentials did not seem promising for the upper echelons of Harley Street. He was an Afrikaans-speaking Lithuanian Jew from Stellenbosch, who moved to London with a heavy South African accent and very uncertain prospects but who, in time, became the much loved, much respected and much enjoyed doctor of Marlene Dietrich, David Ben Gurion, Golda Meier, six Arab sheiks, at least two Rothschilds, Sidney Lipworth, Isaiah Berlin and through me, Jacqueline du Pré, Daniel Barenboim, Pinchas Zukerman, Itzhak and Toby Perlman, John Williams and many more.

His distinguishing characteristics were his enthusiasm, his profound interest in medicine, his absolute need to help people and his tenacity. His greatest virtue, at least for me, was the degree to which he cared. He really cared and he never let that slip. Over a period of about six years he sent me to dozens of specialists and consultant physicians and finally – despairing – delivered himself of the following:

> Dominee, (that's what he called me, the Afrikaans word for a man of the cloth) we do not understand your metabolism. We are forced to the conclusion that you are a nervous, creative type, doomed to suffer and Western medicine cannot help you.

Len Selby knew how to be funny even in the serious moments. His sense of humour was often entertainingly self-deprecating and always well timed: 'You know it's a funny thing, in all the years that I've been here I completely lost my South African accent.' These words delivered, of course, with an even thicker South African accent than usual. Why did he keep it? Perhaps because he wanted to stay true to his humble origins.

When Len retired he wrote to me in his difficult to read doctor's handwriting:

I have wanted to be a doctor since I was a small child and I have achieved that ambition. I have enjoyed every day of it and I wish it could go on forever but I am 80 years old and it would not be fair to my patients to carry on. Come and have a *gesels* from time to time.*

* Gesels is the Afrikaans word for a chat.

Eventually, sadly, tragedy overtook him. Len suffered a series of strokes which in time robbed him of all ability to communicate. I nevertheless maintained a tenuous relationship even when conversation was no longer possible. Along his way he earned both respect and affection from almost everyone who had anything to do with him and none more than his wife, Val, who for many long years, visited him on very nearly every day when he was no longer able to live at home and, in the end, did not even know his own name. Val, despite impossible difficulties, maintained the loving relationship and the care until the day Len died. Her dedication was deeply touching.

Unsurprisingly, Len's last gesture to humankind was to donate his body to science for medical research.

32

Evgeny Igorevich Kissin

The BBC Promenade Concert, Shakespeare, the Verbier Festival, the Albert Hall encores, Yankev Glatshteyn, 'Mozart'

•

In November of 1990 the music agent Hans Dieter Göhre invited me to shoot a recital by Evgeny Kissin in a studio in Munich. I accepted the invitation. Kissin was nineteen years old and the first thing that struck me when we met was his earnestness – far beyond his years – so evident that I found it both impressive and touching.

The second was the way in which Göhre and his staff used the Russian intimate form of Kissin's first name, 'Genya', in addressing him. In Russia that is a common way of expressing affectionate respect but it did not seem appropriate in the light of Kissin's magisterial talent and his serious attitude to the work that we were proposing to do together.

In response, I immediately called him Evgeny Igorevich, which in Russian means Evgeny son of Igor. The Russians use the patronymic to indicate formal respect and respect seemed to me to be much more fitting and likely to produce good results than any forced attempt at an intimacy which had not been earned. To me 'Genya' sounded patronizing.

In the event my name for him has endured and I call him Evgeny Igorevich to this day, despite having grown ever closer both to him and to his family. For me the use of the name is also a way of remembering the highly-charged atmosphere of the Munich studio and the excitement of our first work together.

The world loves to discover new stars and the time was obviously right for the kind of portrait film that we had pioneered (to use Jeremy Isaacs' description of our work) with my super gifted young friends.

I proposed the idea of a full length Allegro film to Evgeny Igorevich and he agreed but his teacher, Anna Pavlovna Kantor, expressed grave doubts. She felt a huge responsibility and was justifiably cautious – better no film than a bad one. I did not blame her.

It took a while to win her confidence but she continued to take fright at the slightest hint of imperfection in his playing. I remember her sitting in a corner in a cloud of gloom after a recital which we filmed at the Festival of La Roque d'Antheron near Aix en Provence. There had been some minor problems with some almost unplayably difficult passages. Despite my reassurances she remained gloomy for the rest of the evening while I rejoiced at having found people who cared so much.

We had made a tentative start with Anna Pavlovna's co-operation. There is even a great moment when she waves to the camera in La Roque d'Antheron. I knew then that we had passed the Anna Pavlovna test.

Our way of filming was at that time entirely new to Kissin but he very soon responded with a warmth that was surprising in the light of his youthfulness and his reserved manner. I was impressed as well by the speed at which his command of English developed – and the quality in his use of it. This came from a very real need in his professional life, his voracious reading, and his prodigious memory.

I remember him in a check-in queue at London airport reading *The Tempest*. I asked how he was getting on with the elevated language. Instead of answering he fired a question at me, a popular Jewish device which is not untypical of him:

'Do you believe that all the plays attributed to Shakespeare were written by one person?'

'That is what we've been told.'

'Well, I don't.'

He went on to tell me the number of words in the vocabulary used by Francis Bacon, who was recognized as having the largest vocabulary in England in his time. He then gave me the size of the vocabulary that is actually used in the plays which is considerably greater – a noteworthy statistic. It turned out that Kissin had been mightily impressed by the work of the Russian Shakespeare scholar Ilya Gililov who had spent half a lifetime studying the subject and had come to the conclusion that the plays were the result of the labours and the games of the Poets of Arden, starting with Philip Sidney and his wife and daughter. Although Gililov's theory was discredited by English scholars and critics alike, Kissin was so deeply convinced that he offered to give a series of lectures on the subject at the Verbier Festival and to bring Gililov from Russia to participate. He asked whether I would go with him to help him organize and present it and I did so. We had fun, raised some big questions and had an enlivening time.

We have sometimes been asked why the artists who appear in our films seem to be more friendly than when they appear in the films of others. As far as I know there are two possible answers to that question. The first is the style of the film making itself and the unusual closeness of our cameras to the subject. The second is the trust and affection which we try to develop between the artist and every member of the crew. That trust works in both directions and the camera somehow sees it.

After filming in Gstaad with Evgeny Igorevich, Gidon Kremer and the Hagen Quartet we asked the BBC for permission to film the encores at the BBC Prom Concert on the 10th of August 1997. Kissin was scheduled to play the first solo piano recital in the entire 103-year history of the London Promenade Concerts. It was a Sunday afternoon in the second hottest August since records began but Kissin nevertheless drew the biggest Prom audience in all of those 103 years. As if that were not enough, he ended his recital with the longest succession of encores ever performed at the Proms. We filmed it all and, by the end, the whole of the back of Kissin's white jacket was visibly wet through with sweat, adding a certain authenticity to our historic record of a great event. We were lucky to be there and to be so generously received by the BBC, by Evgeny Igorevich and by Anna Pavlovna – imperfections and all.

In the editing we made two separate television films: an Allegro-style portrait film *The Gift of Music*, and *The Albert Hall Encores* as a separate performance film. By contrast, for the DVD, we told the story exactly as it happened by putting the two together, without a break, making a hundred-and-four-minute story.

A few years later a similar opportunity occurred when he played a recital in the Roman Theatre at Orange in the South of France. Amazingly, we were again able to release two television recitals which included some spectacularly difficult music and without having to retake a single note.

Like Jacqueline du Pré, Evgeny Igorevich has a gift for relevant surprise. When we were making the film *We Want the Light* on the subject of the Jews and German music and we needed a moment of poetic reflection, he produced, instantly, in Yiddish and from memory the following words by Yankev Glatshteyn (translation follows).

S'hot zikh mir gekholemt
Goyim hobm Mozartn gekreytsikt
Un im begrobm in an eyzl-keyver.

Nor yidn hobm im gemakht far Gots-mensch
Un zayn gedekhenish gebensht.

Zayn apostol bin ikh iber der velt geloffn
un bakert yeder eynem vos kh'hob getroffn
Umetum vo kh'hob gekhapt a Krist,
Hob ikh im geshmadt oyf a Mozartist.

Vi vunderlekh iz fun getlekhn mensch
Zayn musikalisher testamant,
Vi durkhgenogglt mit gezang
Zaynen zayne likhtike hent.

In zayn grester noyt,
Hobm beym gekreytsiktn zinger
Gelakht alle finger

In zayn veynendikhsten troyer,
Hot er noch mer vi zikh alleyn
Lib gehat
Dem schokhns oyer

I dreamed the gentiles crucified Mozart
and buried him in a donkey's grave
but the Jews made of him a man of God
and blessed his memory.

I, his apostle, travelled the world
and converted all whom I encountered
and whenever I met a Christ
I baptised him a Mozartist.

How wondrous is the musical testament
of this god-like man.

How through-nailed with song
are his bright hands.

In the greatest need of this crucified singer
were laughing - all his fingers
And in his most weeping grief
he cared more for the sounds in his neighbour's ear
than he cared for himself.

The Glatshteyn poem remains burned into our memories. I recited it in full when we won the Jewish Cultural Award 2003/2004 for our film *We Want the Light*. We have a plan to recite alternate lines as a duo when and if some suitable occasion arises.

Karim Said

Daniel Barenboim, Edward Said, the Purcell School

•

When we were asked by WDR in Cologne to make a film about the complex relationship between the Jews and German Music (the project that came to be named *We Want the Light*), I asked Daniel Barenboim to give us an extended interview. He said, 'Of course, but I could not give you enough time before I go to Weimar, so come there. You will get to know the West-Eastern Divan and you will have fun.' Then, as I was going out of the door, he added, with a questioning Barenboim look, 'You realize, Cristobalin, that you cannot do this in under twelve programmes.' Being brave and foolish by nature I said, 'We will have to find a way.'

I went to Weimar and, on the second day, Daniel invited me to a student concert. It took place in a gymnasium hall where the audience was sitting on the same level as the piano and surrounding it. When the concert ended Daniel got up, walked over to the piano and said, in German, 'Ladies and Gentleman, we have a surprise for you. You will now hear an encore played by someone who did not appear in the concert.' Unusual, one might say, but then Daniel Barenboim is a master of the engaging surprise. He called, 'Karim' and out walked a diminutive 11-year-old, Karim Said, made a cursory bow, sat down at the piano, and launched, with no hesitation, into Mendelssohn's *Rondo Capriccioso*.

The piece is not easy by any means, but it begins with two pages of slow chords. We had barely heard the first page when I asked myself,

'How is it possible for an 11-year-old boy to create so much magic from a few slow chords?' At exactly that moment, Daniel, evidently responding to the same things that were making such an impression on me, leaned on my shoulder and said, 'What you cannot learn, he already knows.' I decided that we should try to make a film about this Karim Said who 'already knows'.

As soon as the concert was over I hurried backstage, intent on learning more about this young fellow's personality, his background, and most of all, his relationships with his parents and his teachers. I needed to know, before all else, whether Karim Said would be able to contribute and cooperate in the way that film making requires.

I found the personality as sane and as appealing as the playing had been magical. I told him that we had made several films with young artists – although none quite so young as eleven. The two youngest had been Pinchas Zukerman when he was nineteen and Jacqueline du Pré when she was twenty-two. I asked whether he would be interested to do such a thing and I can see the answer now. An eager face looked up at me with questioning eyes and confirmed the message, 'Yes I would like to do that.'

As early as we dared on the following morning we telephoned his parents in Jordan to ask for approval. Unsurprisingly, they were not in favour. They insisted that Karim still had far too far to go and said that neither the demands of making a film nor the consequences of living with it once it had been made, would be good for their son.

Some correspondence followed. I tried to persuade them that I was not planning to make a sensationalist young-artist television splash but an honest account on film of Karim's progress and the development of his impressive gifts. I added that, provided the presence of the cameras did not disturb him, we would, for the most part, be filming things that he would be doing anyway.

Without telling me, his parents consulted a cousin, the philosopher and musician, Edward Said. He was much respected by all who knew him and, as luck would have it, he had seen and liked quite a number of our films. He was in favour. We were given the go-ahead.

Daniel Barenboim then proposed Karim to the Purcell School in Hertfordshire which helped the project hugely. The Purcell School is a wonderfully vibrant and productive place that was exactly right for him at that moment. Also, it brought him within easy reach of London, where we were based. We started filming immediately and Karim blossomed in front of our cameras, winning friends among the crew, and the Purcell School pupils and staff along the way.

Karim assured me that he was not camera shy and we were soon to see him live up to his claim. From the start his relationship with the camera was lively, to say the least, and he welcomed it and responded to it. There is plenty of evidence for that in the finished product. The camera liked what it saw. His openness and uninhibited interaction with the camera contribute a great deal to the film.

When Karim was 14 he managed, with his irresistible conviction, to persuade an impressive number of fellow students to form a voluntary orchestra and to rehearse quite regularly in what little free time they had. He then had the idea of giving a concert with that orchestra to raise money for the school library. He was given permission. He organized it all himself, arranged and conducted the rehearsals and then conducted the concert without the score. Naturally, we filmed it.

Here is a transcript of a sequence in the film with members of the orchestra – every one of them older than Karim and at an age where age difference is usually a great divider.

Nupen (out of vision):	What is the name of this orchestra?
Orchestra members:	The Beethoven Orchestra.
Nupen (out of vision):	And who called it the Beethoven Orchestra?
Orchestra members:	Karim!
Nupen (out of vision):	Whose idea was it?
Orchestra members:	Karim's idea.
Madeline Bradbury Rance:	Karim is very charismatic and very persuasive as a person. He will run up and grab you in the middle of the corridor and say 'Mandi, would you like to come to the rehearsal tonight? And could we have just 15 minutes to look over bowings for the Beethoven? And have you got any ideas about this?' He's very sweet.

Nupen (out of vision):	Is he good to work with?
Orchestra members:	Yes, and he's very funny. He's very funny.
Mica Levy:	I guess I joined the orchestra because I thought that it's pretty good that he's managed to organise all of this and he is so interested in doing it and it's sort of crazy having a school full of musicians and not using them as much as you can, so I see the logic in the way it's working and I think it has come out pretty well.
Caroline Aide:	On Tuesday, in our rehearsals, he had us all concentrating to such a high degree and we were all together, we were all playing musically and it made all your hairs go up on your arms and you felt like.... Oh, wow, this is inspirational.
Madeline Bradbury Rance:	That would be the second movement
Caroline Aide:	Yes, the second movement. It gets you every time.
Pavel Mansourov:	The bit where we were all out of tune?
Caroline Aide:	No, no, the bit with the fugato and the opening of the second movement.
Madeline Bradbury Rance:	With the cellos and the violas. It's always best with the cellos and the violas.

(The rehearsal of the Beethoven 7th Symphony continues)

Karim (sings):	So can you just make sure that it's going forward. Yes, the first one should be a little bit stronger than the next one (sings) but don't exaggerate it as much as you did because it is not an authentic Bach performance. So can we just go (sings) going towards the next ornament please. A little bit more romantic.
Helen Smith:	I feel like he knows my part as well as I do.
Madeline Bradbury Rance:	And he conducts from memory.

Helen Smith:	Yes, he conducts from memory which is completely amazing. I think that's just incredible, that he knows where everyone is in their parts as well.
Pavel Mansourov:	As long as he doesn't make *us* play from memory it's all right.
Caroline Aide:	I think with Karim that he has such passion for Beethoven that he can pull it off.

One of the guests at the concert was Lady Evelyn Barbirolli who knew a lot about conducting as a high-level performer herself, also as the wife of the great conductor John (Giovanni Battista) Barbirolli, and as a member of many competition juries. She said that she had never seen so natural a talent for conducting at such an early age.

Among the reassurances which I gave to Karim's family when I was trying to win their approval for making the film, was that we would not release it on DVD. There were three prime reasons for that: first, because it was too early in the development of his career, then because, with no established reputation behind him, there would not be sufficient public demand for sales to recover the considerable cost of producing a professionally made DVD, and finally because DVD has a quality of permanence about it while television is essentially fleeting, and his parents felt that so permanent a record at so early an age would be inappropriate.

On the other hand we all felt that television exposure would do no harm precisely because of its essentially ephemeral nature: most television programmes disappear forever as soon as the last end credit has gone by at the end of the first broadcast. So we offered the film to the BBC. They kept us waiting for two years but eventually broadcast it in a prime time slot on BBC FOUR on 14 November 2008.

Some years later Karim told me that he was being asked by agents and concert promoters to give them something of himself on video and he asked, rather tentatively, whether we could supply extracts from the film.

The world had changed and Karim had changed. He was giving regular concerts both as pianist and conductor and was in the process of forming a chamber music ensemble which he calls the Da Vinci Players. We took the plunge, produced a commercial DVD, and it is doing exactly what we always intended it to do: bringing Karim – and the pleasure which he gives through his gifts – to a wider audience.

Since the prime idea was to show the development and progress of his talent, the process took us seven years. We called the film *Karim's Journey* and it has won two international prizes: The Special Jury Award at the Sole e Luna Film Festival in Palermo in 2009 and Bronze Medal at the New York Film and Television Festival in 2010.

We did not expect these awards because the film is deliberately modest in its claims but it did not win the prizes for its claims. It won them for being true to his artistic persona which has its very individual appeal and which is what really matters most.

34

Daniil Trifonov

The Wigmore Hall debut recital, the philosophy
The Magics of Music, the Castelfranco Veneto Recital

•

In March of 2012, Lady Annabelle Weidenfeld invited me to the Wigmore Hall debut recital of Daniil Trifonov and to supper at her home afterwards. She told me that I would hear piano playing such as I had not heard before.

I had known Annabelle since she had been a new and glamourous arrival in the offices of the music agency Ibbs and Tillett and so I knew that she had real experience behind her to back her claims, but I heard something more in her voice – her enthusiasm for Trifonov came positively bubbling down the line. She suggested that I should make a film about him of the kind that we had pioneered with Jacqueline du Pré and my other young friends. I replied that my close personal relationships with the artists in those films had contributed an essential ingredient to their success and I had no means of knowing whether I could develop the same intense friendship and trust with her 22-year-old prodigy. I nevertheless accepted the invitation to the concert and the supper.

During the Wigmore recital I heard a combination of delicacy in the tender moments and a contrasting fire in the dramatic moments that took my breath away. Annabelle's claim was vindicated. The most impressive thing for me was the continuity – the way it all hung together so seamlessly – the story-telling quality that made everything belong, both to all that had gone before and to everything that followed.

That is one of the essentials of great music-making, of course, but the degree of it was breathtaking.

At supper after the recital Annabelle sat us together and we engaged immediately in intense conversation. What impressed me first was Trifonov's glorious intelligence, his speed of comprehension and his fascination with detail. This brought the conversation to life but his questions led me into territory which I try always to avoid. He asked what kind of film I would make and, at the risk of frightening him off entirely, I said that I did not yet know – that it was too soon to know, that I had learned that it is a mistake to try and describe a film before it is made. I could tell him only that I would try to make it, first and foremost, an honest account of his astonishing gift and his artistic persona. I described the importance of the cutting room where a film can either come alive or drain away into the quicksands of film editing. I explained that films have to grow and live in the making, and that decisions made away from the cutting room can be dangerous and sometimes even fatal. I quoted Fellini's words 'If you know your craft, the film will tell you what to do – in the cutting room.'

I had no need to fear. My worries fled away like lightning. Trifonov understood immediately and his response brought sunshine with it. He said that my words echoed precisely his own convictions about musical performance and he confirmed it by email a few days later:

> Your philosophy is something that is very close to the way I believe in working on the music and then in performing it. Ideas come and get accepted or rejected but everything is in the service of music of its life, spirit and also its communicative opportunities. And your expression of the artwork being made in the making is the exact goal performer should have on the stage. Sometimes listeners may attend performance where artwork has been made at home and then being only exposed on the stage in the manner of 'Museum of dead butterflies' according to the expression of my teacher. Music has to be treated as the art of alive moment.

That response was enough to tell me that we had a real chance of doing something worthwhile together. We started corresponding about where to film and what music to include – how to be in the right places at the right times when interesting things might happen – how to begin our voyage of discovery. Annabelle went in search of funding for our bold adventure.

Unhappily, television was no longer paying what it had thought appropriate for more than twenty years and production costs were rising as a result of the High Definition digital revolution. I feared that we would not receive the broadcast fees that both the BBC and German television had paid us for every film we had made during all those years. I knew that even if we received broadcast acceptances from both of those countries there would still be a financial shortfall. I said so and Annabelle came running to the rescue: 'We will find you a Russian oligarch.' We carried on in hope.

In the event, oligarchs proved to be thin on the ground and unenthusiastic about music and musicians. They preferred football and other sporting activities. We had already started spending money, however, and so we were in trouble but we had built so much hope for the project that I could not begin to think of abandoning it. We decided to go ahead and hope for manna from heaven. That turned out to be simultaneously brave and foolish but the enthusiasm held and when we started filming – in Castelfranco Veneto, near Venice – and without financial support of any kind, Trifonov's intelligence and his humour held fast every inch of the way.

We were struck constantly by the speed of his thought, his readiness to understand and comply with whatever we asked him to do, the rapidity with which he was willing to make changes and do retakes, his patience with the time that it took to set up the complex technical requirements of film – all new to him. He allowed the cameras to come closer than we had ever dared to go before and so we were able to shoot everything from the most intimate standpoint of the performer rather than from that of the audience. But most of all, we were struck by the richness of his mind, the poetry in his playing and in his thoughts about it.

Film and music thrive on fertile imaginations. Although Daniil's manner in public is quiet and modest, one of his many surprises in performance is the way in which he gives his wondrously fertile imagination such uninhibited free rein. There is an entertaining sequence in which, without a word of warning, and totally unprepared, he gives his imagination freedom to accompany his interpretation of Ravel's small boat on an unpredictable ocean. A spontaneous running commentary accompanies flawless virtuoso pianism while looking directly at the camera and not the keyboard.

Something similar happens in another sequence in which he remembers his discovery of the virtues of practising in a swimming pool – the water providing a useful physical resistance to his fingers – not quite as good as practising on a keyboard but a great deal better than practising in thin air.

In answer to the question of when he first discovered that he could do things on the piano which others cannot do, his reluctance to show off prompts the reply, 'I am just playing the piano. There are people doing even more crazy things.'

As Daniil says in the finished film, his first interest in music, which surfaced, uninvited, at the age of five, was for composition, rather than performance. When we learned that he would give the first performance of his first piano Concerto at the Cleveland Institute, Ohio, on the 23rd of April 2014, we had no choice but to borrow money and go there. Both the concerto and his virtuoso performance of it generated enthusiastic responses from the critics and the public alike and the sequence added considerable colour to our film. It is always heartening to be present when young talent is finding its audience – a recurring theme in our portrait films.

The Cleveland trip gave us the opportunity to include in our film Daniil's then girlfriend, now his wife, Judith Ramirez, also a pianist, whose very considerable and touchingly reticent charm adds yet another important element to our story. Films are made by teams and we were lucky to be able to bring together several of the best film makers I know because we needed a large crew to shoot the performances in the way that we did. Every member of the crew responded to Daniil's magic and the responses of both Daniil and Judith in turn contribute significantly to what comes off the screen to the viewer.

Some films draw strength from affections developed along the way and this was certainly one of them. It went on to win three international prizes, including the International Classical Music Awards DVD of the Year.

35

Caroline and Matthew Percival

My mother was loved by many people and when she died I was inundated with letters of condolence. I wanted to answer each one in full but had no chance of doing it without help. I went to a secretarial agency in St John's Wood, called Harpers Secretarial, which had done typing for me in the past and met the strikingly beautiful Caroline Percival who, unfortunately, passed the work on to a colleague. The encounter with Caroline had, however, left a lasting impression.

Some time later I needed a script typed and took the work round to Harpers. Once again I landed with Caroline Percival but again she turned me down, telling me this time that the business no longer did work of that kind. I retreated, regretfully, but as I reached the door she suddenly relented and offered to do the typing in her own time, after work. I was later to learn that the change of heart was prompted by my crestfallen look.

I have often been touched by the spontaneous, generous gesture and try always to pick up the spirit of it in response and so, when the time came to collect the script, I went armed with a bottle of Champagne and two glasses in the hope that they would extend the time of the contact. We got on immediately and conversation was easy, fired by palpable chemistry of the kind that makes one dizzy. Caroline Percival had winning ways and my gratitude for her generosity rapidly developed into something a great deal warmer and more stirring.

I invited her to supper. She said that it was a policy of the company not to accept private invitations from clients. But then, once again, suddenly relented saying that since I was not a conveyancing client, perhaps it would be permissible after all. She offered Friday of the following week. I left elated and with my script elegantly done.

Caroline relates that when she got home clutching her mostly empty Champagne bottle, the telephone was ringing. She picked it up and heard my voice saying, 'To hell with next week. How about tomorrow?'

Tomorrow it was and we have been together ever since – amazingly, with not a single cross word in the first ten years – unlikely though that sounds. We had both suffered too much in the past to allow any cloud to impinge on our happy relationship and we shied away from every whisper of tension. In time that had to change, of course, but we will both be forever grateful for those ten cloudless years which brought us so close together and helped us to recover from our past losses.

The relationship with Caroline was so unbelievably cloudless that when the subject of marriage came up – as it did from time to time – we both drew back because we did not want anything to change. We each had a lurking fear that formalising the relationship might rob it of some of its welcome freedom.

That unnecessary worry eventually retreated and after sixteen years together, we decided to take the plunge.

We chose Mallorca for the wedding because we had friends there who lived and worked on the land and whom we felt lived the sanest lives we had so far encountered. As with most of the important changes in my life, our friendship with that farming family happened as a consequence of a most unusual sequence of events.

We had discovered Mallorca when we were planning to make a film about Rachmaninov with Vladimir Ashkenazy. I applied to Boosey and Hawkes for a licence to use Rachmaninov's music which was still in copyright at the time. We were asked to negotiate with a woman who demanded such spectacular clearance fees as were way beyond our possibilities. When I tried to explain that we were not intending to make a cinema film and that television budgets for independently produced documentaries made it impossible for us to pay the sum demanded, she responded with 'You need us. We do not need you' and terminated the meeting.

I was lost. The strength of the rebuttal flattened me for some days. But the shoot dates with the Swedish Radio Symphony Orchestra and Vladimir Ashkenazy had already been booked and were fast approaching. I decided to switch the project to Tchaikovsky because the size of the orchestra which we had booked was right, because Tchaikovsky's music is great and because it was out of copyright. Within days of that thought dawning, Caroline and I fled to Mallorca with a suitcase full of books about Pyotr Ilyich Tchaikovsky.

We rented an isolated house in the gentle landscape of south-east Mallorca and we spent all our waking hours looking for our story. We came up with a plan. More significantly we found that we not only lived well together, we also worked well together – a blessing which has remained with us to this day and for which I will be forever grateful.

Soon after we started, we saw a man and woman harvesting almonds in the adjacent field and so we went there to say *Muy buenos días*. The couple and their family were soon to become close and much admired friends. Every Sunday, without fail, the entire family, grandfather Francisco Estelrich Antich, grandmother Catalina Rigo Barcelo, son Xisco Estelrich Rigo, daughter Cati Barcelo Verger, granddaughter Catalina Estelrich Rigo and grandson Toni Torres Barcelo, plus grandchildren as they were born, came together for the main meal of the week. Before long we received a standing invitation to join them, which has continued to this day.

It was enlivening to be in their presence. They seemed to know more about how to live than city dwellers. They switched from Mallorquin to Castillian Spanish much of the time to make us more welcome. Mallorquin is a tough one to pick up on the fly.

Before committing ourselves, Caroline and I consulted our London friends about the venue for the wedding. All the close ones welcomed the idea of a few days on the sunny island to celebrate with us.

When the time came Caroline and I were married in the Ayuntamiento of Felanitx in the presence of our old friends from London and our new friends from Mallorca. The entire ceremony was conducted in Mallorquin which added a certain piquancy to the occasion and the feast took place in a country restaurant called

Es Clos (The Keys) where we were served with an affection and an unpretentious diligence that I have never seen equalled in any other restaurant. It was a happy occasion and marriage did nothing to upset our sunny relationship.

When I fell in love with Caroline she was living in a spacious three-storey flat in St John's Wood High Street, London with her 11-year-old son, Matthew. As is normal with such arrangements Matthew considered himself to be the master of the house and was not at all enthusiastic about my arrival on the scene.

Among his other virtues, Matthew can be very funny and the first manifestation of his humour – and tentative acceptance of the new situation – appeared when he asked his mother, 'What is it about this Christopher that reaches the parts which the others cannot reach?' That was an adaptation of a television advertisement for Heineken beer that was current at the time. Not bad for an eleven year old! That gift of insight with humour was to serve Matthew well in time.

He was also gifted at cricket, football, tennis, table tennis, competition cycling and snooker and, as with most talented sportsmen, was decidedly competitive. These characteristics soon turned out to be unexpectedly useful. The tension between us eased because he was better at all of those things than I was and winning was important to him. By contrast, I play sport to have fun and to give some fun to my opponent. That matters to me much more than winning although some of my grand gestures did go where they were supposed to go anyway and I did win sometimes.

This difference of approach provided a useful basis on which to build a new relationship with Matthew. There was, however, one dramatic moment which potentially threatened everything. The St Johns Wood High Street flat had a spare room just big enough to accommodate a half-sized snooker table which Caroline had provided before I came on the scene. Matthew and I spent many hours in there but one evening a huge row developed. I can't remember what the basis of it was and I can't even think of any situation on a snooker table that could merit quite such a passionate difference of opinion. Of course, we were both solidly convinced that we were right. As a result no solution was to be found and the temperature rose dramatically – until Matthew stormed off and disappeared into his room for the rest of the evening. Caroline, wise as ever, instructed me to do nothing at all but wait for the next evening and then behave as if nothing had happened. I did so, and my relationship with Matthew moved onto another level. We have continued to build on that ever since and grown steadily closer over the years.

Having no children of my own, I have never felt like a father or step-father to him – and never wanted to. I have disliked hierarchy since I was seven or eight, doubtless because of my egalitarian father and grandfather and the discrimination that was everywhere around me in the South Africa of my youth which so disturbed me. I felt it wrong to demand subservience or physical recognition of social superiority over another person as a matter of skin colour or of social right in the course of everyday life. I wanted to be Matthew's friend, not his step-father, and we succeeded in that.

Matthew's true father suggested that he should follow his example and become an accountant. Neither Caroline nor I thought that that would be the right thing but I was reluctant to suggest film or television because it is such a horribly uncertain road.

Then, out of the blue, when we were living in the south of France for a while, Matthew suddenly announced that he would like to make a film about truffles, truffle hunting and truffle hunters. He told us that he had done some encouraging research and that truffle hunters were a very strange, idiosyncratic and interesting lot. He had discovered also that the sums of money which changed hands between the hunters and their aficionado clients were nothing short of fantasy spectacular.

He had been working with me for some time both filming on location and in the cutting room. He was quick to learn and understand the essential rules. All that I had to do was to pass on what I had learned from the Features Department Producers in BBC radio – to whom I owed so much. A good apprenticeship makes all the difference in this game.

We hired a camera and off he went, aged nineteen, into the wilds of Provence, to make his first film – entirely on his own. Chapeau Matthieu! He shot all the material himself and did all the interviews, but films are made or broken in the cutting room, even if only because it is the last stage in the process. In practice there is much more to it than that. It is in the cutting room that a film's best intentions are either potentiated or lost. And so when editing time came we did it as a threesome, including Peter Heelas with whom I had made all my films from day one. Matthew came up with the title *Truffle Passions – Unearthing the Black Diamond*. It turned out well.

On the strength of his Truffles film Matthew joined an independent documentary production company and progressed steadily and quickly from being a runner to being Executive Producer and Commissioning Editor at CNN, London, which is where he is now.

Caroline and I have continued to work together peacefully ever since our Tchaikovsky adventure and I have been thankful time and again for her amazingly quick and accurate assessments of character. That great gift has saved us from what could have been dangerous mistakes on more than one occasion.

I am permanently thankful to her also for her spectacular gift for cooking which manifests itself on at least five evenings every week and which I have long thought was the source of the surprisingly good health I enjoyed for so many years.

But there is much more to it than the practical blessings. There is the love which cannot be faked, cannot be manufactured and which illuminates the relationship constantly. This has a lot to do with the fact that we met at a moment when both of us had suffered life-changing losses, losses which have made us permanently grateful for spiritual kindnesses and generosity.

Caroline calls it chemistry and claims to have recognized it from the first meeting – such are the miraculous workings of feminine intuition. I see it differently; as a blessing from whatever gods there be – as unexplainable in the way it touches the heart as the workings of music when it is at its best and most powerful – totally beyond all explanation and as close to the soul as we ever can get.

36

Why?

When we began to make films about my musician friends and their music-making we responded to the established television appetite for facts and figures about our heroes. We responded to the when and the where and the who of documentary. We looked at their doings and their habits, their dazzling and unexplainable talents and the seemingly exotic nature of their lives. This was all very interesting and television-appealing. But it was not long before I realized that we had in front of us something of even greater interest and value than the when and the where and the who – namely, the why?

Why can the black dots which Franz Peter Schubert put on white paper 188 years ago stir the heart so profoundly and draw instant and unexpected tears to the eyes? Tears that not only come from the deepest places within us but places that seem to have links in some way to the eternal. Tears that flow, before the mind has even begun to process any thought about why those sounds can mean so much to what we call the soul – an effect that in my case not only produced tears but, at times, left me physically shaking. It does not happen very often but when it does, we do not forget it, an effect wonderfully remembered in Kenneth Clark's famous words, 'Once art touches the soul in that way, it calls that soul back for the rest of its days.'

A huge question presented itself: could we possibly make films about the why of such mysterious magics rather than the documentary facts and figures? I knew that it was impossible for any film to attempt direct answers. I felt that the only thing to do was to try and plant seeds that would invite the television viewer to find his or her own way to that mysterious place.

I did not want to use actors to represent our heroes because I felt that reconstructed physical events would draw the viewer's attention to the everyday rather than to the spiritual – and the spirit was very precisely the place where I wanted to go.

Then we discovered that by placing the often poetic words of our protagonists *out of vision*, in places which resonated actively with their music, or with images related to their spiritual lives or artistic aspirations, the result often added light and love to the unexplainable power of their music.

That was a great discovery and that is the road that we took with our films about Respighi, Brahms, Mussorgsky, Bizet, Sibelius, Paganini, Cristobal Halffter, Schoenberg, Piazzolla, Schubert, Tchaikovsky and *We Want the Light*.

I was not surprised to find that the most open-hearted formulation of the workings of this magic came from Lotte Lehmann, addressing her audience at the end of her unforgettable farewell recital in Town Hall, New York:

> You were the wings on which I soared, and if sometimes it was possible for me to take you with me on my flight into beauty and into a better world, then perhaps I have achieved a fraction of what I wanted to give you.

DVD Contents

Short excerpts from the following films

1968 Vladimir Ashkenazy: The Vital Juices are Russian (34")

1969 The Trout (Barenboim, Perlman, Zukerman, du Pré, Mehta) (23")
title sequence (21")

1966 Double Concerto (Ashkenazy, Barenboim, English Chamber Orchestra) (12")

1982 Jacqueline du Pré and the Elgar Cello Concerto (19")

1967 Segovia at Los Olivos (15")

1970 The Ghost (Barenboim, Zukerman, du Pré) (35")

1975 Pinchas Zukerman: Here to make Music (22")

1978 Itzhak Perlman: Virtuoso Violinist (I Know I Played Every Note) (12")

1979 Elegies for the Deaths of Three Spanish Poets (Cristobal Halffter) (44")

1995 Remembering Jacqueline du Pré (35")

1977 Andrés Segovia: The Song of the Guitar (1'01")

1973 Carmen: The Dream and the Destiny - Domingo, Tourangeau, Krause (22")

1978 Pinchas Zukerman and Itzhak Perlman - Grand Duo (21")

1984 Jean Sibelius 1865-1957 Part 1: The Early Years (35")

1991 Nathan Milstein: Master of Invention (19")

1982 Jacqueline du Pré and the Elgar Cello Concerto (17")

1983 Modest Mussorgski: Pictures at an Exhibition (29")

1988 Tchaikovsky's Women (46")

1997 Paganini's Daemon (35")

1998 Evgeny Kissin: The Gift of Music (22")

1998 Evgeny Kissin at the Royal Albert Hall (37")

1994 Franz Peter Schubert: The Greatest Love and the Greatest Sorrow (47")

2004 We Want the Light (1'57")

Total running time: 13 minutes

Filmography

1966   Double Concerto (Ashkenazy, Barenboim, English Chamber Orchestra)
Golden Prague Award, 1967
Prix René Cidalc, Monte Carlo, 1967

1966   Isaac Stern with the LSO

1966   Mozart for New Year's Eve

1967   Melos in America

1967   Segovia at Los Olivos

1968   Vladimir Ashkenazy: The Vital Juices are Russian

1969   The Trout (Barenboim, Perlman, Zukerman, du Pré, Mehta)
TZ Rose, 1970
Diapason d'Or for the year 1991

1970   Barenboim on Beethoven

1970   The Ghost (Barenboim, Zukerman, du Pré)

1971   John Williams at Ronnie Scott's

1972   Ashkenazy Plays Beethoven (Essex):
Sonata No. 8 in C minor Opus 13 (Pathétique)
Sonata No. 31 in A flat Opus 110

1973   Carmen: The Dream and the Destiny (Domingo, Tourangeau, Krause)

1973   Mozart by Zukerman

1974   The Amadeus Quartet plays Beethoven

1975   Pinchas Zukerman: Here to make Music
International Emmy Nomination, 1976

1977   Andrés Segovia: The Song of the Guitar
Prix du Public, Besançon, 1977
Diapason d'Or for the year, 1991

1978   Itzhak Perlman and Pinchas Zukerman. Grand Duo 1

1978   Pinchas Zukerman and Itzhak Perlman. Grand Duo 2

1978   Bach D minor Partita – Perlman at St. Johns

1978   Bach E minor Partita – Perlman Plays Bach

1978   Brahms Violin Concerto (Itzhak Perlman, Lawrence Foster, Philharmonia Orchestra)

1978 Itzhak Perlman: Virtuoso Violinist (I Know I Played Every Note)

1979 Elegies for the Deaths of Three Spanish Poets (Cristobel Halffter)
      British Academy International Award, 1979
      International Emmy Award, 1979
      RAI Prize at the Prix Italia, 1980

1980 Vladimir Ashkenazy Recital No. 1
      Beethoven Hammerklavier Sonata Opus 106

1980 Vladimir Ashkenazy Recital No. 2:
      Chopin twenty-four Preludes Opus 28

1981 Vladimir Ashkenazy Recital No. 5:
      Beethoven: The last two Sonatas Opus 110 and 111

1981 Through Roses (Marc Neikrug) and German version
      Gold Award (music category) International Film & Television Festival of New York, 1982

1982 Ottorino Respighi: A Dream of Italy

1982 Jacqueline du Pré and the Elgar Cello Concerto
      Diapason d'Or for the year 1991

1983 Johannes Brahms 1833-1897. Three films (Zukerman, Neigrug)
      Gold Award (music category) International Film & Television Festival of New York, 1983

1983 Modest Mussorgski: Pictures at an Exhibition (Ashkenazy, Swedish Radio Symphony Orchestra)
      Diapason d'Or for the year 1991

1983 Vladimir Ashkenazy Recital No. 3:
      Beethoven, Sonatas Opus 101 and 109

1983 Vladimir Ashkenazy Recital No. 4:
      Chopin – Two Nocturnes Opus 27 Nos 1 and 2
      Sonata in B minor Opus 58

1983 Vladimir Ashkenazy Recital No. 6:
      Chopin 2 Nocturnes Opus 9 Nos. 1 & 3
      Polonaise in F sharp Opus 44
      Impromptu in F sharp major Opus 36
      Scherzo No. 3 Opus 39

1984 Jean Sibelius 1865-1957 Part 1: The Early Years
      Jean Sibelius 1865-1957 Part 2: Maturity & Silence
      Silver Award (music category) International Film & Television Festival of New York, 1984
      Special Jury Award, Banff Television Festival, 1985
      DVD of the Month, Gramophone Magazine Awards, 2006

1984 Schubert Sonatinas and Arpeggione Sonata (Zukerman, Neikrug)
Sonatina 1, 2 & 3, Arpeggione Sonata

1985 Variations on a theme of Corelli – Sergei Rachmaninoff – Introduced and played by Vladimir Ashkenazy

1985 Ashkenazy Plays Rachmaninoff (Six Etudes Tableaux Opus 39)
No. 1 in C major
No. 2 in A minor
No. 3 in F sharp minor
No. 4 in B minor
No. 5 in E flat minor
No. 9 in D major

1985 Ashkenazy Plays Rachmaninoff (Six Etudes Tableaux & Corelli Variations)

1985 Ashkenazy Plays Schumann (Papillons, Etudes Symphoniques)

1985 The Language of New Music (Schoenberg, Wittgenstein)
Silver Award (music category) International Film & Television Festival of New York, 1985

1985 Isaac Stern in Dublin

1986 Murray Perahia plays Beethoven

1986 Nathan Milstein in Stockholm

1986 Ashkenazy Plays Schumann (Lugano) (Etudes Symphoniques)

1987 Ashkenazy Observed
Diapason d'Or for the year 1991

1988 Tchaikovsky's Women (Part 1)

1989 Peter Ilych Tchaikovsky (Part 2): Fate

1991 Nathan Milstein: Master of Invention (Some memories of a quiet magician): Part 1

1991 Nathan Milstein: Master of Invention (Some memories of a quiet magician): Part 2

1991   Johann Sebastian Bach: The Goldberg Variations played by Daniel Barenboim

1993 Kreutzer Sonata (Milstein, Pludermacher)

1994 Franz Peter Schubert: The Greatest Love and the Greatest Sorrow
Nominated at the Banff Television Festival, 1994
Czech Crystal Award at the Prague Festival, 1994

1995 Remembering Jacqueline du Pré

1997 Paganini's Daemon

1998 Homage to Astor Piazzolla

1998 Evgeny Kissin: The Gift of Music

1998 Evgeny Kissin at the Royal Albert Hall

1999 Gidon Kremer: Man of Many Musics (First come the sounds)

2001 Who was Jacqueline du Pré?

2002 Evgeny Kissin at the Chorégies d'Orange: Bach & Schumann

2002 Evgeny Kissin at the Chorégies d'Orange: Mussorgski & Encores

2004 We Want the Light
Winner of the Jewish Cultural Award for Film and Television, 2004
Winner, Best Editing, New York Film and Television Festival, 2004
Preis der deutschen Schallplattenkritik

2005 The Purcell School

2005 Jacqueline du Pré in Portrait
Elgar Cello Concerto with Daniel Barenboim and the Philharmonia Orchestra, 1982
Beethoven's Trio The Ghost with Pinchas Zukerman and Daniel Barenboim, 2004
DVD of the Year Award at Midem, Cannes 2005

2008 Karim's Journey

2008 Jacqueline du Pré – A Celebration
Who was Jacqueline du Pré? 2001
Interview with Jacqueline du Pré, 1980
DVD of the Year Award at Midem, Cannes 2008

2009 Everything is a Present. The Wonder and the Grace of Alice Sommer Herz

2011 Nathan Milstein and the Bach Chaconne

2015 Daniil Trifonov: The Magics of Music
ICMA DVD of the year, 2016
Silver Award, New York Film and Television Festival, 2015
Accolade Global Film Winner, 2015

2015 Daniil Trifonov in Castelfranco Veneto

2017 Jacqueline du Pré; A Gift Beyond Words
A new compilation to mark 30 years since her death